POLITICS OF SCALE

Explorations in Heritage Studies

Series Editors:
Ali Mozaffari, *Deakin University*
David C. Harvey, *Aarhus University*

Explorations in Heritage Studies responds directly to the rapid growth of heritage scholarship and recognizes the trans-disciplinary nature of research in this area, as reflected in the wide-ranging fields, such as archaeology, geography, anthropology and ethnology, digital heritage, heritage management, conservation theory, physical science, architecture, history, tourism and planning. With a blurring of boundaries between art and science, theory and practice, culture and nature, the volumes in the series balance theoretical and empirical research, and often challenge dominant assumptions in theory and practice.

Volume 1
Politics of Scale
New Directions in Critical Heritage Studies
Edited by Tuuli Lähdesmäki, Suzie Thomas and Yujie Zhu

POLITICS OF SCALE
New Directions in Critical Heritage Studies

Edited by
Tuuli Lähdesmäki, Suzie Thomas and Yujie Zhu

First published in 2019 by
Berghahn Books
www.berghahnbooks.com

© 2019, 2023 Tuuli Lähdesmäki, Suzie Thomas and Yujie Zhu
First paperback edition published in 2023

All rights reserved. Except for the quotation of short passages for the purposes of criticism and review, no part of this book may be reproduced in any form or by any means, electronic or mechanical, including photocopying, recording, or any information storage and retrieval system now known or to be invented, without written permission of the publisher.

Library of Congress Cataloging-in-Publication Data

A C.I.P. cataloging record is available from the Library of Congress

British Library Cataloguing in Publication Data

A catalogue record for this book is available from the British Library

ISBN 978-1-78920-016-4 hardback
ISBN 978-1-80073-638-2 paperback
ISBN 978-1-78920-017-1 ebook

https://doi.org/10.3167/9781789200164

Contents

List of Figures and Tables	vii
Foreword David C. Harvey and Ali Mozaffari	ix
Introduction. Heritage and Scale Tuuli Lähdesmäki, Yujie Zhu and Suzie Thomas	1

PART I. SCALED CONCEPTUALIZATION OF HERITAGE

Chapter 1. Politics of Scale: Cultural Heritage in China Yujie Zhu	21
Chapter 2. The 'European Significance' of Heritage: Politics of Scale in EU Heritage Policy Discourse Tuuli Lähdesmäki and Katja Mäkinen	36
Chapter 3. The Dynamics of Scale in Digital Heritage Cultures Rhiannon Bettivia and Elizabeth Stainforth	50

PART II. SCALE IN HERITAGE INSTITUTIONS AND POLICIES

Chapter 4. Managed Landscapes: The Social Construction of Scale at Angkor Rowena Butland	65
Chapter 5. The Politics of Border Heritage: EU's Cross-Border Cooperation as Scalar Politics in the Spanish-Portuguese Border María Lois	81
Chapter 6. Broadening the Scope of Heritage: The Concept of Cultural Environment and Scalar Relations in Finnish Cultural Environment Policy Satu Kähkönen and Tuuli Lähdesmäki	95

PART III. SCALE IN HERITAGE PRACTICES

Chapter 7. Locals, Incomers, Tourists and Gold Diggers: Space, Politics and the 'Dark Heritage' Legacy of the Second World War in Finnish Lapland   113
    Suzie Thomas

Chapter 8. Becoming Mediterranean: The Intangible Cultural Heritage of Klapa Singing in Identity-Building and Nation-Branding Discourses   126
    Eni Buljubašić and Tuuli Lähdesmäki

Chapter 9. Tuning in to Radio Heritage in Newfoundland   140
    Michael Windover and Hilary Grant

Afterword. The Politics of Scale for Intangible Cultural Heritage: Identification, Ownership and Representation   156
    Kristin Kuutma

Index   171

Figures and Tables

Figures

1.1 Heritage administrative system in China.   24

1.2 Heritage policies and regulations at different administrative levels.   26

1.3 Upscaling and downscaling heritage in China.   30

4.1 Map of the Angkor World Heritage Site, showing the Angkor Zoning and Environment Management Plan (ZEMP).   74

5.1 In this commercial panel, quality Eco-raya is displayed as a marker of the BIN-SAL territory. Eco-raya's logo combines the two countries' flags, with the lighter character being the symbol of both spellings (*Raya,* in Spanish and *Raia,* in Portuguese), in a sort of hybrid vowel.   86

5.2 On the DVD cover, the colours of the flags of the two countries are used to write the title.   87

7.1 Map of Finland and surrounding area showing: 1. Inari; 2. Rovaniemi; 3. Oulu. Areas of Finland ceded to the Soviet Union: a. Petsamo; b. Salla-Kuusamo; c. Karelia.   117

9.1 Prime Minister Louis St. Laurent speaking at welcoming ceremonies, 1 April 1949.   141

9.2 Newfoundland Ranger Sergeant Ernest Clarke (Regt. #57), between 1935 and 1950.   145

9.3 Mr Joseph Smallwood signing the agreement that admitted Newfoundland into Confederation, Hon. A.J. Walsh, chairman of the Newfoundland delegation, is at the right, 11 December 1948. 151

Table

4.1 Spatial descriptions for 'Angkor' by ICC contributor and year. 73

 Foreword

David C. Harvey and Ali Mozaffari

Across the academy as a whole, *scale* is often taken for granted and seen along naturalized or fixed lines. Indeed, perhaps like *heritage*, the manner in which scale appeals to the common senses and a desire to anchor oneself provides it with a power and traction that is easy to overlook. Accepted as second nature and as part of the background context through which analysis can be organized, scale becomes prone to becoming a tool of domination. In this background guise, scale often either evades critical scrutiny, or leaves many critical readings of heritage slightly muted in its scalar engagement. Scale, however, is far more important than merely providing a useful device within which to categorize and organize, and should not be seen as a quasi-explanation for *how things are*. Rather than perceiving scale as a static or neutral setting, therefore, the chapters in this volume interrogate scale as a continual process of (re)construction, thus disrupting presumptions about the fixity of power or the efficacy of hierarchical management systems. Indeed, while scale is often at the heart of how domination is facilitated and inequalities legitimated, it might also be possible to make astute interventions in how power geometries operate through an intelligent and sensitive understanding of scalar politics. Whatever one's critical ambitions, scale should never be ignored, and we feel that this edited volume makes an important contribution in our examination of what scale *does* and how heritage and scale interact in a fluid and contingent manner. This edited volume brings together an exciting mix of established and emerging scholars. Not content to deploy scale as an 'answer', they bring a dynamic blend of creative and critical insight to bear. This is the first book-length collection of work specifically on the relations between heritage and scale, and will make a significant contribution to wider debates within both heritage studies and more widely within the humanities and social sciences.

Issues of heritage reside within many of the most pressing issues around the world today, whether connected to changing climates and environmental crises, or with anxieties over identity politics and strident exclusive populism, the seemingly endless intermittent conflicts of displaced people and refugees, and the alarming rise of social and economic inequalities. Quite rightly, critical heritage scholars have responded, especially through work that has interrogated how borders are produced, performed and embedded. This book adds to these bodies of work and, crucially, points towards a need to do more than be 'critical', but to think how heritage studies can make positive interventions. We are delighted to have *The Politics of Scale: New Directions in Critical Heritage Studies* published in the Berghahn 'Explorations in Heritage Studies' book series.

David C. Harvey
Ali Mozaffari
13 March 2018

David C. Harvey is Associate Professor in Critical Heritage Studies in the Department of Archaeology and Heritage Studies at Aarhus University, Denmark, and Honorary Professor of Historical and Cultural Geography at the University of Exeter. His work has focused on the geographies of landscape, heritage, memorialization, identity and creative practice. He has contributed to some key debates about processual understandings of heritage, extending the temporal depth of heritage, the outlining of heritage-landscape and heritage-climate change relations, as well as the opening up of hidden memories through oral history. His most recent work includes *The Future of Heritage as Climates Change: Loss, Adaptation and Creativity* (Routledge, 2015), edited with Jim Perry, and *Commemorative Spaces of the First World War: Historical Geographies at the Centenary* (Routledge, 2018), edited with James Wallis. He is co-editor of Berghahn's *Explorations in Heritage Studies* book series.

Ali Mozaffari is Fellow of the Australian Research Council (DECRA) in the Alfred Deakin Institute, at Deakin University, Australia and Adjunct Research Fellow with the Australia-Asia-Pacific Institute, at Curtin University, Australia. The focus of his work is on the politics of heritage, social movements and the making of cultural heritage, heritage and the built environment, and histories and design of architecture in Iran and more broadly in West Asia. His recent work includes 'Designing a Revolutionary Habitat: Tradition, Heritage and Housing in the Immediate Aftermath of the Iranian Revolution – Continuities and Disruptions', *Fabrications* 28, no. 2 (May 2018): 185–211, co-authored with Nigel Westbrook and the edited volume *World Heritage in Iran: Perspectives on Pasargadae* (Routledge, 2016). He is co-editor of Berghahn's *Explorations in Heritage Studies* book series.

Introduction
Heritage and Scale
Tuuli Lähdesmäki, Yujie Zhu and Suzie Thomas

Scholarly research of cultural heritage has faced paradigmatic changes during the past few decades. These changes have occurred in part as a reaction to diverse social, political, economic and cultural transformations of societies and traditional foundations of nation states. Today's world, characterized by networked agencies, global cultural flows, cultural hybridity and movement of people within and across borders, contextualizes the idea of heritage in new ways. It challenges its previous core function as a bedrock of monocultural nation-building projects, a continuation of elitist cultural canons, and as upholding Eurocentric cultural values. As a part of this transformation, consensual heritage narratives about the nation and national identity have been questioned and contested through various identity claims below and above the national narrative – and within it (e.g. Ashworth, Graham and Tunbridge 2007, Labadi 2007; Smith 2006). A range of communities, defined either geographically or by cultural, social, economic, ethnic, religious, or linguistic experiences, have increasingly asserted the legitimacy of their collective identities and of their heritage as this identity's manifestation (Smith 2006). These developments have brought heritage research into a new critical phase.

During the last decades of the twentieth century, academic fields within humanities and social sciences took increasing interest in uneven power relations, hierarchical power structures, explicit and implicit politics of dominance and oppression, silenced narratives and alternative, emancipatory and empowering identity projects. Critical research stemming from postmodernism, poststructuralism and Foucauldian perspectives on power gave ground to and strengthened new academic disciplines of Postcolonial,

Racial, Gender, New Museology and Subaltern Studies. The theoretical frame of this critical research also renewed disciplines that more explicitly focus on the study of cultural heritage. In Cultural Heritage Studies, the change from the previous emphasis of conservation and preservation of heritage (although these questions are also still debated) to complex questions of the power that heritage entails and produces has generated a field of study and a scholarly approach called Critical Heritage Studies. Rather than asking 'what do we do to heritage', scholars within this field, such as Smith (2006) and Harrison (2013), have posed the question 'what does heritage do/how is heritage used?' They perceive the ideas, practices and processes of heritage as inherently political, emerging within complex power relations and open to change and contest (Graham and Howard 2008; Harrison 2013; Smith 2006).

The exploration of power relations in Critical Heritage Studies focuses particularly on several 'grand narratives' that have dominated the meaning making and practices of heritage for centuries. Nationalism, imperialism, colonialism, Western triumphalism, social exclusion based on class and ethnicity, cultural elitism and the fetishizing of expert knowledge have all had a crucial impact on how cultural heritage is discussed, used and managed. These ideas and ideologies have arguably influenced what has been understood and defined as cultural heritage by privileging old, grand, prestigious, expert-approved sites, buildings and artefacts that sustain Western narratives of nation, class and science (Smith 2012). Critical Heritage Studies seeks to question and unravel the previous and still existing hegemonic power structures in heritage and scrutinize the workings of power in heritage from a broad interdisciplinary perspective.

The recent studies on cultural heritage perceive the concept as a presentist process: it is not a passive act of preserving things from the past but 'an active process of assembling a series of objects, places and practices that we choose to hold up as a mirror to the present, associated with a particular set of values that we wish to take with us into the future' (Harrison 2013: 4). The concept of heritage itself is understood in this critical perspective as a complex and relational phenomenon that draws together and joins various social and cultural entities, such as material objects, places, values, ideas, emotions, memory and identity. Several scholars (e.g. Dicks 2000; Kirshenblatt-Gimblett 2004; Munjeri 2004; Smith and Akagawa 2009) have emphasized how these tangible and intangible dimensions of heritage are inevitably intertwined. Heritage is about the entanglement of these diverse dimensions and their 'manufactured' effect on people, a constant process of meaning making and cultural production that Kirshenblatt-Gimblett (2004) defines as a 'metacultural' operation. For her, fostering, preserving and producing heritage are processes that take place on a meta level, such as in diverse national and international heritage policy processes.

Although Critical Heritage Studies seeks to explore the mechanism of power in heritage and question the essentialist notions of stable meanings and Eurocentric values of heritage, the critical view of heritage scholars has rarely scrutinized a core issue that produces these mechanisms and notions: the issue of scale. When heritage sites are nominated to the UNESCO (United Nations Educational, Scientific and Cultural Organization) World Heritage List, for example, the world heritage status that is bestowed upon them gives a site significance at different scales. The site's value locally may be transformed by the world heritage status, while it also gains a global 'outstanding universal value'. The relationship between this status and nation states – especially with sites that have contested histories or heritage – can also lead to experiences of transnational conflict and contestation (e.g. Liwanag 2016). Despite these recognizable issues of scale, most heritage research does not necessarily identify scale as a central issue.

Scale and scalar relations play a crucial role in the production and meaning making of heritage – thus scale can be seen as one of the core concerns of Critical Heritage Studies. Although scale has been broadly discussed in geography, a further critical analysis of its constructive and performative nature is needed in order to understand the power hierarchies in heritage and in various conflicts related to its meanings, ownership, preservation and management. What is scale? Does it relate only to issues of space, magnitude and level, or are there, as we suggest, also more nuanced ways of considering this term? The recent growth of concerns within heritage policy and practice, and the increasing attempts to preserve and govern heritage, necessitate reconsidering the scales of heritage.

Scalarly structured entities and their relationships are interconnected and constantly transforming, both historically and theoretically. Massey (2005) has conceptualized space as a relational construction that simultaneously includes diverse scalar dimensions and multiple meanings, both shared and personal. Similarly, heritage can be perceived as a multilayered and multi-scalar phenomenon. Certain layers of heritage meanings are activated in certain discourses, policies and practices at different scales. Thus, the same heritage practice, object or site can have several scalar meanings and be used to foster and promote several scalar identities or feelings of belonging to different scalarly organized communities. In diverse processes of heritage making, the idea of heritage is commonly fixed to both real and imagined scalarly structured and defined territories: heritage is perceived and narrated as reflecting not only locally, regionally and nationally framed meanings but also those of supranational entities, such as cross-border or transnational regions or continents. However, scale does not only determine the relationships of territories and territorialized cultural features and identities. It also influences non-territorial social and cultural divisions; for example, public and personal, young and old, official and unofficial, minority and majority, and normative and unorthodox (see Ashworth and Graham 2005; Ashworth, Graham and Tunbridge 2007; Kean 2008).

In the volume, the heritage-scale relationship is perceived as a domain of power and politics. Instead of defining scale as a singular unit, such as local, national or global, the contributors emphasize a plural and dynamic understanding of scale and its relationship to heritage. The volume deploys the concept of 'politics of scale' to analyse the power struggles during the processes of production, reconfiguration and contestation within and among scales of heritage. The key questions that this volume addresses are:

- What understandings of scale influence interpretation and meaning making of heritage?
- How is the idea of scale used by heritage institutions to govern heritage, legitimize authority and produce hierarchies in heritage?
- What kinds of workings of power, politics and policies are implicated through the scaled nature of heritage?
- How are heritage discourses reinforced through scale, and how do they affect other scaled divisions, such as political divisions, minority-majority relationships, citizenship or notions of 'otherness'?
- How do conflicts and struggles within heritage discourses emerge, and how do they move between and along scales?

Definitions of Scale

In geography, the notion of scale has been discussed within diverse theoretical frameworks. The concept of geographical scale indicates socio-spatial organization within a bounded geographical area – usually labelled as size (such as province or continent) or level (such as global, national, regional, local and even household) (Marston 2000). Besides these 'technical' definitions, recent research also includes more nuanced elaborations. Below, we discuss four conceptualizations for understanding and utilizing the concept of scale that are critical in underscoring the power relations in heritage. These conceptualizations function as our point of departure in developing politics of scale as a theoretical and methodological approach.

Scale as a Hierarchy

In previous heritage studies, scale has been commonly discussed in relation, and as connected, to spatial entities that are hierarchically structured. In these views, the notion of scale is intertwined with the idea of hierarchy –

whether the hierarchy itself is perceived as 'natural' or 'constructed'. For example, Graham, Ashworth and Tunbridge (2000: 4) defined scale as follows: 'Scale: an intrinsic attribute of places is that they exist within a hierarchy of spatial scales. Places therefore have a heritage at local, regional, national, continental and international scales, while, in turn, a particular heritage artefact can function at a variety of scales.' Others have explained heritage as 'exist[ing] within nested spatial-scale hierarchies' (Ashworth 1994: 13). In this kind of scalar hierarchy, local, regional, national, continental and global levels form a spatial system in which each 'broader' scope is understood as transcending the previous 'narrower' scope (Ashworth and Graham 1997: 382).

As Graham, Ashworth and Tunbridge (2000) note, the same heritage artefact can function simultaneously at different territorial levels. However, the structure of these territorial levels is stable in this conception. The notion of scale in this conceptualization follows a hierarchical order similar to a Russian 'matryoshka' nesting doll. Heritage is understood as being able to include 'multi-scalar' meanings, and yet the concept of scale is still seen as being structured along pregiven and fixed scalar units, such as village/town/city, a municipality, a region, a nation or a continent.

Approaching heritage through a nested spatial hierarchy relies on essentialist notions of spatial entities and their scaled 'order'. Thus, various studies on spatial meanings of heritage seem commonly to entail a stiff and categorical notion of scale. This kind of approach to scale hinders perception of the complexity of a heritage-scale relationship and prevents viewing scale as a relational social construct and an instrument of power. Indeed, many of the previous studies on the spatial meanings of heritage have been excessively place-bound, ignoring the relational nature of spatial borders and the fluidity of ideas related to territorial entities, as Harvey (2015) claims. Harvey emphasizes how the relationship between the idea of heritage and scale can be perceived as an open, plural and relational process detached from physical distance, proximity or essentialist claims to territorial hierarchy. Thus, with this volume we aim to deconstruct the idea of a hierarchical order of scale, and scrutinize the power relations included in this idea, and the processes in which it is maintained.

Scale as an Instrument of Power

The 'Russian doll' structure of scale discussed above has several implications. It creates uneven power relations among different scales, cements diverse social, political, economic and cultural hierarchies, and upholds the dominance and inequality included in these hierarchies. The Russian doll structure of scale also formats the power relations between social actors. Different social actors within this structure have different weights of influence. Some are more powerful than others. This uneven development is based on the structural relationship between institutions and the resources of power, capital and information that social actors use to produce the scale in which they act or seek to act (Smith 1990). This uneven development results in a process of hierarchization and re-hierarchization (Swyngedouw 1997). The process changes the geometry of social power by strengthening the control of some while disempowering others (Swyngedouw 1997).

Swyngedouw (1997: 148) points out that it is often capital (assets, financial or otherwise) that moves upward (upscaling) while the regulation moves downward (downscaling). Similar trajectories can be identified in heritage governance and administration from various parts of the globe (see Zhu's chapter in this book). In these developments, top-down administrative systems have been established to reinforce heritage governance at 'lower' scales. As a result, the processes of heritage making are influenced and manipulated by discourses produced at the 'higher' scales of power, although the local heritage actors are those who in practice implement these processes.

Scale as a Process

The notion of scale as a process stems from studies exploring the social production of space. The idea of the relational and processual nature of space is the core concept in Lefebvre's (1991) studies. For him, the same space contains various social spaces that all are present in a multilayered way in our physical environment. The production of space(s) brings about a constant reshuffling and reworking of social spaces at different scales (Brenner 2001; Lefebvre 1991). Researchers have also emphasized the constructivist and social-constructionist understandings of the nature of scale. Scalar configurations are thus seen as the outcome of complex socio-spatial processes that regulate and organize social power relations (Swyngedouw 1997, 2000). Scaling the 'material' intertwines with scaling the 'social': scalar structure of material culture includes and produces scalar social structures. Embedded in geographical constructions, scales become arenas in which socio-spatial power choreographies are enacted and performed (Swyngedouw 2004). Thus, various scholars have focused their interest on scale as a social production, social relation and conflict (Marston 2000; Smith 1990). Here, scale is not a fixed force or existing resolution but a constant process of formation, transformation and rescaling (Brenner 2001; Swyngedouw 1997).

In Critical Heritage Studies, heritage is commonly understood as a process. Connecting the processual notions of heritage and scale enhances a deeper understanding of the politics of scale in heritage. In some studies, scale has functioned as an analytical tool to understand the connections and activities of international and transnational movements in these processes (e.g. Graham, Ashworth and Tunbridge 2000).

Scale as a Network

Latour (1996) and Castells (1996) suggest that the world's complexity should not be thought of as levels, layers, territories or spheres but rather networked together. The conception of 'network' stimulates discussion about the flow of objects, people, ideas and technology as an interconnected complexity. Different from scales that address boundaries and hierarchies, the conception of network helps us to view relations and connections between diverse units (Marston, Jones and Woodward 2005). In this view, the constant movement from local to global (and back to local) is based on the idea and politics of connectivity. This politics is actively utilized by various internationally acting organizations and institutions who engage in constructing transnational or interurban networks to enhance their power, authority and legitimacy related to other scales. This is particularly the case in Europe, where many transnational or trans-regional networks link together across the boundaries of local, regional and national state territories.

Following Brenner's (2001) views, we emphasize how the networks of connectivity and hierarchical scales of heritage governance are mutually constitutive. In each scale, heritage-related networks are established to develop common interests and knowledge across certain boundaries. Heritage actors active in these networks exchange information through formal meetings or informal contact. A well-known example of this kind of heritage network is the International Council on Monuments and Sites (ICOMOS). Established in 1965, ICOMOS is an international network of heritage and conservation practitioners and specialists who also act as government officials and heritage consultants. At the regional level, several non-European heritage networks have been established to promote cultural uniqueness and regional identities, such as the Aga Khan Trust for Culture, the Islamic Educational, Scientific, and Cultural Organization in the Muslim World, and the Caribbean Community and Common Market in the Caribbean region (Salazar and Zhu 2015).

In following these views, scale can be perceived as a strategically constructed tool deployed to produce and reproduce power relations in various ways. Processes of scale formation/transformation are cut through by all manner of fragmenting and differentiating processes of empowerment and disempowerment, such as nationalism, localism, class differentiation and competition (Swyngedouw 1997). Processes of scale formation are, thus, social practices that effectively 'harness powers and instrumentalities at other scales' (Jonas 1994: 258).

Although geographers have brought the concept of scale to heritage research, the idea and concept of 'politics of scale' has remained underdeveloped in this field and has thus hindered deeper analyses of the workings of scales of heritage and their production through continued sociopolitical contestation. In this volume we perceive politics of scale as a crucial concept and a theoretical and methodological approach to trace the 'power geometries' (Massey 1993) of how heritage works.

Heritage and Politics of Scale

In geography, Smith (1990) initiated the concept of politics of scale, which was later deployed by people such as Herod (1997) and Swyngedouw (1997), in social-spatial production research. Geographers use this concept to explain the transformation in political governance (such as global-local relations), the rise of supranational organizations and regulation, and the shifting importance of nation state.

Revisiting the definition of 'politics of scale' enables us to broaden our understanding of heritage and 'what heritage does'. Brenner has suggested an important revisit to the concept. According to him, politics of scale can refer to 'the production, reconfiguration or contestation' both within one scale (the singular) and among different scales (the plural) (Brenner 2001: 599). The singular form indicates a struggle or contestation in a boundary setting, such as in producing a place, locality, region or nation. The plural form, as he rephrases it as a 'process of scaling', does not focus on a production of a singular unit as such but rather on 'hierarchization and rehierarchization' among multiple spatial units through interscalar transformation (Brenner 2001: 600). Indeed, a number of studies have examined how, for example, diverse social movements struggle to shift the scale of their political contests and how people use scale to take advantage of certain interscalar political conditions (Herod 1997; Smith 1990). Herod (1997) illustrates how labour unions have negotiated local, regional and national contracts to strengthen their bargaining positions. Similar 'processes of scaling' or 'interscalar transformations' take place in various contests and struggles related, for example, to gender, lesbian, gay, bisexual and transexual rights, and abortion.

In the field of heritage, the plural form of politics of scale (or as Brenner phrased it, process of scaling) is poorly recognized and examined. Notwithstanding this, politics of scale in heritage do exist. For example, there commonly exists more or less active resistance from 'lower' scales to negotiate with or among different scales for cultural or property rights. The idea of ownership – to whom does heritage truly belong – is one of the critical issues of politics of scale. The concept of politics of scale helps with theorizing heritage; the recognition of scale as an instrument of power and a tool of hierarchization and re-hierarchization brings to the fore the essentiality of scale to heritage.

One of the core concepts in Critical Heritage Studies is 'Authorized Heritage Discourse' (AHD), initiated by Smith (2006) a decade ago. With this concept, Smith refers to a heritage discourse that 'takes its cue from the grand narratives of Western national and elite class experiences, and reinforces the idea of innate cultural value tied to time depth, monumentality, expert knowledge and aesthetics' (Smith 2006: 299). For her, the authority of this discourse is heavily anchored within state-sanctioned agencies and international bodies such as UNESCO and ICOMOS, who qualify objects, ideas and places as heritage and legitimize dominant narratives about them. Smith, however, also emphasizes how heritage discourse is disputed and mutable. Relations among different scales in the processes of heritage making are not always cooperative and harmonious but contested and competitive – in a sense of dissonance framed by Tunbridge and Ashworth (1996). Similar to the actions of various social movements, subordinate groups use the scale of 'local', 'community' or even 'home' to negotiate and resist control from the heritage discourse.

Critical Heritage Studies emphasizes that the values of heritage in the discourse of supranational organizations are deeply rooted in a European conservation tradition (Winter 2014). This tradition can be traced back to the eighteenth century, when the first modern ideologies of conservation – followed by efforts of preserving cityscapes of major European historical cities, such as Rome and Paris – took place (Glendinning 2013). The strategy of using heritage to develop 'national consciousness' emerged concurrently in some European countries, but it became a dominant heritage discourse during the nineteenth century alongside the rise and spread of nationalism and modernity (see Harrison 2013). Following the founding of broadly accepted and internationally operating heritage organizations from the mid twentieth century onwards, such as UNESCO and ICOMOS, heritage has entered into the scale of the global. This scalar dimension intersects with the discourse of universalism. UNESCO and its advisory board in particular have established the heritage discourse of a 'universal value' that is promoted in its conventions and policy texts. This discourse legitimates the significance of the global scale of heritage and disseminates UNESCO's value system around the world. The World Heritage List and the rules of inclusion to and exclusion from it are UNESCO's core mechanisms to gain and reinforce its global-scale authority.

In the twenty-first century, as Smith (2006) notes, heritage has, thus, become a 'universalizing' discourse. Although this discourse claims to be 'universal', it nonetheless relies on and recycles various Eurocentric values. The development and promotion of the notion of 'authenticity' as a core heritage value is an often-discussed example of this kind of legitimated Eurocentric conception. It became an important issue of heritage management and conservation after the launch of the 1964 Venice Charter for the Conservation and Restoration of Monuments and Sites. The application of authenticity was further universalized after the 1972 World Heritage Convention and further globally applied through other international policy documents, such as the 1994 Nara Document on Authenticity.

The construction of a heritage-scale relationship is, and has always been, a process of constant negotiation and contest. Dominant, dominated and *alternative* heritage discourses are not embedded in one or two scales but interacted with and negotiated among different scales. The universalizing discourse of UNESCO is also a transforming and negotiated process including actors at different scales. States parties, international pressure and soft power diplomacy have an increasing impact on the World Heritage Committee and its decision-making process of adding heritage sites to the World Heritage List (Luke and Kersel 2012). International heritage policies do not automatically transfer the power of heritage making over to the international heritage bodies. International heritage policies are finally enacted and put into practice by states and their national heritage actors, who implement the heritage policies on the national level (Bendix, Eggert and Peselmann 2012; Lähdesmäki 2014). Each state translates the key terms of the UNESCO Conventions in different ways, resulting in 'domestication of global standards', as Bortolotto (2012: 277) has noticed.

Recent studies on cultural heritage have sought to deconstruct heritage discourses by disclosing its political attempts and criticizing the power hierarchies included in it and produced by it. Particularly, studies have focused on a national frame of reference as the main arbiter of values and promoter of heritage discourses (Harvey 2015). The dominant heritage discourses and the management of heritage are predominantly arranged along a hierarchy of spatial scales in which a national framework has played – and still commonly plays – a central role. Heritage functions as a tool to create and rethink national consciousness and unity and to promote economic and social development. No countries can seemingly live without national museums, archives, monuments, historical narratives, or heritage-related agencies, laws and policies. The national frame functions as the most common scalar level in the promotion of a communal identity and the communal meanings of heritage (Graham, Ashworth and Tunbridge 2000: 259). The promotion of a national identity has a more established tradition compared with, for example, the supranational scale of community building (Ashworth 1994: 13).

Nation states, national-level actors and national meanings of heritage have a core role also in the international heritage discourses, policies and practices. Despite the development of international heritage networks, nation states remain important as facilitators and agents of structuring globalization. Nation states jostle for recognition, authority and control alongside new forms of political power in both transnational and regional networks. Nation states are interested in the stability of the national scale, as this scale facilitates heritage governance and can enable capital accumulation. Furthermore, tensions emerge and re-emerge between the global and the national.

In the global scale of the heritage industry, the dominance of the nation state as a scale of governance is little diminished (Leitner, Pavlik and Sheppard 2002). The World Heritage system gives a licence to transform heritage into a soft power to carry out nationalism through legitimizing heritage conservation and commercialization activities. The World Heritage Centre is an international secretariat in need of both economic and political support from its states' parties. As Meskell et al. (2015) indicate, the World Heritage decision making adopted by the World Heritage Committee is less followed by its advisory bodies; instead, it is increasingly influenced by the political and economic interests of nation states in the Committee. An example of this is the success by some Asian countries in promoting the new category of Intangible Cultural Heritage, a UNESCO designation established in 2003.

In addition to the broadly discussed challenges of the national and global scales of heritage, various scholars have become interested in 'downscaling' their research focus. Recent heritage research has explored topics such as community, family or even personal heritage (Harvey 2015). However, in heritage discourses and practices, micro and macro scales of heritage commonly merge and affect each other. While the dominating heritage discourses seek to control the meanings and practices of heritage on the scale 'below' it, heritage is at the same time created by the actors representing these 'lower' scales – and their interests. Indeed, the actors on the 'lower' scale interpret and reinterpret the 'upper' scale heritage discourses from their own point of view and thus influence the form in which it is disseminated and transferred into heritage practices. The politics of scale functions as a crucial theoretical and methodological approach to scrutinize this multi-scalarity of heritage discourses, as the mechanisms through which heritage operates appear to be more elusive and less structural. Heritage often includes 'an attribute of dissonance, not only in a sense of identity and meaning, but also in terms of scale' (Harvey 2015: 579).

Concepts, Institutions, Policies and Practices – Politics of Scale in Action

In this volume, contributors apply the notion of scale to diverse processes of heritage making and the workings of power included within them. Politics of scale here means both a theoretical concept and a methodological approach to heritage-scale relationship and the effects that this relationship produces. This approach is founded on interwoven theoretical discussions that emphasize the constructed, processual, fluid and relational nature of heritage-scale relationship and the critical understanding of the hierarchical and uneven power structures in the production of this relationship.

The book is divided into three distinct parts to focus on particular aspects of scale and its politics, although the parts are also closely interrelated. The chapters interrogate multifaceted meanings of scale that are not only about levels such as global, national and local but also about spatialized social and cultural borders and border crossings and about scale in digital platforms. The examples of heritage discussed, theorized and problematized within this volume are diverse, from intangible cultural practices through to cultural and historic environments and digital heritage. The contributors are diverse in their disciplinary backgrounds, with perspectives grounded in art history, cultural studies, geography, heritage studies, linguistics, literature, museum studies, political science and sociology. Similarly, the examples and debates come from across the globe. The parts are divided roughly to focus on scaled conceptualization of heritage; scale in heritage institutions and policies; and scale in heritage practices. The book is not intended as a simply linear resource, however, and readers are invited to explore the chapters in relation to each other and in whatever ordering and grouping they wish.

The chapters in 'Part I: Scaled Conceptualization of Heritage' discuss diverse attempts to conceptualize heritage and the use of different concepts in varying heritage discourses, analysing the politics that the scaled nature of these concepts entail. The notion of scale is very apparent from a spatial point of view, with heritage discussed at site-specific, national, regional and (with the concept of World Heritage) global levels (Jones, Jones and Hughes 2016). Different forms of 'heritage' are scrutinized; not only World Heritage sites (Zhu) but also the regional idea of European cultural heritage recognized through the mechanism of the European Heritage Label (Lähdesmäki and Mäkinen) and the growing phenomenon of digital heritage (Bettiva and Stainforth).

Yujie Zhu explores the theme of heritage contestation through the lens of the politics of scale with his analysis of cultural heritage production and consumption in China. In this chapter we see the impact of global heritage discourses and policies on localized levels favouring some voices while ignoring others, and we encounter the 'jumping among scales' that takes place as heritage variously 'up-' and 'downscales'. Zhu examines these phenomena through the case study of the Old Town of Lijang World Heritage Site.

Working with a continental scale, Tuuli Lähdesmäki and Katja Mäkinen consider the role of politics of scale in the development of the European Union's (EU's) European Heritage Label. They problematize the tensions between various national identities and narratives across Europe and the efforts of this initiative to select sites that may be interpreted in particular ways to attempt to achieve a 'pan-European'-scaled objective. This inevitably leads to the favouring of certain voices and narratives over others, fitting to the European Commission's political agenda of creating unity and enhancing (cultural) integration in Europe, among other things. Rhiannon Bettivia and Elizabeth Stainforth focus on digital heritage – from digitized heritage collections being placed online through to the upscaling impact on potential audiences that digitization offers. Similar to Lähdesmäki and Mäkinen, they also note regional- and national-scale political agendas at play in their examples of Europeana and the Digital Public Library of America, in their positions as large-scale heritage aggregators.

In 'Part II: Scale in Heritage Institutions and Policies', authors discuss the policies and politics of heritage management structures – ranging in scale from local municipal heritage authorities to the implementation of UNESCO-endorsed international policy – and their explicit and implicit uses of scale in meaning making, governing and managing heritage. Scale as an instrument of power is particularly relevant to this part, as the different hierarchies of policy and heritage agency structures influence heavily the conceptualization and management of the heritage in question.

The heritage management strategies deployed at Angkor Wat World Heritage Area in Cambodia are critiqued by Rowena Butland, who teases out the connection of heritage 'value' to the social constructs at play and the inevitable inclusion or exclusion of different stakeholders or interest groups and their particular values through an institutionalized and policy-regulated form of cultural heritage management. Harking back to Zhu's example in Part I, this is another case of global-scale policy and practice having an at times troubling, and certainly transformative, influence on local heritage management.

María Lois considers cross-border and transnational scales of heritage making in the context of EU-funded programmes, especially the supranational BIN-SAL border region in Spain and Portugal. She notes how the EU cross-border politics become also scalar politics through the process of heritage meaning making. Satu Kähkönen and Tuuli Lähdesmäki also present an example from within Europe, focusing on local scales in the Nordic countries, and Finnish municipality levels of scale in particular, to discuss the holistic approach to heritage put forward through the concept of cultural environment. They also note, within the notion of politics of scale, a porosity of spatial borders owing to the ambiguous and flexible nature of the very concept of cultural environments. The border-based and in some cases border-free contexts explored in both of these chapters present ample challenges for policy writers and decision makers.

The 'Part III: Scale in Heritage Practices' chapters discuss various practices through which scaled nature and hierarchical structures of heritage are created, maintained and transmitted but also questioned, deconstructed and proposed as alternatives seeking to dismantle these hierarchical structures. They perhaps take a more applied perspective, drawing especially upon the notion of scale as a process and scale as a network. We see also the impact of the researchers on practices on their case studies, be it at a local, national or regional scale. Suzie Thomas reflects upon her and her research colleagues' research practice in relation to the 'dark' heritage legacy of the Second World War in Finnish Lapland in a scaled manner, presenting insight not only into the heritage being researched but also the contribution to the up- or downscaling of that heritage by the very act of research itself.

Eni Buljubašić and Tuuli Lähdesmäki investigate the evolving nature of Dalmatian klapa singing and how this UNESCO-labelled intangible cultural heritage practice has become politicized in Croatia's reconfiguration of its national identity as Mediterranean, scaled within an EU-orientated context. The example is a dynamic one, illustrating also the fluidity of heritage politics and the rapidity with which identities related to different scales can change and evolve. National and regional identity scales also figure in Michael Windover and Hilary Grant's study of 'radio heritage' in Newfoundland, Canada. They identify the different scalar configurations of radio broadcast in Newfoundland during and after its transition from a British colony to a Canadian province. Aspects as nuanced as the regional accents of radio presenters through to the significance of the takeover of radio broadcasts by the national Canadian Broadcasting Corporation in Ottawa have had an impact on the socio-economic and political conditions in Newfoundland, inevitably intertwined with scales of heritage and identity. As they note, '[r]adio made Newfoundland a global village.'

Finally, Kristin Kuutma concludes the volume, drawing together and reflecting upon the theoretical discussion of politics of scale as presented in the previous parts. Reflecting especially on the concept of intangible cultural heritage, framed through UNESCO policies in particular, she discusses how these theoretical views and approaches link to other aspects of Critical Heritage Studies and influence identification, ownership and representation of heritage at interscalar levels.

This edited volume offers a refreshed frame for the continuously evolving field of Critical Heritage Studies by discussing how heritage and scale interact in the processes of heritage making. We demonstrate the numerous ways in which scale, and especially politics of scale, influence concepts of policy affecting (and practices influencing and evolving) heritage. The volume seeks to respond to needs in current heritage research by providing a global, interdisciplinary and critical exploration of the scaled nature of relationships involved in the production and meaning making of heritage. By developing 'politics of scale' as both a theoretical and methodological approach, this volume contributes to the understanding of how heritage discourses and practices affect and produce other scaled divisions in culture and society. Meanwhile, the project is by no means a conclusion to this avenue of enquiry but rather aims to stimulate and further debate and conversation.

Acknowledgements

The introduction and editing of this volume are related to research projects funded by European Research Council, decision no. 636177, EUROHERIT, and Academy of Finland, decision no. 274295, EUCHE (Lähdesmäki); Australian National University and Zhejiang University, China (Zhu); and Academy of Finland, decision no. 275497 (Thomas).

Tuuli Lähdesmäki (PhD, DSocSc) is an Academy Research Fellow and Adjunct Professor at the Department of Music, Art and Culture Studies, University of Jyväskylä (JYU), Finland. Lähdesmäki specializes in heritage, culture and identity politics, particularly in the European context. She currently leads the research projects 'European Cultural Heritage in the Making: Politics, Affects and Agency' (EUCHE), funded by the Academy of Finland, and 'Legitimation of European Cultural Heritage and the Dynamics of Identity Politics in the EU' (EUROHERIT), funded by the European Research Council. She is the Co-PI in JYU's research profiling area 'Crises Redefined: Historical Continuity and Societal Change' (CRISES).

Yujie Zhu (PhD) is a Lecturer at the School of Archaeology and Anthropology, the Australian National University. He is the author of *Heritage and Romantic Consumption in China* (Amsterdam University Press, 2018) and the co-editor of *Sustainable Tourism Management at World Heritage Sites* (UNWTO 2009). He has also published more than thirty articles that appeared in leading anthropology, tourism, and heritage journals, including *American Anthropologist, Annals of Tourism Research,* and *International*

Journal of Heritage Studies. In addition, Yujie is the vice chair of the IUAES Commission on the Anthropology of Tourism and the vice president of the Association of Critical Heritage Studies.

Suzie Thomas (BA, MA, PhD) is Professor of Cultural Heritage Studies at the University of Helsinki, Finland. She is interested in non-professional and so-called alternative engagements with cultural heritage, 'dark' heritage and heritage crime. She worked as a Postdoctoral Researcher on the Academy of Finland Project 'Lapland's Dark Heritage: Understanding the Cultural Legacy of Northern Finland's WWII German Materialities within Interdisciplinary Perspectives' (decision number 275497) and is now Principle Investigator of Academy of Finland Consortium Project 'SuALT: Collaborative Research Infrastructure for Archaeological Finds and Public Engagement through Linked Open Data' (decision numbers: 310854, 310859 and 310860). She teaches masters-level courses in Cultural Heritage Studies and Museum Studies.

REFERENCES

Ashworth, G. 1994. 'From History to Heritage – From Heritage to Identity', in G. Ashworth and P. Larkham (eds), *Building a New Heritage: Tourism, Culture and Identity in the New Europe*. London: Routledge, pp. 13–30.

Ashworth, G. and B. Graham. 1997. 'Heritage, Identity and Europe', *Tijdschrift voor Economische en Sociale Geografie* 88(4): 381–88.

———. 2005. 'Senses of Place, Senses of Time and Heritage', in G. Ashworth and B. Graham (eds), *Senses of Place: Senses of Time*. Aldershot: Ashgate, pp. 3–14.

Ashworth, G., B. Graham and J. Tunbridge. 2007. *Pluralising Pasts: Heritage, Identity and Place in Multicultural Societies*. London: Pluto Press.

Bendix, R., A. Eggert and A. Peselmann. 2012. 'Introduction: Heritage Regimes and the State', in R. Bendix, A. Eggert and A. Peselmann (eds), *Heritage Regimes and the State*. Göttingen: Universitätsverlag Göttingen, pp. 11–20.

Bortolotto, C. 2012. 'The French Inventory of Intangible Cultural Heritage: Domesticating a Global Paradigm into French Heritage Regime', in R. Bendix, A. Eggert and A. Peselmann (eds), *Heritage Regimes and the State*. Göttingen: Universitätsverlag Göttingen, pp. 265–82.

Brenner, N. 2001. 'The Limits to Scale? Methodological Reflections on Scalar Structuration', *Progress in Human Geography* 25(4): 591–614.

Castells, M. 1996. *The Rise of the Network Society: The Information Age: Economy, Society and Culture Vol. I*. Malden, MA; Oxford: Blackwell.

Dicks, B. 2000. *Heritage, Place and Community*. Cardiff: University of Wales Press.

Glendinning, M. 2013. *The Conservation Movement: A History of Architectural Preservation: Antiquity to Modernity*. London: Routledge.

Graham, B., G. Ashworth and J. Tunbridge. 2000. *A Geography of Heritage: Power, Culture and Economy*. London: Hodder Arnold Publication.

Graham, B. and P. Howard (eds). 2008. *The Ashgate Research Companion to Heritage and Identity*. London: Ashgate.
Harrison, R. 2013. *Heritage: Critical Approaches*. New York: Routledge.
Harvey, D. 2015. 'Heritage and Scale: Settings, Boundaries and Relations', *International Journal of Heritage Studies* 21(6): 577–93.
Herod, A. 1997. 'Labor's Spatial Praxis and the Geography of Contract Bargaining in the US East Coast Longshore Industry, 1953–1989', *Political Geography* 16(2): 145–69.
Jonas, A. 1994. 'The Scale Politics of Spatiality', *Environment and Planning D: Society and Space* 12(3): 257–64.
Jones, T., R. Jones and M. Hughes. 2016. 'Heritage Designation and Scale: A World Heritage Case Study of the Ningaloo Coast', *International Journal of Heritage Studies* 22(3): 242–60.
Kean, H. 2008. 'Personal and Public Histories: Issues in the Presentation of the Past', in B. Graham and P. Howard (eds), *The Ashgate Research Companion to Heritage and Identity*. Aldershot: Ashgate, pp. 55–69.
Kirshenblatt-Gimblett, B. 2004. 'Intangible Heritage as Metacultural Production', *Museum International* 56(1–2): 52–65.
Labadi, S. 2007. 'Representations of the Nation and Cultural Diversity in Discourses on World Heritage', *Journal of Social Archaeology* 7(2): 147–70.
Lähdesmäki, T. 2014. 'Transnational Heritage in the Making: Strategies for Narrating Cultural Heritage as European in the Intergovernmental Initiative of the European Heritage Label', *Ethnologica Europaea* 44(1): 75–93.
Latour, B. 1996. 'On Actor-Network Theory: A Few Clarifications', *Soziale Welt* 47: 369–81.
Leitner, H., C. Pavlik and E. Sheppard. 2002. 'Networks, Governance, and the Politics of Scale: Inter-urban Networks and the European Union', in A. Herod and W. Wright (eds), *Geographies of Power: Placing Scale*. Hoboken, NJ: Wiley-Blackwell, pp. 274–303.
Lefebvre, H. 1991. *The Production of Space*. Oxford: Blackwell.
Liwanag, M. 2016. 'The Case for Ethical Guidelines: Åreventing Conflict in the Selection of World Heritage Sites', in H. Silverman, E. Waterton and S. Watson (eds), *Heritage in Action: Making the Past in the Present*. Cham: Springer, pp. 19–32.
Luke, C. and M. Kersel. 2012. *Cultural Diplomacy and Archaeology: Soft Power, Hard Heritage*. London; New York: Routledge.
Marston, S. 2000. 'The Social Construction of Scale', *Progress in Human Geography* 24(2): 219–42.
Marston, S., J. Jones and K. Woodward. 2005. 'Human Geography without Scale', *Transactions of the Institute of British Geographers* 30(4): 416–32.
Massey, D. 1993. 'Power-geometry and a Progressive Sense of Place', in J. Bird, B. Curtis, T. Putnam, G. Robertson and L. Tickner (eds), *Mapping the Futures: Local Cultures, Global Change*. London: Routledge, pp. 59–69.
———. 2005. *For Space*. London: Sage.
Meskell, L., C. Liuzza, E. Bertacchini and D. Saccone. 2015. 'Multilateralism and UNESCO World Heritage: Decision-making, States Parties and Political Processes', *International Journal of Heritage Studies* 21(5): 423–40.
Munjeri, D. 2004. 'Tangible and Intangible Heritage: From Difference to Convergence', *Museum International* 56(1–2): 12–20.

Salazar, N. and Y. Zhu. 2015. 'Heritage and Tourism', in L. Meskell (ed.), *Global Heritage: A Reader*. New York: John Wiley and Sons, pp. 240–58.

Smith, L. 2006. *Uses of Heritage*. London: Routledge.

———. 2012. '2012 Manifesto', *Association of Critical Heritage Studies*. Retrieved 6 December 2016 from http://www.criticalheritagestudies.org/history/.

Smith, L. and N. Akagawa. 2009. 'Introduction', in L. Smith and N. Akagawa (eds), *Intangible Heritage*. London: Routledge, pp. 1–10.

Smith, N. 1990. *Uneven Development: Nature, Capital, and the Production of Space*. Oxford: Basil Blackwell.

Swyngedouw, E. 1997. 'Neither Global Nor Local: "Glocalization" and the Politics of Scale', in K. Cox (ed.), *Spaces of Globalization: Reasserting the Power of the Local*. New York/London: Guilford/Longman, pp. 137–66.

———. 2000. 'Elite Power, Global Forces and the Political Economy of "Glocal" Development', in G. Clark, M. Gertler and M. Feldman (eds), *The Oxford Handbook of Economic Geography*. Oxford: Oxford University Press, pp. 541–58.

———. 2004. 'Scaled Geographies: Nature, Place, and the Politics of Scale', in E. Sheppard and R.B. McMaster (eds), *Scale and Geographic Inquiry: Nature, Society, and Method*. Malden, MA: Blackwell Publishing, pp. 129–53.

Tunbridge, J.E. and G.J. Ashworth. 1996. *Dissonant Heritage: The Management of the Past as a Resource in Conflict*. New York: John Wiley.

Winter, T. 2014. 'Beyond Eurocentrism? Heritage Conservation and the Politics of Difference', *International Journal of Heritage Studies* 20(2): 123–37.

PART I

SCALED CONCEPTUALIZATION OF HERITAGE

CHAPTER ONE

Politics of Scale
Cultural Heritage in China
Yujie Zhu

Since Graham, Ashworth and Tunbridge (2000) introduced the concept of scale into cultural heritage in their seminal work *A Geography of Heritage*, scale has been widely used in heritage studies. Their critical view of heritage studies has stimulated increasing research on politics of cultural heritage. Scholars illustrate that heritage making is not only embedded in the nation state but has extended to stakeholders at different scales, such as UNESCO and its advisory board (Meskell et al. 2014), the regional heritage government (Cheung 2003) and the local community (Brumann and Berliner 2016; Perkin 2010).

However, most of the studies examine scale as a fixed unit or existing category with certain spatial boundary such as 'the local, regional, national and international'. Such an approach fails to investigate the nature of cultural heritage phenomena as a process of 'scale jumping' and social relations of empowerment and disempowerment (Swyngedouw 1997). Scale should not be treated within certain boundaries but is constituted and reconstituted around relations of capitalist production, social reproduction and consumption (Marston 2000: 221). For instance, despite the power of transnational organizations and their relations with state parties, there is also a growth of regionalism and 'localism' in the cultural heritage industry. Regional organizations have sprung up in South Asia, Africa and the Caribbean and promoted their regional heritage identity against the hegemonic European conception of cultural heritage. The adoption of the 2003 UNESCO Convention for the Safeguarding of the Intangible Cultural Heritage demonstrates another example: several Asian countries were able to jointly exert influence on the World Heritage Committee, impose new ideas of heritage conservation in the texts, and create heritage categories according to their own local practices (Labadi 2013). These phenomena indicate that the power structure of the cultural heritage industry is not fixed; rather, it refers to a process of reconfiguration and contestation among different scales.

This chapter deploys the notion of 'politics of scale' to examine the nature of cultural heritage phenomena as a sociopolitical process of contestation. The concept was initiated by Neil Smith (1990) in *Uneven Development* and later was widely used by radial geographers in a broader range of social activities and struggles, such as capital accumulation, state regulation and social strategies (Herod 1997; Swyngedouw 1997). Neil Brenner (2001: 599) defined this notion as 'the production, reconfiguration or contestation' both within one scale (the singular) and among different scales (the plural). As Brenner defined, the singular form indicates a struggle or contestation in a boundary setting, such as a place, a locality, a region or a nation. The plural form, which he rephrased as a 'process of scaling', does not focus on a production of a unit as such but rather on hierarchization among multiple spatial units through interscalar transformation and mobilization (Brenner 2001).

I believe Brenner's definition and usage of 'politics of scale' (particularly the plural form) effectively captures the dynamic of politics of cultural heritage as sociopolitical processes and transformations. One step further, I use the notions of 'upscaling and downscaling' to illustrate how global cultural values and norms are internalized towards national, community and personal forms of cultural heritage and how local or grass roots actions are externalized and become national and even international actions. Such an approach will facilitate a deeper investigation of politics of cultural heritage through the mobilization of scalar narratives and practices.

This chapter examines in detail the case of China to illustrate how politics of scale contribute to heritage studies as a critical approach. Examining the production, governance, practice and consumption of cultural heritage in China, I will address the following perspectives of scalar effects on cultural heritage: 1) how scale is used by cultural heritage institutions to legitimize their authority and produce hierarchies among scales; 2) how global heritage discourses affect national and local scales through the process of downscaling; and 3) how local struggles emerge to negotiate with heritage authorities through jumping among scales.

This chapter is based on long-term research on Chinese heritage policy and ethnographic study at the Old Town of Lijiang, a World Heritage Site. In the following discussion, I argue that the Chinese administrative system facilitates the reinforcement of the structure of heritage governance. The adoption of the World Heritage System in China establishes the hierarchy among current spatial units based on the administrative levels (local, provincial, national and international). Due to the uneven power relations among different scales, the Chinese government effectively adopts the authorized heritage discourse and implements policies in lower scales without substantive challenges. In other words, the state-led heritage institutionalization has crystalized the system into a scalar fix by creating new hierarchies of cultural heritage.

Through the case study of Lijiang, I further illustrate how heritage officials construct and legitimize their commercial-led heritage discourse, where ethnicity is manufactured and stimulated for tourism promotion and marketing. As the dominant force in designing heritage projects, the state and the commercial agents produce and disseminate the legitimacy of official narratives without considering voices from other participants. Local ethnic communities deploy the idea of World Heritage to increase their bargaining power to negotiate such authorized discourse. However, the scalar political strategies are temporary and embedded in its certain spatial form – a place, a region or a nation. The decision making of cultural heritage polices are thus still based on the existing interrelation among heritage institutions. These contestations cannot reshuffle the hierarchy among different scales or rescale the state spatiality.

Hierarchies in Heritage Governance

Since China joined the 1972 UNESCO Convention Concerning the Protection of the World Cultural and Natural Heritage (World Heritage Convention), nominating World Heritage sites has become a national strategy to construct a national identity that fosters social solidarity, control of ethnicity and economic growth (Zhu 2018b: 22). By designating 'traditional culture' (*chuantong wenhua*) as a national or even a World Heritage, the Chinese government emphasizes the significance of the nation as a distinct group deserving world recognition and respect.

China's cultural heritage is administered by a strong hierarchical and centralized state administration (Blumenfield and Silveman 2013), although heritage agencies have undergone a process of reframing and reorganizing in recent decades. Since the foundation of People's Republic of China (PRC) in 1949, the Ministry of Culture (*wenhuabu*) has taken up the responsibility of creating cultural policies, including managing national museums and archives. The State Bureau of Cultural Relics (*guojia wenwuju*), another state-level department, was established in 1988 (and later changed its name to the State Administration of Cultural Heritage or SACH[1]). As an institution focusing on the conservation of cultural relics, SACH is in charge of tangible cultural heritage. The World Heritage nominations are prepared by the SACH and approved by the World Heritage Committee of UNESCO. Concurrently, the Ministry of Construction (which later changed its name to the Ministry of Housing and Urban-Rural Development) manages natural and mixed heritage sites. All of these departments are directly under the State Council (*guowuyuan*) of PRC. More recently, since China joined the Convention for the Safeguarding of the Intangible Cultural Heritage (ICH Convention) in 2004, the Ministry of Culture established a new department to take charge of intangible cultural heritage in 2008.

To understand heritage governance, we must address the current administrative system in China (see Figure 1.1). The country runs on a Leninist party-state political system: each national level institution has its counterparts on the provincial (*sheng*), municipal/prefecture-city (*shi/dijishi*) and county (*xian*) level. For instance, the counterparts of the Ministry of Culture include the Provincial Department of Culture (*sheng wenhuating*), the Municipal Bureau of Culture (*shi wenhuaju*) and the County Bureau of Culture (*xian wenhuaju*).

After the PRC adopted the World Heritage Convention and the ICH Convention, China quickly learned and applied the inscription system to different administrative levels. For instance, the national list of Intangible Cultural Heritage (ICH) was established and approved by the Ministry of Culture. In addition to the national ICH List, there are also lists of ICH at the provincial, municipal and county level. The ICH Lists of provincial, city and county levels are supervised by the Provincial Department of Culture.

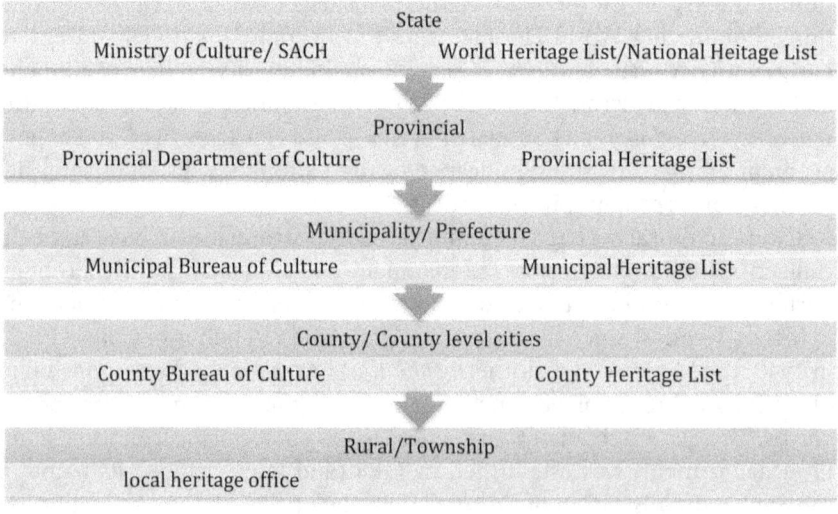

Figure 1.1 Heritage administrative system in China (designed by Yujie Zhu).

At the local level, most heritage sites set up heritage offices to prepare the nomination procedures. Once they have been enlisted as World Heritage Sites, these offices will become the authorized administrative body that manages heritage sites and oversees the conservation and promotion. My studies of such local heritage institutions in Lijiang (Zhu 2016a), Xi'an (Zhu 2018a) and Emei (Zhu and Li 2013) demonstrate that these local heritage institutions integrated administrative functions that were formerly regulated by different heritage-related agencies, such as the local bureaus of cultural heritage, construction and tourism. All the institutions at low levels have a dual reporting system: one is the horizontal – they need to report to the local government on their respective level, as they are part of the administration; and the other is the vertical – they also report to the corresponding body at the level above; for instance, the municipal to the provincial.

Downscaling: The China Principles

Heritage institutions in China have adopted international heritage concepts and applied them to their own system. The current administrative structure established a scalar fix to legitimize the national control over the heritage industry's different heritage sites. In other words, the hierarchical power structure gives agency to state heritage institutions to transfer heritage concepts and values from international through national to lower levels. The top-down approach reinforces the capability of heritage governance to implement heritage practices such as inventorization, the establishment of criteria for inclusion and heritage nominations as well as legal conservation and management.

In 2000, China ICOMOS and The Getty Conservation Institute jointly adapted the international conservation laws (particularly the Burra Charter) to Chinese national policies on the basis of links with Chinese culture and history and published the Principles for the Conservation of Heritage Sites in China, known as the China Principles[2] (Zhu 2016b). Approved by the Chinese State Administration of Cultural Heritage, the China Principles link the international conservation concepts with present legislations and national guidelines of heritage conservation. For instance, the China Principles advocate a minimum of intervention in the conservation process, a concept aligned with the Venice Charter and the Burra Charter (Qian 2007).

The China Principles have become a cultural-political tool to establish heritage discourses through training and implementation (see Figure 1.2). For instance, to be listed as a regional or national heritage or to get funds from central heritage institutions, local heritage institutions have to address how they incorporate the official interpretation of 'authenticity' from the

Figure 1.2 Heritage policies and regulations at different administrative levels (designed by Yujie Zhu).

Principles in local conservation and management. Local authorities also use this concept to legitimate their heritage practices and fulfil their political and economic agenda (Zhu 2015).

The transformation of conservation knowledge into practices is often associated with academic support from research institutions and heritage experts at related levels to legitimize policymaking. For instance, the Chinese Academy of Arts and the Chinese Academy of Cultural Heritage works with the Ministry of Culture and SACH on tangible and intangible cultural heritage. At the provincial level, heritage institutions get support from the provincial Academy of Social Sciences or local universities/colleges. At the local level, in Lijiang, for instance, the Naxi Culture Research institution works closely with the Lijiang World Heritage Conservation and Management Bureau.[3] This government-led, scholar-supported approach justifies the heritage practices of the local authorities to search for maximal political and economic interests.

In addition, national institutions often organize 'trainings sessions', such as conferences, in order to transmit international heritage knowledge and best practices to lower levels. These conferences are often organized by one or two international organizations, such as UNESCO, ICOMOS, IUCN or the World Tourism Organization. Depending on the theme of the conference, heritage institutions at the national level (e.g. SACH, Ministry of Construction or China National Tourism Administration) normally act as the co-organizer. The conferences are also sponsored by related administrative institutions at the provincial level and directly hosted by local heritage offices. The conference programmes exhibit similar structures: they start with an opening ceremony conducted by representatives from the organizers. According to the scalar hierarchy, the opening speeches usually take this order: international representatives then officials from national, provincial and local levels. At the end of the opening ceremony, conference participants are positioned to take a group photo based on the hierarchy of scales and the Chinese administrative ranks: international experts and officials from national and provincial institutions sit in the first row, and other participants from local heritage offices stand behind. The main contents of the conference are presentations in a similar scalar structure: international speakers start first as keynotes, following with presentations by invited Chinese heritage experts from renowned universities and, last, case studies by local officials from different cultural heritage sites. Additional panels or group discussions may take place after these presentations. International heritage experts participate in different panels to lead discussions with the assistance from the Chinese experts. On this occasion, it is often the local officials who ask questions about their practices of heritage conservation and management; and the international experts answer questions by mainly introducing international heritage concepts and experiences like sustainable development and community participation. The scalar hierarchy influences the whole conference, including the order of seats in the official dinner, the way of toasting and name card exchanging, and the overall setting of the conference room.

At the end of these meetings, the host organization, with the assistance of international experts, often adopts a local heritage declaration (such as Beijing Declaration in 2007 or Xi'an Declaration in 2005) to reinforce or echo the China Principles. The exception was the Declaration of Qufu – a 'Consensus on the China-specific Conservation Theory and Practices of Historic Buildings' written in 2005 by a number of conservation practitioners. Instead of complying with the international conventions, the Qufu declaration encourages a localization approach in which 'experiences and concepts need to be analysed, digested, and absorbed according to the actual situation in China' (Qufu Declaration 2005).

Scalar Mobilization: Old Town Lijiang, World Heritage Site

Located in the south west of China, the prefecture level city of Lijiang lies in the north of Yunnan Province. In 1997, Lijiang Old Town (*lijiang gucheng*) became the first ethnic minority area in China to be inscribed as a UNESCO World Heritage Site. As the main ethnic group living in this region, the Naxi people still maintain a number of traditional cultural activities in their daily life. Since the inscription of the town, the local heritage office, the 'Lijiang Old Town Conservation and Management Bureau', has been put in charge of implementing the conservation law and the master plan, facilitating marketing and business development. This new agency in Lijiang has become the exclusive authority on heritage governance (Zhu 2016a).

As in other municipalities, the bureau is to follow the China Principles on heritage conservation and management. As part of their work, the two officials submit reports to the municipal government of Lijiang and the Provincial Department of Culture in Yunnan. As part of Chinese heritage governance procedures, local authorities obtain the authority to develop their own regulation concerning the decentralization of fiscal and administrative power. To be further trained on these Principles, the director of the bureau and the officials of heritage management have actively participated in various training meetings organized by China ICOMOS and the State Administration of Cultural Heritage.

The local bureau develops its own strategy to interpret the China Principles for the sake of economic growth. For instance, the bureau demolished dozens of concrete buildings that were constructed in the 1950s and instead established a variety of low-rise dwellings with strict control of height and façade in order to recapture the aesthetic features of the town during the nineteenth century. In addition, to make the dwellings appear more traditional, the bureau used timber materials and added ethnic decorations to imitate the traditional appearance of Naxi buildings. Finally, the bureau also rebuilt and widened two main streets in the north of the town, paved the original streets with polished marble and decorated the system of canals with greenery and flowers. As a result, many of the larger buildings on these streets were replaced with many smaller houses (Peters 2013; Zhu 2016a).

After Lijiang was nominated as a World Heritage Site, its tourist industry immediately started to attract commercial migrants. While in 1996 1.06 million domestic and 45,930 international tourists visited Lijiang, in 2015 the numbers had risen to 29.414 million Chinese and some 1.155 million international tourists. Since 2000 especially, Lijiang has received a steady increase not only of migration but also of business investment. Traditional family-run businesses are being overrun by tourist shops that industrially produced goods at considerably cheaper prices. The local craftsmen are exposed to commercial competition; they lack protection for maintaining their ability to produce locally made handicrafts. Local grocery stores and restaurants eventually disappeared, unable to compete with the new souvenir shops and fancy restaurants. As a result, heritage tourism has transformed Lijiang from a historic trade town into a tourism marketplace (Su 2012; Zhu 2012).

These processes crowd out local residents, who are in fact supposed to represent their own culture. During my fieldwork in 2006–2012, I continued to hear complaints from local residents that, for instance, the cost of living has increased incredibly over the last decade and that their peaceful life has been replaced by congestion, noise and pollution (Zhu 2016a). Mr Liu, for instance, a local entrepreneur who has witnessed the transformation of the living environment told me that

> Lijiang is becoming a strange place to me – too many tourists come here, and too many outsiders do business here. The cost is rising at a rapid pace, and everything becomes expensive. It's loud and crowded with people from outside. When I walk on the street of the old town, I feel like a stranger. I can only hear Han Chinese on the street, no more Naxi being spoken. None of my old friends live here. This is also the reason why I have bought the new apartment and moved to the New Town. Most of my other Naxi friends did the same. The old town is not our home any more. (Fieldwork interview)

Su (2012) supports this claim by arguing that tourists and businesspeople have taken over places in Lijiang that used to be central to local people's everyday life. His interviewees echo the claims made above and express the feeling of having lost the traditional lifestyle and community cohesion.

Going against this gentrification, several local scholars have voiced concerns in public media and have argued that local residents need to cooperate in order to protect their homeland (*jiayuan*) from increasing commercialization by the heritage industry. In 2003, for instance, an article entitled 'Lijiang, Whose Old City Is It?' (*Lijiang, shuide gucheng?*) was published in the newspaper *Nanfang Zhoumo* (Southern Weekly). In this article, Ying Yi (2003) raised the question of who owns Lijiang as a World Heritage site: the local community, external businesspeople or the government. The article argued that Lijiang has become a playground for Han Chinese, who engage with both cultural production and consumption (Zhu 2018b). Local residents, who are supposed to represent their own culture, are absent in this crowded market.

The State Administration of Cultural Heritage and UNESCO World Heritage Committee noticed this increasing public criticism. In 2007, these national and international heritage institutions expressed their concern that heritage values might be negatively affected by the uncontrolled commercial projects that are increasingly being carried out within the area. For this reason, the World Heritage Committee requested a joint mission by the World Heritage Centre and ICOMOS in order to assist national and local government departments in identifying and assessing the current conservation and management mechanisms. From January 10 to 19 in 2008, a 'reactive monitoring mission' was carried out in Lijiang.[4]

The evaluation was conducted by a team of experts from the World Heritage Centre and another from the advisory bodies, who were accompanied by several Chinese officials from heritage institutions at the national and provincial level. The experts from UNESCO and ICOMOS raised issues and concerns during the mission. As a result, the local authority, anxious not to lose the World Heritage status, responded quickly in order to maintain the label for further promotion and marketing. By learning from various political rules, social norms and cultural values at the international, national and local levels, the local government developed its own long-term development plan for Lijiang, including an updated conservation plan and a new site monitoring office in 2009 (Zhu 2016a).

Upscaling and Downscaling Heritage in China

By adopting the concept of 'politics of scale', this chapter has studied heritage discourses in China through scalar mobilization (see Figure 1.3). In this process, firstly, the existing Chinese administrative system (national-provincial-municipal-county) reinforces the hierarchy among different scales. The Chinese heritage discourse, as the outcome of heritage institutionalization, then contributes to establishing a particular national image

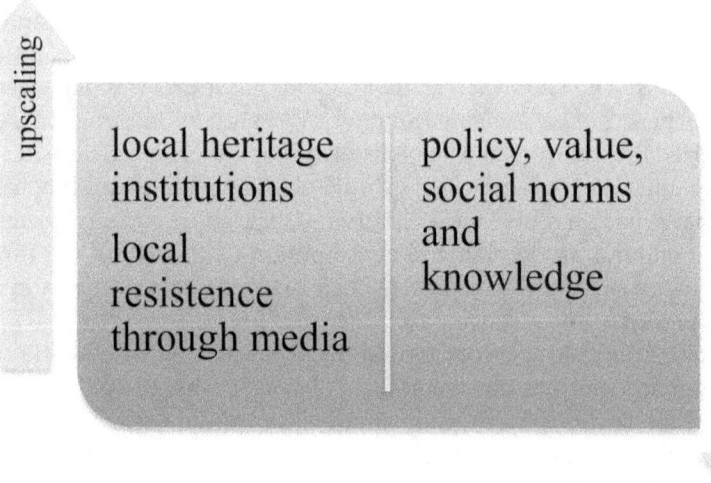

Figure 1.3 Upscaling and downscaling heritage in China (designed by Yujie Zhu).

in the international arena, negotiating cultural and economic exchanges with other countries and strengthening Chinese heritage governance and policy implementation over other scales. Heritage sites need to follow the top-down policies as well as rules and value systems in order to be listed or maintain their heritage status.

Secondly, once a place becomes a World Heritage Site, the local heritage institutions, such as the Heritage Bureau of Lijiang, indeed stand out as 'super agencies' in accumulating funds, redistributing resources and establishing new regulatory institutions to govern the indigenous economic and social activities. I call them 'super agencies' because the title of World Heritage offers them more opportunities to communicate with the national or even the global players. This can be viewed as the result of upscaling occurring during the institutionalization of heritage. However, instead of heritage conservation and protection, the Heritage Bureau deploys the strategy of scale jumping for the purpose of maximizing local economic and social benefits. The economic interests drive local heritage institutions to employ international and national heritage guidelines in local practices.

Thirdly, the case study of Lijiang also illustrated how individuals and social groups could negotiate with local governments in order to defend their interests through upscaling. A variety of groups of people and institutions have different interests in their struggle for the use of heritage. As we have seen in the literature of social movements, people often take advantage of certain political conditions to shift the scale of political contests (e.g. Herod 1997; Smith 1990). For instance, Herod (1997) illustrates how labour unions have negotiated contracts with national, regional and local actors to strengthen their bargaining positions. A similar struggle also happens in relation to gender, homosexuality and abortion.

In Lijiang, the resistance started at the local scale (in the form of daily complaints) and later shifted to the national and international scale (media and UNESCO mission). The use of media in Lijiang shows that this kind of 'scale jumping' can change the power relations between local residents and the authorities. The communication with scholars and social organizations, as well as the use of national media, transformed the local heritage issue into a national/international event. Local resistance was successfully mobilized and upscaled, resulting in an increase of their bargaining power with local authorities (Zhu 2018a).

In addition, local communities often advocate the idea of 'home' as an instrument of power to strengthen their bargaining power in negotiations with the authorities. People like Mr Liu and the author Ying highlighted the significance of 'home' (*jia*) or 'homeland' (*jiayuan*) to legitimize their criticism of the local government. In contrast to the notion of 'locality', a term often claimed or defined by external heritage experts, local people take the term 'home' as a sense of their social belonging. The statement of 'this is my home' from local residents in Lijiang indicates their endeavour to reclaim rights of what heritage should be.

However, as Harrison (2013) argues, it is rare for sites to be listed on the List of World Heritage in Danger, and even rarer to be delisted (this has only happened twice so far). Hence, in the cases like Lijiang, since the current heritage administrative system has been crystalized into a scalar fix, the influence of the international mission is limited. As a consequence, local authorities have the capacity to communicate and bargain with the national and even the international heritage agencies and have more direct power to regulate heritage conservation and management issues.

Conclusion

In this study, I take the interaction between scale and heritage as a new analytical approach to understand heritage as a sociopolitical discourse. The notion of 'politics of scale' sheds light on the process of heritage making in China as a continuous reshuffling and reorganization of spatial scales for empowerment. This analytical approach helps to clarify the role of scale in creating and reinforcing heritage discourses by heritage institutions and policymaking. In this process, the nation state still takes a leading role in the international heritage game. Countries like China borrow and integrate the European-dominant discourse to establish its own authorized heritage system. The scalar structure of cultural institutions facilitates heritage to become a powerful tool of regulation and control.

The top-down approach of policymaking reinforces the uneven development among different scales and fosters the connection between local and global. This process follows the nature of 'politics of scale' that stresses the 'shifting organizational, strategic, discursive, and symbolic relationship between a range of intertwined geographical scales' (Brenner 2001: 600). Despite scaling as a dynamic process of reproduction and reconfiguration, the uneven development among different scales exists to reinforce and impose authorized heritage value on lower scales. The vertical scalar structure works to transfer information, knowledge and capital exchange. Through downscaling, the top-down approach of heritage making still dominates the heritage system despite different forms of resistance and negotiation on the ground.

Following Harvey's (2015) call of *what scale does to heritage*, this chapter also addresses uneven development among different scales of the heritage industry in China. I believe that the analytical tool of 'politics of scale' can be applied as a useful point of departure to understand the political and discursive nature of cultural heritage. Many NGOs have developed various strategies to flatten the hierarchy by inviting local communities to participate in the decision making of heritage management (such as ecomuseum projects and UNESCO stakeholder models in Asia). Being more aware of *what scale does to heritage,* we could potentially create a more democratic communication among different heritage stakeholders in this complex and contested world.

Acknowledgements

This chapter stems from the research project 'Politics of Cultural Heritage in China', which is supported by the Australian National University and Zhejiang University, China. Special thanks to the colleagues from the Australian Centre on China in the World, ANU, for the excellent feedback they provided.

Yujie Zhu is a Lecturer at the School of Archaeology and Anthropology, the Australian National University. He is the author of *Heritage and Romantic Consumption in China* (Amsterdam University Press, 2018) and the co-editor of *Sustainable Tourism Management at World Heritage Sites* (UNWTO 2009). He has also published more than thirty articles that appeared in leading anthropology, tourism, and heritage journals, including *American Anthropologist, Annals of Tourism Research,* and *International Journal of Heritage Studies.* In addition, Yujie is the vice chair of the IUAES Commission on the Anthropology of Tourism and the vice president of the Association of Critical Heritage Studies.

NOTES

1. Since 2018, the State Administration of Cultural Heritage and The State Administration of Tourism have been merged into a new unified institution at the central level.
2. Funded by the Getty Trust, the Getty Conservation Institute works internationally to advance conservation practice through research, education and developing new conservation approaches and strategies. In 2010, China ICOMOS began a revision of the China Principles, which was published in 2015.
3. The Naxi people are the main ethnic group living in Lijiang. They still maintain a number of long-standing cultural activities in their daily life.

4. A 'Reactive monitoring mission' occurs when problems and threats of the site have been brought to the attention of the World Heritage Centre and the report submitted by the states' parties does not dispel the concerns (Brumann 2012).

REFERENCES

Blumenfield, T. and H. Silverman. 2013. *Cultural Heritage Politics in China*. Dordrecht: Springer Science & Business Media.
Brenner, N. 2001. 'The Limits to Scale? Methodological Reflections on Scalar Structuration', *Progress in Human Geography* 25(4): 591–614.
Brumann, C. 2012. 'Multilateral Ethnography: Entering the World Heritage Arena', *Max Planck Institute for Social Anthropology Working Papers* 136.
Brumann, C. and D. Berliner (eds). 2016. *World Heritage on the Ground: Ethnographic Perspectives*. EASA Series 28. New York and Oxford: Berghahn.
Cheung, S.C. 2003. 'Remembering through Space: The Politics of Heritage in Hong Kong', *International Journal of Heritage Studies* 9(1): 7–26.
Graham, B., G.J. Ashworth and J.E. Tunbridge. 2000. *A Geography of Heritage: Power, Culture, and Economy*. Oxford: Oxford University Press.
Harrison, R. 2013. 'Forgetting to Remember, Remembering to Forget: Late Modern Heritage Practices, Sustainability and the 'Crisis' of Accumulation of the Past', *International Journal of Heritage Studies* 19(6): 579–95.
Harvey, D.C. 2015. 'Heritage and Scale: Settings, Boundaries and Relations', *International Journal of Heritage Studies* 21(6): 577–93.
Herod, A. 1997. 'Labor's Spatial Praxis and the Geography of Contract Bargaining in the US East Coast Longshore Industry, 1953–1989', *Political Geography* 16(2): 145–69.
Labadi, S. 2013. *UNESCO, Cultural Heritage, and Outstanding Universal Value: Value-based Analyses of the World Heritage and Intangible Cultural Heritage Conventions*. Plymouth: AltaMira Press.
Leitner, H. 2003. 'The Political Economy of International Labor Migration', in E. Sheppard and T.J. Barnes (eds), *A Companion to Economic Geography*. Chichester: Wiley-Blackwell 450–67.
Leitner, H., C. Pavlik and E. Sheppard. 2002. *Networks, Governance, and the Politics of Scale: Inter-Urban Networks and the European Union*. Oxford: Blackwell Publishers, pp. 274–303.
Marston, S.A. 2000. 'The Social Construction of Scale', *Progress in Human Geography* 24(2): 219–42.
Meskell, L., C. Liuzza, E. Bertacchini and D. Saccone. 2014. 'Multilateralism and UNESCO World Heritage: Decision-making, States Parties and Political Processes', *International Journal of Heritage Studies* 21(5): 1–18.
Perkin, C. 2010. 'Beyond the Rhetoric: Negotiating the Politics and Realising the Potential of Community-Driven Heritage Engagement', *International Journal of Heritage Studies* 16(1–2): 107–22.
Peters, H. 2013. 'Dancing in the Market: Reconfiguring Commerce sand Heritage in Lijiang', in T. Blumenfield and H. Silverman (eds), *Cultural Heritage Politics in China*. New York: Springer, pp. 115–40.

Qian, F. 2007. 'China's Burra Charter: The Formation and Implementation of the China Principles', *International Journal of Heritage Studies* 13(3): 255–64.

Qufu Declaration. 2005. Consensus on the China-specific Conservation Theory and Practices of Historic Buildings. Unpublished manuscript.

Smith, N. 1990. *Uneven Development: Nature, Capital, and the Production of Space.* Oxford: Basil Blackwell.

Smith, L. 2006. *The Uses of Heritage.* London: Routledge.

Su, X. 2012. '"It is My Home. I Will Die Here": Tourism Development and the Politics of Place in Lijiang, China', *Geografiska Annaler: Series B, Human Geography* 94(1): 31–45.

Swyngedouw, E. 1997. 'Neither Global nor Local: "Glocalization" and the Politics of Scale', in K. Cox (ed.), *Spaces of Globalization: Reasserting the Power of the Local.* New York: Guilford Press, pp. 137–66.

Yi, Y. 2003. 'Lijiang, shuide gucheng? [Lijiang, Whose Old City Is It?]', *Southern Weekend,* July. Retrieved 13 September 2012 from http://www.china.com.cn/chinese/feature/368351.htm.

Zhu, Y. 2012. 'Shifting Images: The World Heritage City Lijiang, China', *Heidelberg Papers in South Asian and Comparative Politics* 67: 58–68.

———. 2015. 'Cultural Effects of Authenticity: Contested Heritage Practices in China', *International Journal of Heritage Studies* 21(6): 594–608.

———. 2016a. 'Heritage Making of Lijiang: Governance, Reconstruction and Local Naxi Life', in C. Brumann and D. Berliner (eds), *World Heritage on the Ground, Ethnographic Perspectives.* Oxford: Berghahn, pp. 78–96.

———. 2016b. 'Authenticity and Heritage Conservation in China: Translation, Interpretation and Practices', in K. Weiler (ed.), *Aspects of Authenticity in Architectural Heritage Conservation.* Heidelberg: Springer, pp. 187–200.

———. 2018a. 'Uses of the Past: Negotiating Heritage in Xi'an', *International Journal of Heritage Studies* 24(2): 181–92.

———. 2018b. *Heritage and Romantic Consumption in China.* Amsterdam: Amsterdam University Press.

Zhu, Y. and N. Li. 2013. 'Groping for Stones to Cross the River: Governing Heritage in Emei', in T. Blumenfield and H. Silverman (eds), *Cultural Heritage Politics in China.* New York: Springer, pp. 51–71.

 CHAPTER TWO

The 'European Significance' of Heritage
Politics of Scale in EU Heritage Policy Discourse
Tuuli Lähdesmäki and Katja Mäkinen

Postmillennial Europe has faced various political, economic, social and humanitarian crises that influence how Europeans deal with the past, present and future of Europe. These crises have also shaken the foundations of the European Union (EU) and strengthened criticism of its legitimacy and integration process. Simultaneously, the ideas of European cultural roots, memory, history and heritage have gained a new role in European politics and policies. The EU's increased interest in a common cultural narrative can be perceived as the EU's attempt to tackle some of these recent crises – including identity crises – in Europe. As a response to the rise of new nationalism, right-wing populism and a Eurosceptic and anti-EU atmosphere in Europe, the EU has actively sought to construct and establish a new European narrative based on common values, political ideas, heritage and selected events of the European past upon which Europeans could build their European identity. Memory and heritage have become powerful vehicles for shaping the EU's identity politics (Littoz-Monnet 2012).

The idea of a common European cultural heritage was brought forth already in the 1970s in the official policy discourse of the EU integration. Heritage has also been referred to at the treaty level: the Maastricht Treaty, a founding agreement in the creation of the EU and a deeper European integration, included a treaty article explicitly focused on culture, aimed at 'bringing the common cultural heritage to the fore' (TEU 1992: 24). In the 2000s, the idea of a common cultural heritage was brought out in several EU resolutions, agendas and work plans for culture; it has become a common element repeated in EU cultural policy discourse. Both the European Commission (EC) and the European Parliament (EP) have recently launched several cultural initiatives that explicitly seek to foster and promote a common cultural heritage in Europe and make the idea of it more concrete.

The notion of a common European cultural heritage is extremely problematic. It faces various challenges in Europe, where national narrations of history and cultural memories differ greatly and where global cultural flows and movement of people within and across borders have increased the inner pluralism of the continent. It is impossible to reach any comprehensive definition of a European cultural heritage, as even within a single society, pasts, heritages and identities should be considered as plurals (Delanty 2010). Besides views on the rupture of the grand narrative of nationalism, several heritage scholars have emphasized how nation states still commonly form the fundamental ideological basis, territorialized political sphere, and institutionalized forum of practice for fostering, preserving and meaning making of cultural heritage (see Lähdesmäki, Zhu and Thomas in this volume).

In EU policy discourse, the idea of a common European cultural heritage can be, however, referred to as an unproblematic entity without further discussing the conceptual, ideological and political limitations that the idea entails. References to the idea in the EU's policy documents and official communication material of the EC and the EP form EU-level 'Authorized Heritage Discourse' (AHD) – in Smith's (2006) terms. This discourse is thoroughly political in its attempts to create its objective, a common European cultural heritage, by ignoring the ambiguity and controversy included in the idea and simultaneously retaining its flexibility for various political purposes. Politics of scale has a major role in the formation of the EU-level AHD and the efforts included therein. In EU heritage policy, notions of a European cultural heritage are produced in relation to various scales – local, regional, national and global – either by including these different scales in the European dimension of heritage or by defining it as distinguished from other scales. EU heritage policy discourse includes discussions in which the meanings of heritage are, thus, multilayered or 'multi-scalar'. Such politics of scale can be used in the EU's identity building processes.

This chapter focuses on the politics of scale in the making of a European cultural heritage in EU heritage policy discourse and the implications of the politics of scale for the EU's identity politics. The chapter theorizes the heritage-scale relationship in this discourse by answering the following questions: What kinds of scales are discussed in EU heritage policy discourse? How is the 'European significance' of heritage created in this discourse? What kinds of scalar relationships does this discourse produce? How is scale used as a political tool in it? The chapter seeks to answer these questions by examining the policy documents of the EC's most recent heritage initiative, the European Heritage Label (EHL). Since 2014, the EC has awarded thirty-eight sites with the EHL. In the awarding process, the labelled sites are first preselected by national panels, and the final selection is made by a panel of heritage experts appointed at the EU level.

The data of this study consist of panel reports produced in the final selection process of twenty-nine EHL sites during the first three selecton rounds. For each site, the panel reports have a section titled 'European significance' describing the site's relevance for highlighting the idea of European cultural heritage. These reports enable a critical exploration of what is considered the 'right' type of Europeanness in EU heritage policy discourse and how this is presented and justified. The documents were analysed with qualitative content analysis, utilizing the theoretical framework of linguistic turn and social constructionism in the EU and European Studies that emphasize the use of language, concepts and rhetoric as locations in which meanings are both consciously and unconsciously produced (Checkel 2006; Christiansen, Jorgensen and Wiener 2001; Paasi 2001; Risse 2004; Wiesner et al. 2018; Wiesner, Haapala and Palonen 2017). The chapter, thus, scrutinizes how language produces a European cultural heritage and a heritage-scale relationship in the EHL documents. The chosen method and its linguistic emphasis enables exploration of both explicit and implicit politics and power relations involved in EU heritage policy discourse.

Scales in the Meaning Making of 'European Significance'

Europe and 'European significance' are the explicit scalar focuses of the EU heritage policy discourse. This focus determines the discourse also in the EHL policy documents. According to the decision of the initiative, the EHL shall aim at:

> ... strengthening European citizens' sense of belonging to the Union, ... stressing the symbolic value and raising the profile of sites which have played a significant role in the history and culture of Europe and/or the building of the Union; increasing European citizens' understanding of the history of Europe and the building of the Union, and of their common yet diverse cultural heritage. (EP 2011: 3)

The aims of the EHL focus on the citizens' relationship to the EU. In the policy discourse, the EHL sites assume a function of providing this relationship. To fulfil this function, the sites are expected to have a tight connection to Europe and the EU.

The proposal for the decision of the initiative emphasizes that the main selection criteria for the EHL sites do not include esthetic or architectural values, nor is the point to conserve or preserve the sites (EC 2010a: 2). Instead, the selection criteria underline for example how the sites represent 'their place and role in the development and promotion of the common values that underpin European integration', and in 'European history and European integration, and their links with key European events, personalities or movements' (EP 2011: 4). What is central is the 'European narrative of these sites and their symbolism for Europe' (EC 2010a: 2). No matter how interesting or significant a site is, if it does not succeed in meeting the criteria, such as describing its 'cross-border or pan-European nature' (EP 2011: 4), it cannot be awarded the label. This is underlined also on the EC's website: 'the European Heritage Label focuses on the European narrative and how the sites have contributed to the progress of European history and unity' (EC 2016).

The entire EHL initiative is about scaling cultural heritage into a European framework, and its key aim of highlighting 'European significance' (EP 2011: 3) is extended also and above all to the sites that apply for and eventually are awarded the status of EHL sites (EC 2010a: 2). To understand the politics of scale in the AHD of the EU, it is crucial to explore how the idea of 'European significance' is produced in relation to scale in EU heritage policy discourse.

Common to almost all EHL sites is that their 'European significance' is primarily justified in the panel reports with arguments about the plurality of territorial entities or population groups involved in the site's history. For example, Hambach Castle (Germany) is described as commemorating the Hambach Festival, with participants from Germany, France and Poland advocating for unity in both Germany and Europe. The panel report conceptualizes its 'European significance' through references to the calls for a unified Europe by different national groups and to the cross-border action and context of the site. Indeed, border crossings and cross-border contexts are commonly referred to in the descriptions of the labelled sites. Similarly, Museo Casa Alcide De Gasperi (Italy) has, according to the panel report, a 'transboundary history and location between the Italian and German cultures' (EC 2014: 18). The Historic Gdańsk Shipyard (Poland) is presented as the birthplace of political transformation, first in one country and later in several countries in Central and Eastern Europe. The Pan-European Picnic Memorial Park (Hungary) as a venue of processes that led to the collapse of the Iron Curtain in Europe is presented in the report as a symbol of the end of the Cold War and of a 'borderless Europe' (EC 2014: 20).

Although cultural heritage and its 'European significance' are mostly attached to the plurality of territories – entities that have explicit administrative boundaries that emerge and exist in various social practices, such as culture, governance, politics and economy (Paasi 2009: 467) – the plurality discussed in the panel reports is not only territorial. For example, World War I Eastern Front Cemetery No. 123 (Poland) is described as a cemetery for soldiers from 'different linguistic and religious backgrounds . . . where all soldiers, winners or defeated, were treated with equal respect regardless of the nationality, religion, or military affiliation' (EC 2015: 13). The description of The Imperial Palace (Austria) states that '[t]he Habsburg Empire included a wide range of ethnicities and religions' (EC 2015: 9). As these examples indicate, the reports also refer to linguistic, religious and ethnic plurality, which does not necessarily organize itself along territories.

The panel reports link the 'European significance' of some EHL sites to unions between states, and some of these unions are presented as early models for European integration. For example, Archaeological Park Carnuntum (Austria) is framed as part of the Roman Empire, which is called a 'predecessor of Europe', combining 'different cultures, religions, and geographic areas under one administrative system' (EC 2013: 7). Here Europe seems to be a synonym for the EU. This kind of equating belongs to the political agenda of the EU heritage policy discourse: the rhetoric seeks to naturalize the connection between Europe and the EU as a polity by paralleling them. In the description of the Great Guild Hall (Estonia), the interaction between two economic unions – the Great Guild and the Hanseatic League – is seen as a predecessor of European integration. The Olomouc Premyslid Castle and Archdiocesan Museum (Czech Republic) is introduced as part of Carolingian Europe, and The Imperial Palace as the centre of the Habsburg Empire. National and transnational scales are dominant in these unions and empires, which consist of several states or state-like entities. These sites make it explicit that state unions have existed in the history of Europe, thus making the EU seem a 'natural result' of history. Three sites – Robert Schuman's House (France), Museo Casa Alcide De Gasperi and The European District of Strasbourg (France) – deal directly with the history of EU integration, a transnational process that has been predominantly about cooperation between states, with national-scale actors as key players.

In the case of several sites, such as the Archive of the Crown of Aragon (Spain), The Neanderthal Prehistoric Site and Krapina Museum (Croatia), Archaeological Park Carnuntum, Mundaneum (Belgium), and The Heart of Ancient Athens (Greece), 'European significance' is described through their place in intellectual history. In them, 'European significance' is constructed through non-territorial international exchange that does not locate itself in scales but rather thematically around different spheres of intellectual life. Intellectual history and exchange are also referred to in the descriptions of scholarly sites such as the General Library of the University of Coimbra (Portugal) and Residencia de Estudiantes (Spain). The Historic Ensemble of the University of Tartu (Estonia) is said to have been a 'part of a pan-European network of scientists and participated in cultural exchanges' (EC 2015: 10). Franz Liszt Academy of Music (Hungary) is described as a centre of an international music community, developing 'a living European cultural tradition' (EC 2015: 11).

Although values as such are non-territorial, they can be easily attached to territorial entities and used in producing and imagining territorial communities, such as Europe and Europeans. Indeed, one way to conceptualize the 'European significance' of the EHL sites is to emphasize values that are frequently repeated in EU policy discourse. According to the panel report, Hambach Castle focuses on the Hambach Festival in which liberty, equality, tolerance and democracy were called for. The description of The Historic Gdańsk Shipyard highlights the role of the Solidarity movement 'in the development of freedom, justice, democracy and human rights' (EC 2014: 19). Democracy is brought to the fore in the descriptions of several sites and linked to the emergence of the EU, such as with Museo Casa Alcide De Gasperi and The European District of Strasbourg. Similarly, peace is a recurrent value. For example, Mundaneum is described as both a peace project and an archive that promotes peace through culture and knowledge sharing, and Peace Palace (The Netherlands) is described as having gained its 'European significance' by being the venue of the First World Peace Conference in 1899 and later peace conventions and international institutions. A discussion of values is a way to attach a site to the European scale, as these values are often said to underpin the European integration project. In the decision on the EHL initiative itself, democratic values and human rights are explicitly linked to European integration (EP 2011: 2). However, the emphasis on values in the panel reports is also a means to bring to the fore a micro-scale of heritage; European values are explained as being manifested in the actions of various important European figures. For example, The Heart of Ancient Athens is presented in the report as a venue of the birth and upbringing of persons 'whose intellectual achievements made an indelible mark on the definition of European common values' (EC 2014: 5). Hence, values are used in EHL policy discourse to connect spatial micro- and macro-scales of heritage.

The panel reports describe and contextualize several EHL sites through the processes of establishing or transforming political systems or political institutions and principles. Political systems and institutions produce and are based on their polity that entail defined political borders. These political borders commonly align with territorial borders, such as borders of states or municipalities. The emphasis on political systems, institutions or principles in EU heritage policy discourse can be interpreted as an attempt to create new territorial constructions or rearrange territorial borders, but also as an attempt to affix abstract political ideas to Europe (within or crossing existing borders) in order to present Europe as a cradle of these positive innovations. For example, Sites of the Peace of Westphalia (Germany) concentrates on the Peace of Westphalia (1648), in which 'peace was agreed through diplomatic negations, not force' (EC 2014: 9). As a result of the peace treaties new principles of a political system and international law were adopted, such as sovereign rights for peripheral states. Union of Lublin (Poland) is described as establishing a new political system between the Kingdom of Poland and the Grand Duchy of Lithuania with democratic principles and practices. The 3 May 1791 Constitution (Poland) is highlighted as 'the first constitution democratically adopted in Europe' (EC 2014: 11) with the adoption of division of powers. Hambach Castle is called the 'symbol of the pursuit of democracy in a cross-border context' (EC 2014: 12). The historic Gdańsk Shipyard and Pan-European Picnic Memorial Park tell about moves away from a socialist regime. In the panel report, the Archive of the Crown of Aragon 'possesses one of the oldest testimonies of the creation process of a European state and rule of law including its parliamentary system' (EC 2014: 7). According to the description of The Imperial Palace, the entities included in the Habsburg Empire 'developed an evolved status of citizenship including religious freedom and access to education' (EC 2015: 9). The description of the transformation of political systems and political principles in the reports mainly focuses on the national scale history but also includes a strong transnational emphasis, since the transformation processes entail various kinds of cross-border contexts and focus on different kinds of historical state unions and empires.

The analysis of the panel reports indicates how 'European significance' is constructed by connecting different scalar dimensions. Both the idea of distinct global, national, regional and local scales and their interwoven combinations are used to argue the 'European significance' of several EHL sites. For example, The Neanderthal Prehistoric Site and Krapina Museum is located on the global scale in the panel report by highlighting how the site brings to the fore human development and the genesis of humankind. The global scale also characterizes The Sagres Promontory (Portugal), which is introduced through the history of discoveries. Its scale expands out of Europe; the site is explained to show how European civilization has contributed to 'the global projection that came to define the modern world' (EC 2015: 8). At some of the sites, global or universal phenomena, such as the promotion of peace and human rights in Mundaneum and Peace Palace, are explicitly framed as European projects. Also, several sites, such as The Historic Gdańsk Shipyard and Charter of Law of Abolition of the Death Penalty (Portugal), which have particular national importance, are narrated as European. Numerous references to the sites' cross-border contexts, such as in Hambach Castle and Pan-European Picnic Memorial Park, bring to the fore the regional scale on which the crucial events and action at these sites have taken place. However, the regional scale of these sites focuses on transnational rather than subnational regions, which implies that the political agenda of the EU heritage policy is to produce 'the European' through 'the transnational'. The transnational cross-border regions simultaneously highlight the national scale, as the regions in question are situated on state borders. Residencia de Estudiantes, The Historic Ensemble of the University of Tartu, Great Guild Hall, and Kaunas of 1919–1940 (Lithuania) are examples of sites that focus on a local scale but are presented as a European cultural heritage by emphasizing their international relationships rather than their local meanings. For instance, Kaunas of 1919–1940 is described in the panel report as a 'gateway to contemporary dynamic currents of interwar Europe ... reflecting European interwar modernism' (EC 2014: 15). Here, local and European scales are intertwined: architecture in the city of Kaunas is local, but in the panel report the focus is on the international architectural connections of the city. Obviously, the sites themselves are above all local; a European cultural heritage is pinpointed to very specific local places, thus bringing together a European and a local micro-scale of cultural heritage.

According to the EHL criteria, sites can focus on 'key European ... personalities' (EP 2011: 4), which brings in a personal scale. These criteria are used in justifying the 'European significance' of several sites in the panel reports. For example, the 'European significance' of The Heart of Ancient Athens is emphasized by listing various influential historical personalities known from the city. Also the EHL home museums focus on a personal scale. In addition, a private, intimate or personal scale is evident at sites comprising a hospital, cemetery or student residence. However, the themes tackled in the descriptions of the 'European significance' of these sites mainly concern their official and institutional history.

A crucial scalar dimension inherent in cultural heritage is time. Cultural heritage is always temporally multilayered. Different temporal layers increase the ambiguous nature and complexity of heritage sites and enable the formation of various kinds of interpretations of their meanings. Although the EHL sites include various temporal layers, these layers nevertheless lose their temporal distance from each other and to the present day in EU heritage policy discourse. Various historical processes and phenomena that took place in the past are commonly interpreted in the panel reports as anticipating similar processes and phenomena that occur in the present EU. Particularly historical and present day transnational cooperation, democratic political processes, political integration and societal and political values and principles are paralleled. The past and the present intertwine: in this process the history of the EU (as a process of international cooperation and as a political value community) seems to reach far into the past.

The panel report analysis brought to the fore the relationality of scale and dynamic scalar relations in EU heritage policy discourse. The relevance of different scales varies in the discourse: sometimes, for example, 'the global' is emphasized, while sometimes 'the local' receives more attention. Since the EHL initiative concentrates on 'European significance', different scales are narrated in the discourse as European. At some EHL sites 'European significance' is attached to territorial relations, while at others it is formulated with non-territorial factors, such as values, political principles or intellectual activity and exchange in scientific communities. The intertwining and networking of scales becomes particularly visible when 'European significance' is narrated by describing transnational cooperation and territorial or other kinds of plurality included in the site's history. This is a way to make familiar cross-border cooperation across different times to simultaneously pave the way for present EU integration.

As the 'European significance' of heritage is described in this way in the AHD of the EU, what kinds of representations of Europe are thereby produced in them? In the panel reports, Europe is about values, knowledge and science, and inventing and developing political systems and political principles. Europe is thus presented as an innovative place of influential ideas and positive trajectories. In addition, the panel reports present Europe as a battlefield; some sites are framed as places of peace but also war is commonly referenced. 'European significance' means unions between states at different moments in history, transnational cooperation or, more generally, something to do with the plurality of territorial or non-territorial elements. Among the twenty-nine EHL sites, only three are directly about European integration, but the 'roots' of EU integration are pointed out at many more. The reports' emphasis on transnational encounters builds the history of Europe and the EU as a unified continuum; it creates a teleological narrative of the history of Europe and of the EU as a natural outcome of it.

Politics of Scale in EU Heritage Policy Discourse

The purpose of the EHL initiative is to produce and foster a heritage whose significance and meaning exceeds the national scale and emphasizes the European one. This emphasis indicates how politics of scale is being used in constructing a European identity through a cultural heritage. In scholarly discussion, the idea of Europe, a European identity and European integration have been theorized with various models (e.g. Delanty 2002; Eder 2009; Mayer and Palmowski 2004; Sassatelli 2015). Eder (2009) has modelled the idea of a European identity through three 'stories' that construct the idea in different ways. The post-national story merges national stories into shared stories that rely on the idea of a shared European past and common cultural features; the supranational story stems from the emergence of a distinct story that is decoupled from national stories and instead emphasizes various European-level civic, economic and political mechanisms, such as European citizenship; and the transnational story focuses on the hybridity of Europe and the diversity of its people and cultures (Eder 2009; see also Sassatelli 2015).

The construction of a European cultural heritage in EU heritage policy discourse utilizes aspects of all three of these heuristic and to some extent overlapping models. In the discourse, the idea of a common European cultural heritage transcends the national scale and thus takes a post-national antithetic stand on the traditional national narration of heritage. The EU heritage policy and initiatives themselves represent supranational mechanisms that seek to regulate and govern national-, regional- and local-level heritage actors in the making of a European cultural heritage (Lähdesmäki 2014a, 2014b).

The transnational model of a European cultural heritage emphasizes diversity as its key characteristic. In practice, the construction of the idea of a common European cultural heritage occurs in the EU heritage policy by recognizing the hybridity and diversity of heritage in Europe but, however, by narrating diversity as a starting point for the perception of unity of the European cultural heritage. As a part of this transnational model, the EU is actively attempting to promote transnational cooperation that enhances contacts and activity between EU heritage actors.

The idea of diversity in EU heritage policy discourse is, however, often narrowly defined as national and regional diversity in Europe. Thus, the idea of diversity commonly has a territorial shape in the discourse. The EHL panel reports also bring out a somewhat varied picture of diversity by referring, for example, to multi-ethnicity, multireligiousness and multilingualism. The transnational model of heritage is closely connected to the post-national model in EU heritage policy discourse; the discourse repeatedly brings out expressions related to these two aspects in the same sentence. For example, the decision on the EHL initiative quotes the Treaty on the Functioning of the EU and explains how it 'confers on the Union the task, inter alia, of contributing to the flowering of the cultures of the Member States, while respecting their national and regional diversity and at the same time bringing the common cultural heritage to the fore' (EP 2011: 1). The ideas of diversity and unity are an inter-productive entity in EU heritage policy discourse. Fostering diversity is expected to make cultures more familiar to people; create dialogue between people and cultures; enable perception of common elements among different cultures; and finally produce a sense of communality and a feeling of belonging based on the perceived common cultural elements (Lähdesmäki 2012).

The three stories defined by Eder (2009) explain the idea of Europe by taking a different approach to nation and 'the national'. Nations, nation states and their territorial borders form a starting point in the construction of the idea of Europe and various communal phenomena defined as European, such as European cultural heritage. In this construction, national-scale processes, practices and policies are either objected or adapted to the European level. In fact, the whole practice of building a European communality, the feeling of belonging and identity by fostering a common heritage is borrowed from the nineteenth-century nation-building processes (see Lähdesmäki 2014a; Peckham 2003; Risse 2003).

The politics of scale in EU heritage policy discourse is closely related to the EU's identity politics. Since the EHL initiative's core aim is 'strengthening European citizens' sense of belonging to the Union' (EP 2011: 3), the ideas, values and topics brought forth in the policy rhetoric can be perceived as core elements of the EU's collective identity building. They also function as building blocks that the EU offers its citizens to use in their private identification processes. The EHL applicants must present in their application a clear project of how to communicate their 'European significance' to audiences. In the initiative, the national, regional or local identity building potential of heritage is expected to be extended or even replaced by a European identity project. In the preparation phase of the EHL, national interpretations of heritage were considered a problem to be tackled through the EHL's emphasis on European reinterpretations of heritage meanings. As the EC's Impact Assessment (EC 2010b: 15) of the EHL argues:

> This leads us to a second level of the problem which is that the reading or interpretation of cultural heritage in Europe, including of the most symbolic sites of our shared heritage, is still to a very large extent a national reading. The European dimension of our common heritage is insufficiently highlighted and its potential to stimulate intercultural dialogue is insufficiently exploited.

Conclusions: EU Heritage Policy as Tool for Promoting a European Identity

The analysis brought out how the heritage-scale relationship is extremely complex and relational: different scalar layers merge and criss-cross in the meaning making of a European cultural heritage. This meaning-making process does not follow any simple spatial hierarchy of territories or a nested scalar system but brings forth politics of scale as a dynamic process.

The idea of a European cultural heritage is constructed in EU heritage policy discourse through various territorial and non-territorial elements whose significance in the construction process is situational and thus variable. After the 'European', the most common scalar focus repeated in the policy discourse of the EHL is the national territory discussed in reference to a nation, nation state, state, EU member state or country. Their plurality, interaction and amalgamation produce the core of a European dimension of cultural heritage. When the discourse refers to diversity, regions and their specificities are also included in the construction process. A European cultural heritage is also signified in the discourse through a spatial micro-scale – specific sites are interpreted and explained to represent a European cultural heritage. Occasionally, the heritage is also explained as gaining its 'European significance' by transcending the borders of Europe; heritage proves its 'European significance' by having a global or universal importance or recognition.

In EU heritage policy discourse, a European cultural heritage is typically constructed from various non-territorial ideas, political principles, values and phenomena that are, however, commonly affixed to territorial entities, particularly to states and countries. These ideas and phenomena are explained to be European if several territorial entities are involved in them. However, some of these phenomena, such as European intellectual history, scholarly achievements and scientific views are introduced as European without stressing any particular territorial affiliations.

Besides spatial scales, EU heritage policy discourse is also formed in a relationship to time. The discourse introduces a European cultural heritage through various historical periods and events that are nevertheless commonly interpreted from the point of view of present day EU politics and political processes. Thus, the core temporal focus of the EHL policy documents is on the present day or even the future. The discourse repeatedly emphasizes the importance of engaging young people in fostering a European cultural heritage. This emphasis indicates one of the main political goals of the EU's heritage policy: educating a new generation of Europeans who will share a common European cultural identity.

Acknowledgements

This work was supported by the European Research Council (ERC) under the EU's Horizon 2020 research and innovation program under Grant 636177 (EUROHERIT).

Tuuli Lähdesmäki (PhD, DSocSc) is an Academy Research Fellow and Adjunct Professor at the Department of Music, Art and Culture Studies, University of Jyväskylä (JYU), Finland. Lähdesmäki specializes in heritage, culture and identity politics, particularly in the European context. She currently leads the research projects 'European Cultural Heritage in the Making: Politics, Affects and Agency' (EUCHE), funded by the Academy of Finland, and 'Legitimation of European Cultural Heritage and the Dynamics of Identity Politics in the EU' (EUROHERIT), funded by the European Research Council. She is the Co-PI in JYU's research profiling area 'Crises Redefined: Historical Continuity and Societal Change' (CRISES).

Katja Mäkinen (DSocSc) is a Postdoctoral Researcher at the Department of Music, Art and Culture Studies, University of Jyväskylä, Finland. Interested in the uses and meanings of concepts, she is currently investigating the EU's cultural heritage policy and citizens' participation in temporal-spatial meaning making of cultural heritage as a member of the research project 'Legitimation of European Cultural Heritage and the Dynamics of Identity Politics in the EU' (EUROHERIT), funded by the European Research Council. She is an editor of *Shaping Citizenship: A Political Concept in Theory, Debate and Practice* (Routledge, 2018).

REFERENCES

Checkel, J.T. 2006. 'Constructivist Approaches to European Integration', in K.E. Jorgensen, M. Pollack and B.J. Rosamond (eds), *Handbook of European Union Politics*. London: Sage, pp. 57–66.

Christiansen, T., K.E. Jorgensen and A. Wiener (eds). 2001. *The Social Construction of Europe*. London: Sage.

Delanty, G. 2002. 'Models of European Identity: Reconciling Universalism and Particularism', *Perspectives on European Politics and Society* 3(3): 345–59.

———. 2010. 'The European Heritage from a Critical Cosmopolitan Perspective', *LSE 'Europe in Question' Discussion Paper Series* 19: 1–20.

EC. 2010a. Proposal for a Decision of the European Parliament and of the Council Establishing a European Union Action for the European Heritage Label. COM(2010) 76 final, 2010/0044 (COD). Brussels: European Commission.

———. 2010b. Impact Assessment: Commission Staff Working Document SEC(2010) 197, March 9, 2010. Brussels: European Commission.

———. 2013. European Heritage Label. 2013 Panel report. Brussels: European Commission.

———. 2014. European Heritage Label. 2014 Panel report. Brussels: European Commission.

———. 2015. European Heritage Label. 2015 Panel report. Brussels: European Commission.

———. 2016. European Heritage Label. Frequently Asked Questions. Official Web Site of the European Commission. Retrieved 4 May 2016 from http://ec.europa.eu/programmes/creative-europe/actions/heritage-label/faq/index_en.htm.

Eder, K. 2009. 'A Theory of Collective Identity: Making Sense of the Debate on a "European Identity"', *European Journal of Social Theory* 12(4): 427–47.

EP. 2011. Decision no 1194/2011/EU of the European Parliament and of the Council of 16 November 2011 Establishing a European Union Action for the European Heritage Label. *Official Journal of the European Union* L 303: 1–9.

Lähdesmäki, T. 2012. 'Rhetoric of Unity and Cultural Diversity in the Making of European Cultural Identity', *International Journal of Cultural Policy* 18(1): 59–75.

———. 2014a. 'Transnational Heritage in the Making: Strategies for Narrating Cultural Heritage as European in the Intergovernmental Initiative of the European Heritage Label', *Ethnologia Europaea* 44(1): 75–93.

———. 2014b. 'The EU´s Explicit and Implicit Heritage Politics', *European Societies* 16(3): 401–21.

Littoz-Monnet, A. 2012. 'The EU Politics of Remembrance: Can Europeans Remember Together?' *West European Politics* 35(5): 1182–202.

Mayer, F.C. and J. Palmowski. 2004. 'European Identities and the EU – The Ties That Bind the People of Europe', *Journal of Common Market Studies* 42(3): 573–98.

Paasi, A. 2001. 'Europe as a Social Process and Discourse', *European Urban and Regional Studies* 8(1): 7–28.

———. 2009. 'Regions and Regional Dynamics', in C. Rumford (ed.), *The Sage Handbook of European Studies*. London: Sage, pp. 464–84.

Peckham, R.S. 2003. 'The Politics of Heritage and Public Culture', in R.S. Peckham (ed.), *Rethinking Heritage: Cultures and Politics in Europe*. London: I.B. Tauris, pp. 1–13.

Risse, T. 2003. 'European Identity and the Heritage of National Culture', in R.S. Peckham (ed.), *Rethinking Heritage: Cultures and Politics in Europe*. London: I.B. Tauris, pp. 74–89.

———. 2004. 'Social Constructivism and European Integration', in T. Diez and A. Wiener (eds), *European Integration Theory*. Oxford: Oxford University Press, pp. 159–76.

Sassatelli, M. 2015. 'Narratives of European Identity', in I. Bondebjerg, E. Novrup Redvall and A. Higson (eds), *European Cinema and Television: Cultural Policy and Everyday Life*. Basingstoke: Palgrave MacMillan, pp. 25–42.

Smith, L. 2006. *Uses of Heritage*. London: Routledge.

TEU. 1992. Treaty on European Union (92/C191/01). *Official Journal of the European Communities* NoC 191: 1–112.

Wiesner, C., A. Björk, H-M. Kivistö and K. Mäkinen. 2018. 'Introduction: Shaping Citizenship as a Political Concept', in C. Wiesner, A. Björk, H-M. Kivistö and K. Mäkinen (eds), *Shaping Citizenship: A Political Concept in Theory, Debate and Practice*. New York and London: Routledge, pp. 1–16.

Wiesner, C., T. Haapala and K. Palonen. 2017. *Debates, Rhetoric, and Political Action*. Basingstoke: Palgrave Macmillan.

 CHAPTER THREE

The Dynamics of Scale in Digital Heritage Cultures

Rhiannon Bettivia and Elizabeth Stainforth

In recent decades digital technologies have provided new methods for fostering engagement between cultural heritage organizations and their audiences. At the most basic level, this might involve accessing digitized heritage collections online. Increasingly, there is also an emphasis on reusing and remixing digital heritage content, which signals a shift in the positioning of audiences from cultural consumers to cultural producers (Beer and Burrows 2013). These examples demonstrate how the technical structuring and communication of heritage collections can shape changes in contemporary heritage management and in practices such as collection, preservation, presentation and interpretation.

In this chapter, we investigate the scalar politics of networked digital heritage through examination of the large-scale heritage aggregators Europeana and the Digital Public Library of America (DPLA). Here, the term aggregator refers to an organization that collects, formats and manages digital data from multiple providers and offers federated access to that data via services like online portals (Europeana 2016). Digital aggregators, because of their nebulous geographic location, complicate heritage debates around local, national and transnational scales, especially those that assume the recuperative potential of heritage projects rests in specific localities (Arantes 2007; Coombe and Weiss 2015). Such geographical scaling is troubled by the distributed structures of digital aggregators, which are not spatially bounded in the same way. Europeana and the DPLA provide an opening for further discussion of these issues. The former is comprised of a database and website that offers access to digitized items from over 2,500 of Europe's museums, libraries and archives. The latter, more recent, project is based around a similar model but operates at a national rather than a supranational scale and promotes public access through forging relationships across a range of American libraries and smaller public organizations. It is funded by a combination of US government grant agencies and private research foundations (Darnton 2013). We begin by outlining our approach to scale, informed by the work of Michel Foucault and Tony Bennett, and then go on to assess the technical elements of Europeana and the DPLA in more detail with reference to the policy and strategic planning documents of both projects. We analyse these in relation to the universal ideas they express, namely Europe and the public. We conclude with some reflections on scale and the implications of heritage aggregators for digital heritage cultures.

Scale and Governmentality

In line with the aims of this volume, our examination of digital heritage aggregators will highlight the political dimensions of scale and the interconnectedness of scalar entities through recourse to Foucauldian scholarship on power/knowledge formations. Much of Foucault's later writing on governmental rationality, or governmentality, explored these formations. In a 1982 lecture series, he explained, 'the contact between technologies of domination of others and those of the self I call governmentality' (Foucault 1988 [1982]: 19). Colin Gordon elaborates on this description, explaining practices of government as follows:

> Government as an activity could concern the relation between self and self, private interpersonal relations within social institutions and communities and, finally, relations concerned with the exercise of political sovereignty. Foucault was crucially interested in the interconnections between these different forms and meanings of government. (Gordon 1991: 2–3)

Foucault's work has been influential across a number of disciplines and now comprises a field of inquiry in its own right, loosely labelled governmentality studies. In the realm of cultural studies, too, his approach has been taken up by scholars researching policy and administration. Foremost among these is Bennett, an Australian scholar, whose work on the relations between knowledge practices and governmentality has made a significant contribution to cultural heritage debates, particularly regarding the institution of the museum. Bennett (1990) observes how historical sciences such as anthropology guided museological techniques in the nineteenth century as part of the development of modern modes of liberal government, and stresses the disparity between the museum's democratic rhetoric and the rationality of public instruction constituted in its functioning. In broader terms, his work is directed towards understanding the concept and logic of culture, based on Foucault's methodological principles. In his 2013 publication, *Making Culture, Changing Society*, Bennett distinguishes the emergence of culture as a 'complex':

> The culture complex . . . is, the public ordering of the relations between particular kinds of knowledges, texts, objects, techniques, technologies and humans arising from the deployment of the modern cultural disciplines (literature, aesthetics, art history, folk studies, drama, heritage studies, cultural and media studies) in a connected set of the apparatuses (museums, libraries, cinema, broadcasting, heritage sites, etc.) . . . This complex consists in its organisation of specific forms of action whose exercise and development has been connected to those ways of intervening in the conduct of conduct that Foucault calls governmental. (Bennett 2013: 14)

Bennett's approach is instructive; in applying governmentality to the analysis of culture, he provides a means of investigating the ways in which specific forms of knowledge and expertise give rise to mechanisms, techniques and technologies for the practice of government. This focus is important insofar as our discussion focuses on the practices underpinning notions of 'Europeanness' and 'publicness' in the case studies. Moreover, Bennett's utilization of governmentality supports analysis across the multiple relational sites and contexts of heritage aggregators. Our inquiry into these aggregators is concerned with both their technological features and the multiplicity of their scalar manifestations, which the governmentality perspective addresses.

Also important is Foucault's (1979) identification of practices of government that function via the mutually reinforcing relation of 'all and each'. The presupposition of relative autonomy underpins governmental practice and is at once individualizing and totalizing, operating at both micro and macro levels.[1] Recognition of this mutually reinforcing relation acts as a useful corrective to scholarly critiques of state-sanctioned heritage regimes, which are often situated in opposition to local traditions or personal experiences. As David C. Harvey (2015: 589) cautions, 'it is crucial that we should understand the spatialised geometries of power rather than be blinded by any warming glow of localness'. An analytics of government (Dean 1999) in the vein of the approach we have described positions practices of state and institutional control within a wider framework of practices of self-regulation and differentiation. Furthermore, the move of all and each speaks to our specific concerns about the scalar logic of digital heritage aggregators, which are premised on the empowerment of the user through the centralization of resources in a widely accessible format. This relationship will be explored in more detail below.

Europeana and the DPLA

The emergence of large-scale heritage aggregators such as Europeana and the DPLA has, on one level, been facilitated by the networked structure of the Internet and signals a move towards the standardization of digitized material from across different cultural heritage collections (e.g. those of museums, libraries and archives). The technical metaphors aligned with this model of organization have been traced in a number of ways by media theorists, perhaps most famously by Lev Manovich in the designation of the database as a cultural form; he suggests that the database, through the various non-sequential operations it can perform, offers new ways of structuring knowledge beyond traditional narrative forms (Manovich 1999). Geoffrey C. Bowker proposes a qualification to Manovich's theory, indicating that computerized databases are the outgrowth of a longer movement towards standardization and universal classification, which began in the nineteenth century. He writes that contemporary practices are characterized by the 'greatly increased centrality of the past for the operation of the state . . . and greatly increased technical facilities for such reworking (of the past) with the development of database technology' (Bowker 2005: 32). Europeana and the DPLA both utilize database technology. However, they express an ambiguity of purpose on the subject of centralized resources. In its latest strategic plan, Europeana defines itself as a platform, 'a place not only to visit but also to build on, play in and create with' (Europeana 2014: 10), while the DPLA has, from the beginning, stressed the need to incorporate a blend of centralized and distributed models of access (DPLA 2011: 2). Furthermore, neither project stores digital content, instead aggregating digital object metadata and pointing to the institutional sites where these objects are held (Darnton 2011).

Background

Before discussing how Europeana and the DPLA function and the ideas they embody, it is first important to clarify the distinct set of social and geopolitical circumstances out of which these projects developed. The original impetus for the Europeana initiative was to safeguard Europe's cultural heritage after the announcement of the Google Books Project in 2005 (Purday 2009). There were worries that Google would end up digitizing and privatizing a large volume of European print works, and so the proposal was made for an equivalent programme – a 'European digital library' – that was open access, with non-exclusive rights (European Commission 2005). Funded by the European Commission (EC), the prototype database was launched in November 2008. The database provided access to digitized content (initially around

4.2 million items) from across European museums, libraries and archives via the website www.europeana.eu (see Marton 2011). Since then, it has continued to accumulate content, and 30 million items were available through the online portal by 2015 (DPLA 2015a). The scale of the target matches the project's ambition to be a comprehensive and representative source for Europe's cultural heritage. As the former Chair of the Europeana Foundation Board, Elisabeth Niggemann, wrote, 'Europeana will become the trusted source of Europe's collective memory' (Europeana 2011: 4). This expression of an explicitly European memory culture is connected to the aims of the EC to promote unity through the creation of shared values and cultural symbols, such as the European flag and the Euro (Macdonald 2013). In much the same way, the EC's cultural heritage projects are intended to forge and popularize a cohesive European identity.

The DPLA project was launched later than Europeana, in April 2013, although Robert Darnton, a member of the Directors' Board, recalls the initial presentation of the idea at a 2010 conference: 'The DPLA, we resolved, would be "an open, distributed network of comprehensive online resources that would draw on the nation's living heritage from libraries, universities, archives, and museums in order to educate, inform, and empower everyone in the current and future generations"' (Darnton 2013). In a similar way to Europeana, the project was originally conceived as a public, non-commercial alternative to Google Books, influenced by the principles of the American public library movement in the nineteenth century (Darnton 2013). In the years following 2010, a combination of public and research librarians and experts in the fields of libraries, technology, law and education collaboratively established the DPLA infrastructure (DPLA 2016). By the time its website went live, the project had amassed a substantial amount of digital content, primarily from larger institutions such as Harvard, the New York Public Library, the Smithsonian and HathiTrust. However, it remains committed to enabling smaller public libraries to contribute items from their own collections and is now run as a registered non-profit organization (DPLA 2016).

Technical Framework

Despite their different remits and time frames, DPLA developers have worked with Europeana from the early stages of the project to make their systems interoperable. There are several factors involved in this process. As mentioned, both are aggregators, meaning that they aggregate digital object metadata and direct users to the institutions where these objects are held via a website, portal or application program interface (API).[2] The digital objects are hosted from the institutions' sites rather than from the aggregators themselves. The broad term digital object is understood to encompass a range of artefacts, including thumbnail images, digital photographs of artworks and other visual material and digital scans of text and print works. Metadata refers to the descriptions of those digital objects to facilitate their discovery online. Europeana's first experiments in creating a metadata standard flexible enough to accommodate library, archive and museum holdings resulted in European Semantic Elements (ESE), which was followed in 2013 with the European Data Model (EDM) (Kenny 2015). Much technical effort went towards the development of the EDM, with the aim of creating enriched metadata and greater compatibility between discrete digital collections. For example, the EDM allows for the representation of contradictions, so that different descriptions of digital objects can coexist via proxy elements. This function is important, particularly in the cultural heritage sector in relation to provenance, which can be contested. Hence, the EDM accommodates needs at various scales: programmers are satisfied by a tool that more or less conforms to accepted standards because they can program with it or for it. Meanwhile, cultural heritage organizations have a measure of autonomy in that they can present their own interpretive framework for their collections.

The DPLA metadata application profile (DPLA MAP) is based on the EDM and also aims to unify digital content from a range of institutions (DPLA 2015b). As well as enabling interoperability between the two aggregators, these standards facilitate the linking up of collections at different scales, e.g. national and smaller regional museums, libraries and archives. As Darnton (2013) observed, 'within a generation, there should be a worldwide network that will bring nearly all the holdings of all libraries and museums within the range of nearly everyone on the globe'. Yet, despite the potential of global standardization, each project is defined in more abstract scalar terms, specifically through ideas of Europe and the public. In both cases, these reflect uncertain locations and identity structures that complicate their respective supranational and national boundaries. This issue raises questions about the local contexts the standards are intended to reach; as Bowker et al. (2010: 102) query, 'to what extent is a metadata standard designed generic enough to represent a domain ("reach or scope") while aiming at fitting local structures, social arrangements, and technologies ("embeddedness")?'. In order to draw out the relationship between abstract and more local expressions of Europeanness and publicness, it is necessary to examine how each project engages with its audiences.

Audiences

The earlier reference to Europeana's presentation of itself as a platform is linked to its strategic aim to meet 'rising user expectations' and provide ways to interact with and reuse the material people encounter via the database

(Europeana 2014: 10). The original assumption was that aggregating and making digital heritage content available online would automatically lead to higher engagement, and this was not the case (Europeana 2011). Nick Poole acknowledged that '"access" as a principle has failed almost entirely because it is passive – we have had to learn to move on from passive provision of access to proactive engagement with audiences'; he suggested that 'the next challenge is not mass-digitisation or mass-preservation, but mass-curation of the sheer volume of cultural content' (Poole 2014). Poole was the Chair of the Europeana Network (2010–2014) and the Chief Executive Officer of the Collections Trust up until 2015, the organization that managed the UK aggregator for Europeana cultural heritage data. As such, he was involved in the writing of Europeana's 2020 Strategy, which presents a similar view that digital heritage needs to be made meaningful to people through curation and creative open use (Europeana 2014).

Some of Europeana's more recent projects have attempted to address these concerns. A notable example is Europeana 1914–1918, an initiative to commemorate the centenary of the First World War. It brings together collections from the Europeana database in conjunction with documents and memorabilia gathered from individuals and digitized at several European roadshows. There is also an online collections form on the website, where personal stories and images can be uploaded. Europeana 1914–1918 goes some way towards meeting Poole's call for 'mass-curation' of cultural content because it looks at the broader context and impact of the First World War, inviting individual and collective contributions and making them available in the curated space of the website. In addition, all the material is available for reuse, which allows for adaptation of the content.

Underlying the model of curation and creative reuse, however, is the rationale for Europeana itself, which is related to the EC's aim of promoting a shared European culture and has been described as a form of soft power (Shore 2006). Therefore, the increased focus on individual stories and experiences could also be read as a revision of its strategies for political cohesion, employed when previous approaches failed to engage audiences in anticipated ways. This suggestion brings us back to the terrain of Foucault and governmentality. As Rosemary Coombe and Lindsay M. Weiss observe, it is in keeping with governmental strategies to seek to foster regulated freedom in persons and locales: 'The cultivation of personal autonomy is one means through which such technology does its social work' (Coombe and Weiss 2015: 45). Another way of framing the EC's aims is through Anna Tsing's notion of effective generalization. She writes:

> Generalization to the universal requires a large space of compatibility among disparate particular facts and observations. As long as facts are apples and oranges,

one cannot generalise across them. One must first see them as 'fruit' to make general claims. Compatibility standardizes difference. It allows transcendence: the general can rise above the particular. For this, compatibility must pre-exist the particular facts being examined; and it must unify the field of enquiry. The searcher for universal truths must establish an *axiom of unity* – whether on spiritual, aesthetic, mathematical, logical, or moral principles. (Tsing 2005: 89)

So, while the centenary of the War has been an occasion for the articulation and exploration of different cultures of memory and forgetting, it also has a sufficiently large space of compatibility, as a pan-European catastrophe, to act as an effective generalization.[3] Generalizations standardize difference and fold particulars into universals in the online heritage space of Europeana. While this may be a productive process with respect to fostering mutual understanding, the stakes are important: the memorial culture around the War has a minimum consensus – an axiom of unity in Tsing's terms – yet the idea of a federal Europe does not. As Marc Abélès (2004: 5) discerns, 'on the contrary, the word "federation" seems to repel most of the (EU) member states'. Such generalizations again draw attention to the issue of standardization and the embeddedness of politics in technologies like Europeana. Here, it is Europeana's users that are implicated in the process; the project targets different 'locals' – different potential actors, local institutions and populations, down to individual contributors – to support its transnational identity claim, which is in line with the governmental rationality of the EC.

The DPLA also combines universal and local scales in its public vision. Understandings of publicness have historically been defined in relation to various manifestations of the private; the domestic space of the home was crucial in marking this divide and separating privacy and intimacy from the duties of public life. In a similar way, the establishment of publicly funded and maintained institutions has come to represent a defence against the widespread privatization and marketization of fundamental services (Chun 2016). Such places are generally regarded as trustworthy, in part due to their public service remit. Bennett's work demonstrates how the idea of the public was at the heart of a developing definition of the museum in the nineteenth century: the museum's rhetoric 'is, in the main, characterised by two principles: first the principle of public rights sustaining the demand that museums should be equally open and accessible to all; and second, the principle of representational adequacy sustaining the demand that museums should adequately represent the cultures and values of different sections of the public' (Bennett 1990).

This historical contextualization has parallels in the history of US public libraries (Pawley and Robbins 2013), the namesake of the DPLA. However, although the DPLA positions itself as a digital continuation of the traditions embodied in public libraries, it is interesting to note that there has been some ambivalence about the project from library practitioners. The report from an early working group meeting registers apprehension about the relationship between the DPLA and public libraries: participants 'expressed concerns that a DPLA may inadvertently take public funding away from existing public libraries, while others pointed out that a DPLA could help drive attention to public libraries. Many participants emphasized that a DPLA will support, not replace, existing public libraries' (DPLA 2011: 4). As the extract suggests, the DPLA and public libraries meet at the intersection of knowledge organization, even while the form of publicness at issue seems more historically aligned with physical spaces than technical infrastructures. This apprehension reveals a number of tensions around conceptions of publicness and its entanglement in ongoing debates about public goods and diminishing public funding for institutions like public libraries and state museums.

The DPLA would later clarify its use of the term public to denote a 'critical, open intellectual landscape ... in the face of increasingly restrictive digital options' (DPLA 2016), much as Europeana was conceptualized as a public endeavour that would provide an alternative to corporate entities like Google. Here, the DPLA acknowledges the growing privatization of digital cultural content, although it also points towards a shifting understanding of the term *public*, embedded as it is within the privatized infrastructure of the Internet. Such restrictions partly explain its commitment to supplementing the services that public libraries provide, with activities including digitization, metadata creation and enhancement, hosting and community outreach programmes (DPLA 2016). These support the aims of the initiative to link up collections at local and national scales, which is facilitated by its use of the metadata application profile (DPLA MAP). A differentiation in services also serves to allay the fears of public libraries and other institutions the DPLA relies on to provide digital objects and metadata for aggregation: it casts the publicness of the DPLA in a different light to that of the traditional public library, thus attempting to remove the possible competition for resources anticipated in the excerpt above.

In the assertion that the DPLA makes America's riches 'freely available to the world' (DPLA 2016), it is possible to detect the influence of older notions of public space as 'an emptiness that enables free and equal speech' or access (Massey 2005: 152). As Darnton (2013) put it, 'what could be more utopian than a project to make the cultural heritage of humanity available to all humans?' Yet, while these lofty ambitions seem partially realizable via the infrastructure of a digital public space, that is not to say that access to the infrastructure itself will be similarly democratic or far reaching. Therefore, to return to Tsing's theory, it may be that the public is a sufficiently effective generalization to achieve compatibility among a range of institutions and actors. In practice though, the DPLA must go beyond the development of technology that makes digital heritage widely discoverable and address the unevenness of public rights in different localities, and at different scales. Its grassroots organization and hosting of outreach events demonstrate some of its methods for achieving that. These efforts involve openness of process and ongoing negotiation about the general or local shape of public entities. Only through such negotiation can the potential for more productive and equitable scalar relationships be created.

Conclusion

In this discussion of digital heritage aggregators, we have compared the formation of the Europeana project with that of the DPLA. In their technical development, there are clear parallels; indeed, the data model created by Europeana was reused and adapted for the DPLA. The motives underlying this decision are numerous, some of which have been alluded to previously. For example, the interoperability of European and transatlantic digital heritage collections allows for broader searches and cross-comparison with a larger range of sources. Technical solutions are primarily focused on how such outcomes can be achieved. However, there are also a set of questions to be asked regarding what is lost in the process of standardizing content and the relative losses and gains of effective generalizations (Tsing 2005). Focusing on the needs of individual users does not always counteract this tendency of standardization, since, as Foucault's work shows, techniques of government can be both individualizing and totalizing (1979). Likewise, what has been described as the democratizing effect of heritage aggregators (Darnton 2011) can, at the same time, obscure the political gestures implicit in their conceptual framing.

We would argue for a critical and reflective approach to these entities, one that makes visible the political and ethical decisions taken in developing universal standards (Bowker and Star 1999). Just as the organization of knowledge in museums, libraries and archives has had powerful socially differentiating effects (Bennett 1990), so the workings of digital heritage aggregators have significant implications for contemporary organizational practices. This short study provides a way into thinking about the digital mediation and structuring of such practices and about the multiple scales at which heritage aggregators operate. By emphasizing the interconnectedness of these scalar dimensions, it makes a distinctive contribution to understanding the politics of scale in digital heritage cultures.

Rhiannon Bettivia (PhD) is a Postdoctoral Research Associate at the University of Illinois, Urbana-Champaign, USA. Her research examines the politics and discourses of the growing subfield of digital preservation and investigates new methodologies for preserving the interpretive framework for digital materials. She has published in the *International Journal of Digital Curation* about her work on the IMLS grant *Preserving Virtual Worlds II*, among other publications and presentations in the fields of information science, digital humanities and communications. She also teaches in the areas of digital preservation, metadata and the role of libraries and information in society in the School of Information Sciences at the University of Illinois.

Elizabeth Stainforth (PhD) is a Lecturer in Heritage Studies at the School of Fine Art, History of Art and Cultural Studies, University of Leeds, UK. Her research investigates digital heritage and memory cultures, and she is interested in theories of utopia for developing critical studies of history and heritage. She has worked as an Associate Editor for *parallax* journal and published articles in journals including *Museum and Society, The Journal of Curatorial Studies* and *Digital Humanities Quarterly*. She previously worked for Leeds University Library, where she was involved in projects with the Digital Content and Repositories Team, Special Collections and the Stanley & Audrey Burton Gallery.

NOTES

1. The mutually reinforcing relation of all and each is a relationship we address in more detail elsewhere. See, for example, Bettivia and Stainforth (2015).
2. An API is a web service that can be used to access data and incorporate it into new applications, e.g. other websites.
3. Steffi de Jong (2011) has noted a similar move in the presentation of Second World War narratives, suggesting the war is remembered as a tragedy 'in which all Europeans appear equally as victims' (De Jong 2011: 378).

REFERENCES

Abélès, M. 2004. 'Identity and Borders: An Anthropological Approach to EU Institutions', *Twenty-First Century Papers: On-Line Working Papers from the The Center for 21st Century Studies* 4: 1–26. Retrieved 14 November 2016 from https://www4.uwm.edu/c21/pdfs/workingpapers/abeles.pdf.

Arantes, A.A. 2007. 'Diversity, Heritage and Cultural Politics', *Theory, Culture and Society* 24(7–8): 290–96.

Beer, D. and R. Burrows. 2013. 'Popular Culture, Digital Archives and the New Social Life of Data', *Theory, Culture & Society* 30(4): 47–71.
Bennett, T. 1990. 'The Political Rationality of the Museum', *Continuum: The Australian Journal of Media & Culture* 3(1). Retrieved 14 November 2016 from http://www mcc.murdoch.edu.au/ReadingRoom/3.1/Bennett.html.
———. 2013. *Making Culture, Changing Society*. Abingdon and New York: Routledge.
Bettivia, R. and E. Stainforth. 2015. 'All and Each: Dialogues in the Digital Archive', *Connecting Communities: Storytelling & the Digital Archive Conference & Community Showcase, Leeds, March 2015*. Leeds: University of Leeds.
Bowker, G.C. 2005. *Memory Practices in the Sciences*. London: MIT Press.
Bowker, G.C., K. Baker, F. Millerand and D. Ribes. 2010. 'Toward Information Infrastructure Studies: Ways of Knowing in a Networked Environment', in J. Hunsinger et al. (eds), *International Handbook of Internet Research*. Dordrecht: Springer, pp. 97–117.
Bowker, G.C. and S.L. Star. 1999. *Sorting Things Out: Classification and Its Consequences*. Cambridge, MA: MIT Press.
Chun, W. 2016. *Updating to Remain the Same: Habitual New Media*. Cambridge, MA: MIT Press.
Coombe, R. and L.M. Weiss. 2015. 'Neoliberalism, Heritage Regimes, and Cultural Rights', in L. Meskell (ed.), *Global Heritage: A Reader*. Hoboken, NJ: Wiley-Blackwell, pp. 43–69.
Darnton, R. 2011. 'Six Reasons Google Books Failed', *The New York Review of Books*. Retrieved 14 November 2016 from http://www.nybooks.com/daily/2011/03/28/six-reasons-google-books-failed/.
———. 2013. 'The National Digital Public Library Is Launched!', *The New York Review of Books*. Retrieved 14 November 2016 from http://www.nybooks.com/articles/2013/04/25/national-digital-public-library-launched/
Dean, M. 1999. *Governmentality: Power and Rule in Modern Society*. London: Sage.
De Jong, S. 2011. 'Is This Us? The Construction of the European Man/Woman in the Exhibition It's our History!' *Culture Unbound* 3: 369–83.
DPLA. 2011. 'Digital Public Library of America Working Group Meeting'. Retrieved 14 November 2016 from https://dp.la/info/wp-content/uploads/2011/03/DPLA_March2011Workshop_Notes.pdf.
———. 2015a. 'DPLA Strategic Plan: 2015 through 2017'. Retrieved 14 November 2016 https://dp.la/info/wp-content/uploads/2015/01/DPLA-StrategicPlan_2015-2017-Jan7.pdf.
———. 2015b. 'Metadata Application Profile, Version 4.0'. Retrieved 14 November 2016 from https://dp.la/info/wp-content/uploads/2015/03/MAPv4.pdf.
———. 2016. Website. Retrieved 14 November 2016 from https://dp.la/.
Europeana, 2011. 'Strategic Plan 2011-2015', Brussels. Retrieved 14 November 2016 from http://www.pro.europeana.eu/c/document_library/get_file?uuid=c4f19464-7504-44db-ac1e-3ddb78c922d7&groupId=10602.
———. 2014. 'Europeana Strategy 2015–2020', Brussels. Retrieved 14 November 2016 from http://pro.europeana.eu/files/Europeana_Professional/Publications/Europeana%20Strategy%202020.pdf.
———. 2016. 'Glossary', Brussels. Retrieved 14 November 2016 from http://pro.europeana.eu/page/glossary.

European Commission. 2005. Scanned copy of letter by Jacques Chirac and Gerhard Schröder to José Manuel Barroso, 28 April. Retrieved 14 November 2016 from http://ec.europa.eu/information_society/activities/digital_libraries/doc/letter_1/index_en.htm.

Foucault, M. 1979. 'Omnes et Singulatim: Towards a Criticism of "Political Reason"': The Tanner Lectures on Human Values, delivered at Stanford University, 10 and 16 October. Retrieved 14 November 2016 from http://tannerlectures.utah.edu/_documents/a-to-z/f/foucault81.pdf.

———. 1988 [1982]. *Technologies of the Self: A Seminar with Michel Foucault*, L.H. Martin, H. Gutman and P.H. Hutton (eds). London: University of Massachusetts Press, pp. 16–49. Retrieved 14 November 2016 from http://foucault.info/doc/documents/foucault-technologiesofself-en-html.

Gordon, C. 1991. 'Governmental Rationality: An Introduction', in G. Burchell, C. Gordon and P. Miller (eds), *The Foucault Effect: Studies in Governmentality*. London: Wheatsheaf Harvester, pp. 2–3.

Harvey, D.C. 2015. 'Heritage and Scale: Settings, Boundaries and Relations', *International Journal of Heritage Studies* 21(6): 577–93.

Kenny, E. 2015. 'Europeana: Cultural Heritage in the Digital Age', in P. Innocenti (ed.), *Cultural Networks in Migrating Heritage: Intersecting Theories and Practices across Europe*. Farnham: Ashgate, pp. 85–94.

Macdonald, S. 2013. *Memorylands: Heritage and Identity in Europe Today*. London: Routledge.

Manovich, L. 1999. 'Database as Symbolic Form', *Convergence* 5(2): 80–99.

Marton, A. 2011. 'Forgotten as Data – Remembered through Information: Social Memory Institutions in the Digital Age: The Case of the Europeana Initiative'. PhD thesis. London School of Economics.

Massey, D. 2005. *For Space*. London: Sage.

Pawley, C. and L.S. Robbins. 2013. *Libraries and the Reading Public in Twentieth-Century*. Madison: University of Wisconsin Press.

Poole, N. 2014. Unpublished interview with Elizabeth Stainforth.

Purday, J. 2009. 'Think Culture: Europeana.eu from Concept to Construction', *Bibliothek: Forschung und Praxis* 33(2): 170–80.

Shore, C. 2006. '"In uno plures"' (?) EU Cultural Policy and the Governance of Europe', *Cultural Analysis* 5: 7–26.

Tsing, A.L. 2005. *Friction: An Ethnography of Global Connection*. Oxford: Princeton University Press.

PART II

SCALE IN HERITAGE INSTITUTIONS AND POLICIES

 CHAPTER FOUR

Managed Landscapes
The Social Construction of Scale at Angkor
Rowena Butland

The concept of 'scale' is neither neutral nor innocuous (Sheppard and McMaster 2004) but a socially constructed tool that influences the way we perceive and understand human-environment relationships (Marston 2000). As social constructions, geographical scales are not contained by impenetrable boundaries but have porous limits that are continually evolving and changing (Gale 2016). These negotiated boundaries form the interfaces for unique multidirectional relationships between different scales (Mackinnon 2010). An ontology of scales can thus be manipulated to include and exclude objects and networks, and struggles for power and control flow out across multiple scales (Muzaini 2013). It is these characteristics that draw interest in examining the conceptualization and production of scale and deciphering the power structures within scale and scaling processes (Bisht 2018).

It is difficult to discuss heritage and its related concepts without using scaled terminology that implies levels, degrees or extents; for example, local, national and global significance (Lloyd and Morgan 2008). Similarly, an approach to human, environment and heritage relationships that sees the creation of heritage places can be considered as a dialogue of scale (Green and Jones 2018). In constructing a heritage site or area, some form of boundary and hierarchy between the significant and the insignificant is applied to the landscape (Morell 2009). Situating itself within a theoretical framework concerned with the social construction of scale (Marston 2000), this chapter examines how the continual evaluation of heritage objects and locations constructs a scale of 'heritage'. The chapter will firstly address the management of cultural heritage, its emphasis on value, and how this can help to conceptualize a scale of heritage. It will then utilize the Angkor World Heritage Area (Cambodia) to explore the scaling processes at work when heritage professionals define and value the site. The chapter will demonstrate how the boundaries, or frames, of what is 'heritage' shift to reflect various agendas.

Heritage as Scale, Value and a Form of Inclusion or Exclusion

There is a need to recognize the cultural politics and power relationships active in the conservation and interpretation of cultural heritage (Pendlebury 2013). The institutionalization of cultural heritage management, through the embedding of planning legislation and practices, has often encouraged objective, rationalized management (Young 2016); such an approach conflicts with post-positivist theory that encourages a subjective, pluralistic approach to heritage and its interpretation (Borges and Adolphson 2016). This power can be exerted through controlling access to material culture, or it can manifest in an imperialistic assessment of values that ignores local values, ideas and knowledge (Waterton, Smith and Campbell 2006). At the extreme, the power exerted by foreign experts can create a neo-colonial environment, where western conservation ideologies can be imposed on non-western cultures (Lwoga 2018; Winter 2007).

Despite a social justice agenda that promotes participatory planning approaches, resolving the tensions between the interests of governments, cultural heritage planners and local communities remains one of the most controversial issues in culture heritage management (Green and Jones 2018). Dissonance between stakeholders, particularly where livelihoods are involved, can lead to the failure of heritage management projects (Tchoukaleyska 2016). While there is recognition of differences between those who live near a site and those who visit from afar (Chen, Leask and Phou 2016), in practice there is a tendency for the 'scientific' values and decisions of experts to rule over other less vocal groups (Green 2016). Management of heritage landscapes has become spatially differentiated, with areas of high significance through to less significant surrounding spaces (Gillespie 2013). The recognition of these degrees, or scales, of significance will have material and social consequences, as different management practices will be applied to different spaces (Apaydin 2018).

In the context of heritage, value is the most important and desirable quality of an object, place or activity from the perspective of an individual or group (Vakhitova 2015). The values, meanings or significance attached to objects and locations help us develop a sense of place and identity (Tchoukaleyska 2016). Value is so integral to heritage that some see heritage as equating to value: heritage only exists through meaningful interactions between humans and their environment (Loulanski 2006). A more utilitarian viewpoint is that value provides an understanding of the sociocultural contexts of heritage management (Young 2016). A pluralistic viewpoint driven by principles of equity and empowerment recognizes that heritage can have multiple values (Smith 2006). Such significance is not pregiven but results from continuous interactions between an artefact and its spatial-temporal contexts (Loulanski and Loulanski 2014). Thus it is quite possible for values and meanings to not only evolve over time but also to often conflict (Vakhitova 2015).

Considering heritage value as a social construction allows recognition that it is a political tool that can be used to empower different interests and ideologies (Smith 2006). Contemporary heritage management entails the ranking of values as well as decisions of what is and is not to be protected, and these processes are often contentious and political (Pendlebury 2013). Within this context, scale reveals itself both overtly and covertly (Muzaini 2013). Firstly, the question of 'whose heritage?' lends itself to untangling the overt discourse surrounding the scaled agents, who are both the perceivers of heritage and providers of value (Young 2016). This ontology of scales is usually categorized according to physical relationships to a heritage site, with the social construction of local, national and global 'communities' most evident in discussions that link heritage and identity (Green and Jones 2018). Secondly, a more covert hierarchy of scales can be extracted from examining the application of the concept of authenticity to contemporary heritage landscapes (Lloyd and Morgan 2008). A strong focus on assessing and validating values and significance has led to reliance on a test of authenticity (Khalaf 2017). Thus not everything, nor every space, is equally valuable (Lwoga 2018). Heritage itself can be considered a scale, with its boundaries defined by the categorization of locations and items based on how much value they possess (Muzaini 2013).

As if to emphasize the contradiction between heritage rhetoric and management practices, categories of value are often applied freely without consideration for their inherent instability (Fredheim and Khalaf 2016): in particular, intrinsic value and extrinsic value. Intrinsic values are seen as those heritage qualities that do not require any particular experiences or modification to understand them, as they inherently exist in a cultural resource (Parkinson, Scott and Redmond 2016). In contrast, extrinsic values resulting from human perception, utilization or alteration of a cultural resource are seen as extrinsic (Walter 2014). Thus it is assumed that there are naturally occurring values, and it is these that are often seen as most important to protect (Vakhitova 2015). Such an idea is used to legitimate decisions concerning the ranking and conservation of heritage sites and values (Vargas 2018).

As naturalization creates an illusion of intrinsicity, the fact that heritage is something that can be differently perceived becomes lost (Lwoga 2018). Instead, the notion of intrinsic value needs to be recognized as a political tool that assists with the naturalization of certain values and meanings, and not something free of human subjectivities (Apaydin 2018). Governments and key organizations look to heritage professionals, like archaeologists and architects, to rationally and objectively resolve conflicts between competing values (Ferretti and Comino 2015). Heritage managers must make decisions that can both elevate and suppress different interests and ideologies (Borges and Adolphson 2016). At times heritage professionals seem to be raised to lofty levels where they can impossibly remove all bias and similarly perceive the 'true' value of a site (Young 2016). However, there is often no mention of how these values represent those of heritage 'experts' as opposed to the multiplicity of meanings from the wider community (Parkinson, Scott, and Redmond 2016). Thus there is a need to enquire about how much influence the values and meanings of heritage professionals are having on what is being protected and represented (Roux 2017). In addition, there is a need to reveal the way that experts influence and construct the scales of value, particularly through their application of and adherence to the test of authenticity (Muzaini 2013). These scales potentially have important material consequences for heritage sites and surrounding landscapes, in that they dictate spatially differentiated management and protection policies placed on these objects and areas (Caust and Vecco 2017).

The fight for legitimacy by heritage managers has led to authenticity 'testing' that strictly demarcates between the 'traditional' and the 'contemporary' (Lwoga 2018), perhaps denying the natural evolution of an area or an object beyond its founding moment (Smith 2006). These relative yet seemingly oppositional concepts are often used to form sharp formal boundaries between objects belonging to the past and those that are seen as part of the present (Lennon and Taylor 2012). The closer the modern is to the traditional, the more authentic a contemporary culture is judged (Tchoukaleyska 2016).

By falsely limiting the links between past and present, the relationship between heritage professionals and communities becomes more problematic (Roux 2017). The formalization of boundaries by heritage planners to demarcate protected heritage from contemporary space means that inevitably there must be some similar separation by local communities (Gillespie 2013). Achieving a balance between protection and sustainable use of cultural heritage resources remains a difficult and controversial issue (Caust and Vecco 2017). By seeing heritage as part of a modern dynamic cultural system (Lwoga 2018), it is recognized that through the process of living, heritage is fundamentally connected to a sense of place and identification with the surrounding contemporary space (Apaydin 2018). As people will constantly create, transform and experience space and place, the boundaries between old and new places must be recognized as complex, and authentic heritage spaces as similarly multifaceted (Hoelscher and Alderman 2004).

Case Study: The Angkor World Heritage Area (Cambodia)

The Angkor World Heritage Area (Cambodia) incorporates a vast collection of stone temples and monuments that are the remains of a series of capitals belonging to the Khmer empire, which once dominated much of South East Asia (Fletcher et al. 2015). The most famous of these monuments is Angkor Wat. Initially protected under French colonialism (1925) as the Angkor Archaeological Park, the site was inscribed on the World Heritage List in 1992 (Gillespie 2013). The current World Heritage Area merely captures the core area that was the centre of power from 802 AD until 1431 AD (Fletcher et al. 2015). Over the past thirty years, the wider discourse that surrounds Angkor's management has shifted from considering the protection of heritage monuments to the creation of a heritage place and, lastly, a growing desire to ensure the conservation of a vast cultural landscape (Evans and Fletcher 2015). Alongside this, the modern town of Siem Reap has rapidly expanded along the southern border of the World Heritage Area, as tourism to Angkor and its surrounds is one of the main drivers of the Cambodian economy (Chen, Leask and Phou 2016).

Throughout its 'modern' history, Angkor's management has been significantly influenced by foreign governments and international agencies; initially the French and Japanese, then UNESCO and now an eclectic international community (Winter 2007). The International Coordinating Committee for the Safeguarding and Development of the Historic Site of Angkor (ICC) was established under the requirements of Angkor's World Heritage inscription (Peycam 2016). The ICC acts as an advisory body for UNESCO, overseeing and coordinating international efforts to protect and develop the Angkor-Siem Reap region (Heikkila and Peycam 2010). The inaugural meeting was held in Paris in December 1993, subsequently meeting bi-annually (primarily in Siem Reap), with a 10th anniversary summit held in Tokyo in December 2003. International teams working at Angkor are allowed representation through their government representative and/or team leader. There are also a number of international cultural, heritage and development agencies that contribute (Peycam 2016). Whilst participants come from a number of different vocations (archaeologists, art historians, urban planners and environmental scientists), their work at Angkor will be seen as broadly encompassing that of heritage professionals.

The ICC holds considerable sway over the management of Angkor, as it can directly advise UNESCO and the World Heritage Committee of any dissatisfaction with Cambodia's conservation and management of Angkor heritage (Peycam 2016). All international projects must be cleared through the Committee so as to ensure the long-term plans for the site. The ICC has influenced the extent to which modern activities can be undertaken in the areas surrounding the Angkor monuments; it has held the Cambodian government accountable for negotiating adequate financial returns from tourist entry fees and has called upon international teams to explain discrepancies between intentions and actions for archaeological and conservation activities at the site (Winter 2007).

The research presented here is based on textual analysis and was covered in the detailed minutes of the 1993 and 2003 ICC Symposia. The material presented at the ICC consisted of reports from commencing, ongoing and completed international projects, representing attitudes and perceptions concerning Angkor and its management. The main themes of discussion fall into three categories: safeguarding and protection, institutional/governance framework and sustainable development for the local population.

Language and its relationship with the material landscape (Suri and Ekbia 2016) were given deliberate consideration during the textual analysis, with three key questions framing the review:

- What is considered heritage?
- What meanings and values are attached to Angkor?
- What is the spatial definition of the valued space?

Government and other official documentation are created with political, economic and social motivation. As a result, a particular knowledge and understanding of the world will develop through the meanings and representations created. The social and political power of the voices at the ICC (government and international agencies) ensure that these documents, their text and subtext, will inform what people think and do when managing the Angkor World Heritage Area (Peycam 2016). Within the subsequent sections, quotes from the ICC documentation will be cited (as country, year), with 1993 and 2003 referring to the ICC symposium that took place that year (i.e. ICC 1993, ICC 2003).

What Is Angkor?

To reveal how 'Angkor' was spatially perceived, labels for the site (i.e. 'Angkor Wat', 'Angkor World Heritage Area') were collated and organized along an axis reflecting a sense of increasing spatial areas: from perceptions of Angkor as a single temple or isolated monuments to expressions of Angkor as a heritage region or cultural landscape. A comparative analysis of International and Cambodian responses (Table 4.1) revealed that in both years a broad range of labels were utilized. These suggested various spatial conceptualizations of 'Angkor'.

The Spatially Ambiguous

For both the International and Cambodian ICC contributors (in 1993 and 2003), the spatially ambiguous 'Angkor' was a commonly utilized label, requiring the audience to understand how the speaker was envisaging the site. This suggests that perhaps 'Angkor' is not a physical space but is instead an idea. It could, therefore, be a place that is created to fit a perceived purpose rather than a defined location.

The Spatially Non-definitive

Many of the labels required communal understanding of indefinite spatial terms, such as 'region', 'territory' or 'landscape'. These terms can be considered malleable social constructions (Levitt and De La Torre 2016). 'Region' is utilized by governments around the world to include and exclude certain spaces and people, facilitating economic, political and social agendas (Borges and Adolphson 2016). The notion of a cultural landscape was originally introduced to cross barriers and facilitate representation on the World Heritage List for people that did not necessarily differentiate between culture and nature (Lennon and Taylor 2012). Such language nuances become potentially problematic (Felder, Duineveld and Van Assche 2014) when considering that the ICC meetings are simultaneously translated into English, French and Khmer. Similar situations have previously arisen in international heritage management circles and continue to escape a simple solution (Taylor 2012). It could even be argued that the use of the terms 'monuments' or 'Angkor monuments' are similarly ambiguous, as they raise questions relating to which structures qualify, or are considered, as monuments (Tyner, Inwood and Alderman 2014).

A Monumental Landscape

Discussions at the ICC are focused on the management of the Angkor World Heritage Area, so it is perhaps not surprising that labels equating to such an area (such as 'Angkor Archaeological Park' or World Heritage Area) are dominant in both years for both the International and Cambodian contributors to the ICC. However, embedded within this discourse is an Angkor framed as a 'monumental' landscape.

A sense of 'Angkor' being only the central monument of 'Angkor Wat' or of 'Angkor' being a cluster of monuments is not unexpected. The focus within the ICC was on ensuring the immediate safeguarding, conservation and research of the major structures. 'All that remains of that civilisation is its rich heritage of cult structures in brick and stone' (ICOMOS: ICC September 1992). The World Heritage inscription only protected the monuments of the site (Gillespie 2013), and initially there was minimal international funding distributed for external conservation or development projects. By 2003, the ICC discourse suggests an interest in 'Angkor' is more consistent with a landscape idea of heritage: 'The urgent necessity to protect and preserve the monuments and the historic zone in their cultural, socio-economic and ecological dimension has been reconfirmed' (Japan 2003).

There are other factors influencing an interest in a cultural landscape approach to Angkor. Between 1993 and 2003, hostility and conflict within Cambodia decreased (Winter 2007), and thus safety and accessibility increased beyond the core historical areas. The number of foreign teams working at the site also increased, with interest (and finance) extending beyond preserving key monuments (Winter 2007). In addition, international support towards tourism and urban management, as well as environmental monitoring and conservation, accompanies a growing discussion of sustainable development ideologies in Angkor's management (Caust and Vecco 2017). This is a discourse that seeks to successfully integrate heritage management with the livelihoods of those who live in and around the World Heritage Area (Vargas 2018).

The Angkor Zoning and Environmental Management Plan

A second requirement of Angkor's World Heritage inscription was the creation of the Angkor Zoning and Environmental Management Plan (The ZEMP, Figure 4.1). The ZEMP distinguished four different areas, each designed to offer varying levels of protection as well as facilitate sustainable development within the surrounding region (Gillespie 2013). Zone 1 is the core monumental sites: these are the areas that are specifically inscribed on the World Heritage List and are thus afforded the most protection. This area equates to the Angkor Archaeological Park (as well as the outlying temples of the Rolous group and Banteay Srei). Zone 2 is identified as protected archaeological reserves. The purpose of this zone is to protect material found within the zone as well as to offer a physical buffer between modern development and the 'ancient' monuments through attempts to control construction and development. Zones 3 and 4 offer further protection for Angkor's cultural landscape – in particular, its hydrological features. In addition a fifth zone covers the entire Province of Siem Reap (in which Angkor is located). This was an attempt at broadly coordinating archaeological, social and economic outcomes (Heikkila and Peycam 2010).

The spatial identifiers utilized at Angkor can be seen as equating to several of these categories. The ZEMP Zone 1 equates to the Angkor World Heritage Area, or the Angkor Archaeological Area. Within Zone 1 lie Angkor Wat and the Angkor Monuments. This is therefore the most common spatial definition of 'Angkor' utilized within ICC discourse. The Angkor Cultural Landscape is less definitive and thus potentially more problematic. Apart from language nuances, there are also questions as to whether such a definition is equating to Zone 2, Zone 3, Zone 4 or perhaps even further. It thus becomes apparent that there is potential for conflict, negotiation and the manipulation of cultural, economic and political processes when Angkor is spatially scaled within various management practices.

Table 4.1 Spatial descriptions for 'Angkor' by ICC contributor and year.

Collated Reference	Description	Cambodian Contributors		International Contributors	
		1993	2003	1993	2003
ANGKOR	Angkor	18%	17%	23%	27%
SINGLE MONUMENT	Angkor Wat	5%	0%	4%	0%
	Angkor Monument	0%	0%	2%	0%
MULTIPLE MONUMENTS	Angkor Monuments	14%	8%	15%	15%
WORLD HERITAGE AREA	Angkor Park	14%	17%	5%	5%
	Angkor Complex	0%	0%	2%	2%
	Historic Site of Angkor	0%	0%	12%	8%
	Angkor Site	9%	25%	16%	20%
	Sites of Angkor	5%	0%	2%	0%
	Historic Area of Angkor	5%	0%	3%	3%
	Angkor City	5%	0%	1%	0%
CULTURAL LANDSCAPE	Angkor Area	9%	0%	4%	2%
	Angkor Region	18%	8%	9%	8%
	Angkor Core and Periphery	0%	8%	2%	3%
	Angkor Territory	0%	8%	0%	2%
	Angkor Zone	0%	8%	1%	3%

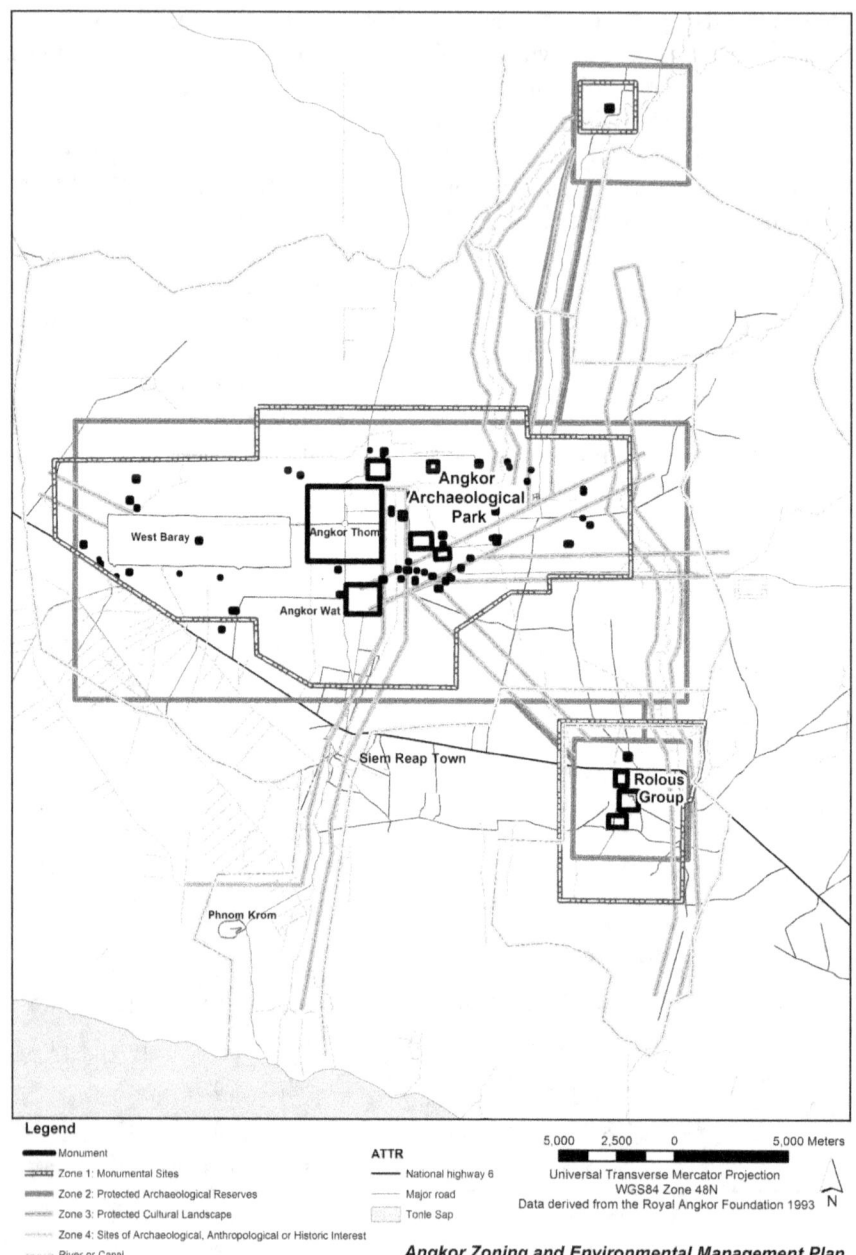

Figure 4.1 Map of the Angkor World Heritage Site, showing the Angkor Zoning and Environment Management Plan (ZEMP). Map created by author.

The Value of Angkor

Two approaches were taken to determine perceptions of the importance of Angkor. Firstly, it was determined whether the values being spoken of were referring to either a local, national or international significance (i.e. the level of value). The analysis then sought to explore the justifications behind Angkor's importance that are utilized within the ICC meetings.

It was expected that discussion at the ICC symposium would be focused on safeguarding and protecting the global significance of the World Heritage Area. However, within the ICC documentation, references to Angkor's national values were most frequent. The reasons for this may lie in the multiple roles Angkor is perceived as playing in the development of Modern Cambodia, in particular as a cultural, social and economic resource (Caust and Vecco 2017). However, it is important to acknowledge that Angkor's global values were also substantially recognized through multiple references to its World Heritage inscription.

International Contributors

Angkor was valued as a national symbol, a monument, which formed a pillar of the national identity: '[Angkor is] Ruins – Vestiges, which bear witness to a rich and glorious past, reflect all those values that are a source for the Khmer people of hope reborn and identity recovered' (UNESCO 1993). Another interpretation of Angkor's significance was as an economic resource. Amongst international contributors, Angkor had a significant role in Cambodia's financial reconstruction through tourism. This was perhaps a result of the ultimate interests of international contributors as being foreign aid donors and capacity builders (whether directly or indirectly) (Peycam 2016).

A joint focus on Angkor as a cultural symbol and as an economic resource created an interesting duality where the site was perceived as having both a passive and an active role in contemporary society. On the one hand, it was understood as a monument to a past civilization and therefore removed from the current population and their daily behaviours. On the other hand, Angkor had an active role as a key to the socio-economic development of the contemporary population, integral to both the economic and social livelihoods of the Cambodian nation. Despite this awareness of Angkor's contemporary role, there was little mention of Angkor's value for the local community. Recognition of Angkor's national and global values suggested a 'monumental' view of Angkor: one that is focused on the significant objects of the historic landscape. Angkor was perceived as monuments of universal human achievement, with responsibilities to support the country in which they were situated: such interpretations of significance elevated the heritage area beyond its surrounding population and landscape.

Cambodian ICC

Angkor's national values were also emphasized within Cambodian contributions to the ICC. As with international contributors there was an emphasis on the national symbolism (historical and identity) of the monuments and their functional importance (such as economic value). There was also a strong assertion by Cambodian contributors of their sense of pride in Cambodia's ownership (and construction) of the site: 'The presence of numerous countries underscores the exceptional and universal value of the Angkor site, symbol of the identity of the Khmer Nation and of its unity, and witness beyond the frontiers and the centuries of the creative genius of humankind' (Cambodia 1993). Underlying these assertions appears to be an emphasis on reminding international participants that Angkor belongs to Cambodia. This discourse could be a reflection of the fact that the 1993 and 2003 ICC meetings did not convene in Cambodia but instead in Paris and Tokyo: such action abstracts Angkor out of contemporary Cambodia and into an international arena.

In an interesting demonstration of the way in which scale concerns connections between different scales, discussions of Angkor's value at a national and local level as an economic resource often emphasized its global significance. Angkor's international appeal was acknowledged, usually through mention of the visitors who 'value' the site: 'Angkor, symbol of the great Khmer civilisation and crowning jewel of mankind's world heritage, is, thanks to tourism and the revenue generated by it, the hope for balanced, sustainable development' (Cambodia 2003). Through tourism, Angkor was understood as an economic resource that will assist in fighting poverty and lead towards the development and reconstruction of Cambodia and Siem Reap. There was also discussion of the capacity building and employment benefits that came from foreign involvement in the site. There thus appeared to be an awareness that Angkor, like other world heritage sites, could not be disconnected from the modern population and contemporary development or its management would fail.

Conclusion: Scaled Values

In defining 'Angkor', International Contributors to the ICC drew attention to the economically productive space. The monuments of Angkor provided a tourist drawcard, creating the image of the past (Caust and Vecco 2017).

Potentially, economic motivations lead not to an integration of heritage with the modern lives and landscape but towards a heritage disconnected from contemporary non-heritage (Lloyd and Morgan 2008). Recognition of the (economic) value of tourism would mean an increasing focus on the behaviours and practices that contribute to the tourist experience (Tchoukaleyska 2016). For example, the cultivation of traditional handicrafts in the villages within the Angkor Park is about expanding the 'authentic' landscape of heritage. There was minimal discussion within the ICC documentation of the local community's experiences and values. Therefore, the definition of a 'heritage' scale would be driven by the expert's perception of what constitutes heritage and acceptable 'heritage' (Bisht 2018). Angkor as a landscape could perhaps be viewed as a reflection of the interest in the economics of the tourist experience (Caust and Vecco 2017; Winter 2007). Creating the complete 'Angkor experience' means that 'Angkor' was conceived as more than the World Heritage Area. The evidence is that it expands to an Angkor Cultural Landscape, representing at least ZEMP zones 1 and 2, if not also zones 3 and 4, thus potentially influencing the relationship between Angkor and the surrounding area.

Cambodian contributors to the ICC also framed 'Angkor' through an economic agenda, but they coupled it with a strong political agenda. A dominant message to emerge was that Angkor belongs to Cambodia, and thus Angkor should be framed with nationalistic (not global or local) purposes in mind. Angkor has been tasked with reconstructing and maintaining both the national economy and identity. The assertion of the Cambodian right to utilize the site as an economic resource emphasized a functional relationship between Angkor and its surrounding area. The labels for Angkor used by Cambodian contributors implied a landscape (or World Heritage Area) dominated by monuments burdened with both symbolic and economic value. A spatial focus on the World Heritage Area, by the national government, reflected a focus on the important income of tourists and the 'touristscape' (Chen, Leask and Phou 2016). The dominant portrayal of Angkor delineated (scaled) relates to the area encompassed by the Angkor World Heritage Area. In their role as a pillar of the national identity, the large monuments within that space provide a tangible symbol of Cambodia (Heikkila and Peycam 2010). The international gaze facilitated by the World Heritage inscription affirms the significance of the monuments in focusing on the large structures that are easily pictured and appreciated for their grandeur rather than their complexity (Vargas 2018). For the Cambodian contributors, Angkor is constructed at a 'monumental' scale: a series of monuments spread across the area of the Angkor Park.

This chapter set out to explore how the evaluation of heritage is a process of scale construction. Focusing on the Angkor World Heritage Area, the chapter demonstrated how scaled terms have been utilized for economic, political and/or social purposes. 'Angkor' was framed as a single monument, an archaeological parkland and a limitless landscape. Most significantly, it was frequently spoken of in a spatially ambiguous manner, raising potential issues with the meanings behind the word. The chapter then considered the different ways that 'Angkor' was defined through the values that are placed on it. The concept of heritage revolves around dynamic values (Parkinson, Scott and Redmond 2016). It is increasingly recognized within heritage discourse that individual experiences influence perceptions of value (Loulanski 2014). As individuals, and as cultural groups, we define the boundaries of valuable space through perceptions of acceptable and authentic behaviours, attitudes and aesthetics, thus facilitating the construction of a scale of heritage.

Rowena Butland (PhD) is a cultural geographer who has worked in Asia, the Caribbean and Australia. Her research has focused on community cultural heritage, heritage and scale, and spatial management of heritage. She is currently exploring the links between psychology and critical heritage studies, in particular the emotional benefits of heritage and psychological experiences that heritage landscapes can bring about.

REFERENCES

Apaydin, V. 2018. 'The Entanglement of the Heritage Paradigm: Values, Meanings and Uses', *International Journal of Heritage Studies* 24(5): 491–507.

Bisht, P. 2018. 'Social Movements and the Scaling of Memory and Justice in Bhopal', *Contemporary South Asia* 26(1): 1–16.

Borges, L.A. and M. Adolphson. 2016. 'The Role of Official Heritage in Regional Spaces', *Urban Research and Practice* 9(3): 290–310.

Caust, J. and M. Vecco. 2017. 'Is UNESCO World Heritage Recognition a Blessing or Burden? Evidence from Developing Asian Countries', *Journal of Cultural Heritage* 27: 1–9.

Chen, C.-F., A. Leask and S. Phou. 2016. 'Symbolic, Experiential and Functional Consumptions of Heritage Tourism Destinations: The Case of Angkor World Heritage Site, Cambodia', *International Journal of Tourism Research* 18(6): 602–11.

Evans, D. and R. Fletcher. 2015. 'The Landscape of Angkor Wat Redefined', *Antiquity* 89(348): 1402–419.

Felder, M., M. Duineveld and K. Assche. 2014. 'Absence/Presence and the Ontological Politics of Heritage: The Case of Barrack 57', *International Journal of Heritage Studies* 21(5): 460–75.

Ferretti, V. and E. Comino. 2015. 'An Integrated Framework to Assess Complex Cultural and Natural Heritage Systems with Multi-Attribute Value Theory', *Journal of Cultural Heritage* 16(5): 688–97.

Fletcher, R., D. Evans, C. Pottier and C. Rachna. 2015. 'Angkor Wat: An Introduction', *Antiquity* 89(348): 1388–401.
Fredheim, L. H. and M. Khalaf. 2016. 'The Significance of Values: Heritage Value Typologies Re-examined', *International Journal of Heritage Studies* 22(6): 466–81.
Freestone, R., S. Marsden and C. Garnaut. 2008. 'A Methodology for Assessing the Heritage of Planned Urban Environments: An Australian Study of National Heritage Values', *International Journal of Heritage Studies* 14(2): 156–75.
Gale, R. 2016. 'Shall We Tell the Minister? Scale Matters in Public Policy: Place is a Geographic Institution', *Geographical Research* 54(3): 245–55.
Gillespie, J. 2013. 'World Heritage Management: Boundary-making at Angkor Archaeological Park, Cambodia', *Journal of Environmental Planning and Management* 56(2): 286–304.
Green, B. and K. Jones. 2018. 'Place and Large Landscape Conservation along the Susquehanna River', *Society and Natural Resources* 31(2): 183–99.
Green, K.E. 2016. 'A Political Ecology of Scaling: Struggles over Power, Land and Authority', *Geoforum* 74: 88–97.
Heikkila, E.J. and P. Peycam. 2010. 'Economic Development in the Shadow of Angkor Wat: Meaning, Legitimation and Myth', *Journal of Planning Education and Research* 29(3): 294–309.
Hoelscher, S. and D. Alderman. 2004. 'Memory and Place: Geographies of a Critical Relationship', *Social and Cultural Geography* 5(3): 347–55.
ICC. 1993. Minutes: First Meeting of the International Coordinating Committee for the Safeguarding and Developing of the Historic Site of Angkor. Paris, France. Paris: UNESCO.
———. 2003. Minutes: Tenth Meeting of the International Coordinating Committee for the Safeguarding and Developing of the Historic Site of Angkor. Tokyo, Japan. Paris: UNESCO.
Khalaf, R.W. 2017. 'A Viewpoint on the Reconstruction of Destroyed UNESCO Cultural World Heritage Sites', *International Journal of Heritage Studies* 23(3): 261–74.
Lennon, J.L. and K. Taylor. 2012. 'Prospects and Challenges for Cultural Landscape Management', in K. Taylor and J.L. Lennon (eds), *Managing Cultural Landscapes*. Abingdon: Routledge, pp. 345–64.
Levitt, P. and R. De La Torre. 2016. 'Remapping and Rescaling the Religious World from Below: The Case of Santo Toribio and Santa Ana de Guadalupe in Mexico', *Current Sociology*, October 2016: 1–9.
Lloyd, K. and C. Morgan. 2008. 'Murky Waters: Tourism, Heritage and the Development of the Ecomuseum in Ha Long Bay, Vietnam', *Journal of Heritage Tourism* 3(1): 1–17.
Loulanski, T. 2006. 'Revising the Concept for Cultural Heritage: The Argument for a Functional Approach', *International Journal of Cultural Property* 13(2): 207–33.
Loulanski, V. and T. Loulanski. 2014. 'The Heritization of Bulgarian Rose', *Acta Geographica Slovenica* 54(2): 401–10.
Lwoga, N.B. 2018. 'Dilemma of Local Socio-Economic Perspectives in Management of Historic Ruins in Kilwa Kisiwani World Heritage Site, Tanzania', *International Journal of Heritage Studies,* January 2018: 1–19.
Mackinnon, D. 2010. 'Reconstructing Scale: Towards a New Scalar Politics', *Progress in Human Geography* 25(1): 21–36.

Marston, S. 2000. 'The Social Construction of Scale', *Progress in Human Geography* 24(2): 219–42.

Morell, M. 2009. 'Fent barri: Heritage Tourism Policy and Neighbourhood Scaling in Ciutat de Mallorca', *Etnográfica* 13(2): 343–72.

Muzaini, H. 2013. 'Scale Politics, Vernacular Memory and the Preservation of the Green Ridge Battlefield in Kampar, Malaysia', *Social and Cultural Geography* 14(4): 389–409.

Parkinson, A., M. Scott and D. Redmond. 2016. 'Competing Discourses of Built Heritage: Lay Values in Irish Conservation Planning', *International Journal of Heritage Studies* 22(3): 261–73.

Pendlebury, J. 2013. 'Conservation Values, the Authorised Heritage Discourse and the Conservation-Planning Assemblage', *International Journal of Heritage Studies* 19(7): 709–27.

Peycam, P. 2016. 'The International Coordinating Committee for Angkor: A World Heritage Site as an Arena of Competition, Connivance and State(s) Legitimation', *Sojurn: Journal of Social Issues in Southeast Asia* 31(3): 743–85.

Roux, N. 2017. '"A House for Dead People": Memory and Spatial Transformation in Red Location, South Africa', *Social and Cultural Geography*, January 2017: 1–22.

Sheppard, E. and R. McMaster (eds). 2004. *Scale and Geographic Inquiry: Nature, Society and Method*. Malden, MA: Blackwell.

Smith, L. 2006. *Uses of Heritage*. New York: Routledge.

Suri, V.R. and H.R. Ekbia. 2016. 'Spatial Mediations in Historical Understanding: GIS and Epistemic Practices of History', *Journal of the Association for Information Science and Technology* 67(9): 2296–306.

Taylor, K. 2012. 'Landscape and Meaning: Context for a Global Discourse on Cultural Landscape Values', in K. Taylor and J.L. Lennon (eds), *Managing Cultural Landscapes*. Abingdon: Routledge, pp. 21–44.

Tchoukaleyska, R. 2016. 'Public Space and Memories of Migration: Erasing Diversity through Urban Redevelopment in France', *Social and Cultural Geography* 17(8): 1101–119.

Tyner, J, J. Inwood and D. Alderman. 2014. 'Theorizing Violence and the Dialectics of Landscape Memorialization: A Case Study of Greensboro, North Carolina', *Environment and Planning D: Society and Space* 32(5): 902–14.

Vakhitova, T. 2015. 'Rethinking Conservation: Managing Cultural Heritage as an Inhabited Cultural Landscape', *Built Environment Project and Asset Management* 5(2): 217–28.

Vargas, A. 2018. 'The Tourism and Local Development in World Heritage Context: The Case of the Mayan Site of Palenque, Mexico', *International Journal of Heritage Studies*, January 2018: 1–14.

Walter, N. 2014. 'From Values to Narrative: A New Foundation for the Conservation of Historic Buildings', *International Journal of Heritage Studies* 20(6): 634–50.

Waterton, E., L. Smith and G. Campbell. 2006. 'The Utility of Discourse Analysis to Heritage Studies: The Burra Charter and Social Inclusion', *International Journal of Heritage Studies* 12(4): 339–55.

Winter, T. 2007. *Post-Conflict Heritage, Postcolonial Tourism: Culture, politics and Development at Angkor*. London: Routledge.

Young, G. 2016. *Reshaping Planning with Culture*. New York: Routledge.

CHAPTER FIVE

The Politics of Border Heritage
EU's Cross-Border Cooperation as Scalar Politics in the Spanish-Portuguese Border

María Lois

This chapter contributes to the debates around the scalar politics of heritage, by approaching the European Union cross-border cooperation programmes. Previous studies have spotted the necessity of unravelling scale as a major dimension in the making of the EU 'geographies of governance' (Murphy 2008; Van der Wusten and Mamadouh 2008). However, the question remains somewhat understudied when considering cross-border regionalization. Using the concept of scalar politics, I analyse the heritage making of the EU's internal borders within the framework of EU funded politics and policies. Understanding heritage 'as a mode of cultural production' (Kirshenblatt-Gimblett 1998: 149), the chapter focuses on the heritagization practices occurring when spaces, individuals, objects, traditions and so on are reconstructed, reinterpreted and affected to produce heritage (Lois and Cairo 2015). Namely, heritage is approached as a discursive construction (Smith 2006) with material and symbolic significances for communities' imaginations and representations. In this process of meaning making, some voices, sites and values are performed as elements of cultural signification.

The empirical focus of the chapter is on the Spanish-Portuguese border, since the simultaneous entry of Portugal and Spain into the European Community in 1986 marketed the border as a space of development, where EU cross-border cooperation politics and priorities and local actors' practices are actively involved in cross-border regionalization policymaking. As previous research has shown (Lois and Cairo 2015; Prokkola and Lois 2016), multiple agencies of heritagization have placed the Spanish-Portuguese border as a contested site of representation.

Drawing on various materials – such as political and planning documents, institutional and media reports and promotional resources, and also fieldwork at border heritage sites and events, including participant observation in the Eco-raya events since 2014 (including interviews and permanent informal conversations and email exchanges with local institutional and non-institutional actors from both sides of the border) – this study examines how border is narrated, performed and exhibited in EU funded programmes. Hence, border areas are approached as discursive sites, where authorities, locales, the tourism industry, visitors, consumers and so on negotiate what is to be narrated and what is to be silenced, and, specifically, which scalar dimensions are to be found in border heritage sites, events and promotional materials. As previously argued (Prokkola and Lois 2016: 15ff.), this process of meaning making should not be approached as one which is single scaled, since border heritagization implies a wide and complex range of actors and institutions that are themselves distinctively scaled. Border heritagization is related to paradoxical narratives, experiences and geographical imaginations, where the border becomes a space of representational syncretism.

Discourse analysis is a suitable method to interpret the data because it transgresses the division between material and immaterial (Rose 2007); in this case, it supersedes material and symbolic dimensions of border heritage making, paying attention to the re-creation of border across local, regional, national or international discursive scales. At the same time, visual representations and performances are read as discursive sites for the production of scaled textual and visual narratives, since 'all visual representations are made in one way or another and the circumstances of their production may contribute toward the effect they have' (Rose 2007: 14).

The chapter proceeds from conceptualizing EU cross-border cooperation as scale and scalar politics to a presentation of BIN-SAL, a case study of a Spanish-Portuguese cross-border region. The analysis focuses on the events of heritage production and the meanings of heritage itself, exploring the scalarity of visual and textual narratives. The chapter closes with an understanding of the politics of heritagization and cross-border governance as a complex scalar universe where the spatial meaning of EU internal borders is constantly negotiated.

EU Cross-Border Cooperation as Scalar Politics

Scale has been at the centre of geographical thinking since the discipline's institutionalization. In the 1980s, political geographers such as Peter Taylor (1982) and Neil Smith (1984) approached the question from a structural perspective, highlighting the material dimension of scale and enforcing its critical potential. The early 2000s debate between Brenner (2001) and Marston (2000) was key to introducing constructivist and symbolic dimensions, enabling the post-structural horizon of a relational and dynamic notion of scale. Trying to overcome the differences between dominating positions on the debate and to relocate politics in the centre of scalar discussions, MacKinnon (2011: 22) argued for paying attention to the scalar politics; the 'specific processes and institutionalized practices that are themselves differentially scaled'. Institutional and non-institutional actors produce, contest, negotiate, remake, and perform space-making narratives, with rhetorical and material effects. Following on, research in Critical Heritage Studies has also contributed to scale's conceptualization. It has stated not only that 'heritage is an inherently spatial phenomenon' (Graham, Ashworth and Tunbridge 2000: 4) but has also approached the relationship of heritage to scale as a relational process intrinsically linked to continuous political negotiation (Harvey 2015).

EU politics and policies have challenged the image of a single political geography of the so-called integration project (Lois 2013). By promoting specific territorial arrangements as scenarios for its aid and action agenda, EU programmes and initiatives enable scales of politics and policymaking other than the sovereign state, overlapping their territorial logic. Political-geographical configurations such as the European Regional Policy (generally referred to as a 'Europe of the Regions') are key for understanding EU spatial politics. In this view, regions are envisaged and promoted not only as institutional structures but also as strategic formations in planning and development agendas such as the Lisbon Strategy. Basically, European development perspectives address regional arenas as an iconic part of its scalar organization. In the mid 2000s, around 75% of EU regulations were implemented on a regional level (Evers 2006: 81, quoted in Lambregts et al. 2008: 46), normalizing the regional scale as a space of policymaking and political action. Regions become the normalized scale on which to stage EU development repertoires (Ray 1999: 525) such as job creation, competitiveness or economic growth (EC 2017). In this scenario, cultural heritage has become an essential guideline of the EU region making (COM 2014/477 final; Lähdesmäki 2014), conceptualized as an economic asset (Aguilar 2005).

In a 'Europe of the Regions' common framework, cross-border regionalization has become a laboratory to test the integration process (Knippenberg 2004). By forging two (or more) border areas of different states, cross-border cooperation programmes with regional and local actors (institutional and non-institutional; public and private) engage in development strategies where the national states are not the main political space or agency. The new regions are drawn as scenarios to plan, develop and build transnational policies, politics and identities. Programmes such as the iconic

INTERREG are, in other words, 'crucial by enabling the formation of new networks and institutions of transnational planning' (Jensen and Richardson 2004: 13). Thus, EU internal borders are pictured and planned as spaces of intervention: the encounter between heritage and cross-border regionalization, as politics and policies of the EU for border areas, qualifies for transborder spatial identities. In other words, borders become the symbolic and material scale of heritage making, and, therefore, a disputed space of narration. Under the umbrella of the EU institutional framework, border heritagization opens spaces of recognition, negotiation or dispute of scaled representations of the border. Cross-border region making not only opens up a process of scale making but also brings to the fore different heritage scales. It connects border politics, policies, narratives, practices and performances. National and regional authorities, municipalities, stakeholders, local action groups, the tourism industry and other actors in EU-funded initiatives reinterpret, remember, forget, reassess and negotiate the scalar dimension of border meaning. The planning, supervision and exhibition of border heritage is unmistakeably political, and 'the scale of heritage interpretation becomes a political act' (Prokkola and Lois 2016: 17).

In the next sections, a Spanish-Portuguese cross-border region (BIN-SAL) and two projects (Eco-raya and BIN-SAL United Heritage) are examined through the lens of scalar politics. Both case studies are understood to be actions oriented to the meaning making of the territory BIN-SAL via heritage, where the border is conveyed at different scales. The aim is not to realize an exhaustive and systematic inventory but to review some textual and visual narratives to approach the political geographies of heritage in policies and practices of EU cross-border governance.

BIN-SAL, a VIP Territory

BIN-SAL is one example of cross-border regionalization because of the cooperation between institutional actors from the nine municipalities located at the Beira Interior Norte (BIN), in Portugal, and the province of Salamanca (SAL), on the Spanish side. This binational collaboration started in 2001, within the framework of Interreg III-A – that is, the EU initiative promoting cross-border cooperation between neighbouring regions for the period 2000–2006. In this case, the transborder region making was projected as a means to transform the common socio-spatial features of the borderland: a dispersed and aging population, underdeveloped infrastructures, high rates of unemployment and underqualified human resources (Caballero and Cortés 2013). In 2006, the Working Community of BIN-SAL was constituted, giving a legal name and enclosing the area of intervention as the BIN-SAL territory. In the subsequent call for action of the EU cross-border cooperation programmes, BIN SAL became VIP BIN SAL, a set of projects and actions under an acronym that stands for 'Valorize, Innovate and Promote the BIN-SAL territory'. Under the umbrella of VIP BIN-SAL, some projects have been specifically oriented to perform and narrate heritage as a resource for regional development, such as the Eco-raya trademark and events; a scenario for the heritagization and performance of borderland culinary commonalities. There is also a promotional DVD entitled *BIN-SAL United Heritage*, a sample of a scaled narrative oriented to region making.

Performing Cross-Border Heritage: Eco-raya Trademark and Events

Defined as 'a cross-border platform to promote the most representative products of the border area' (OADR-AMCB 2010: 6), Eco-raya focuses on agro-food products and events as a means for rural development. The Eco-raya trademark and events have taken shape as seminars to stage regional food and target local producers; as specific events for cross-border cuisine aimed at restaurant owners (as the I Forum of Cross-Border Cuisine Bin-Sal) and in the Eco-raya fair.

The Eco-raya fair is an annual event organized around a regional agro-food small producers' group from both sides of the border. The first fair took place in 2010, on the Spanish side; the 2011 and 2013 editions were on the Portuguese side. In 2014 the Eco-raya binational Working Group (authorities, professionals, stakeholders) decided to establish the fair at a permanent premise, a cattle marketplace in the peri-urban area of Salamanca (Spain). For the 2016 edition, Eco-raya gathered together ninety-three agro-food producers and artisans exhibiting wines, olive oil, pastries, dairies, honey and bread.

As in any culinary heritage event (Bessière 1998), tasting is an essential activity of Eco-raya. Each year, in the lobby of the fairground, several kiosks stage the Portuguese municipalities of the region promoting rural areas as sites to visit, framing them as tourist attractions. The fair becomes a place-making experience, through the tasting and consumption of border products, sites and experiences: folk music from both sides of the border is an essential part of the agenda.

In the first edition of Eco-raya the Working Community arranged a cross-border food and wine pairing (*maridaje misturado*) using products from both sides to find a mixed match. In 2014, the creation of Agro-Raya as a commercial mark of cross-border territorial-based qualification underlined the notion of quality through local agro-food production and evoked the regional aspect of the border. In 2016, some new activities were incor-

Figure 5.1 In this commercial panel, quality Eco-raya is displayed as a marker of the BIN-SAL territory. Eco-raya's logo combines the two countries' flags, with the lighter character being the symbol of both spellings (*Raya*, in Spanish and *Raia*, in Portuguese), in a sort of hybrid vowel. Photo: Maria Lois, 2016.

porated into the fair's agenda. Catering Colleges from the Portuguese and the Spanish sides performed several cooking sessions to promote and sample the local cuisine of both sides. In the last cooking show, cross-border culinary fusion was also ventured. As in 2010, a merging fusion scale was envisaged as the space for BIN-SAL food heritage making. The Eco-raya edition of 2016 also inaugurated BIN-SAL Seminars, a corner to emplace workshops and talks focusing on local issues such as environmental tourism, agricultural innovation or artificial intelligence applied to cheese tasting. In one of the sessions, some promotional videos were shown and discussed by their authors, such as BIN-SAL United Heritage (*BIN-SAL Patrimonio Unido*): the second case study.

Border as Narrative Resource: BIN-SAL United Heritage

Released in 2013, BIN-SAL United Heritage is a promotional DVD produced by all the agencies related to BIN-SAL region making – the Association of Municipalities of the Beira Interior Norte and the province of Salamanca –

with Interreg Spanish-Portugal Programme funds. The DVD presents two pieces. First, there is a short film (six minutes) also titled BIN-SAL United Heritage. In this piece, folk music is used as a background narrative to display images and ideas related to the region, including cultural diversity, history, biodiversity, food heritage and millenary art. This short film works as a synopsis of the main videopiece: a fifty minute story organized around natural, cultural and craft heritage. Following a first-person narrative documentary model where the storyteller is never shot, the film describes and nominates regional heritage, framing it in a multi-scalar universe.

The audiovisual narration starts by setting the BIN-SAL cross-border territory as a place of past wars and conflicts inhabited by different but very similar people (00.54). Referred to as 'sister lands' (1.00), the two sides of the border are framed as place of current cooperation, where old borders hardly exist (1.20). Once the scenario of today's place making is set, the film defines heritage, as 'a wide set of inherited natural and cultural values' (1.25). Understanding heritage as a commonality coming from both sides and as a source of wealth, BIN-SAL heritage is explored through an assemblage of regional images and folk music.

In the case of natural heritage, the video stresses 'biodiversity as heritage value' (3.50), underlining the variety and richness of regional flora and fauna

Figure 5.2 On the DVD cover, the colours of the flags of the two countries are used to write the title. Photo: María Lois, 2017.

and framing the explanation of BIN-SAL landscape as a model of sustainable development; in other words, as a 'genetic heritage' (15.53). Natural heritage is labelled as a 'national monument to care for' (6.00), preserve and conserve. Moreover, to identify BIN-SAL natural heritage, the narration uses the national listing systems to qualify the Natural Park Arribes del Duero (named as International Park on the Portuguese side) and the mountain ranges of Estrela (Portugal) and Candelario. Concurrently, Natura 2000 – an EU-promoted network of nature protection areas that systematizes the designation of protection and conservation areas in member states – are mentioned as markings for some BIN-SAL natural zones (5.30). In short, authorized heritage discourse (AHD – Smith 2006) is mobilized by referring to national and international heritage conventions and listings.

At the same time, cross-border regional commonalities, in particular, are addressed and scaled, such as Campanula da Estrela (6.50) – an endemic flower that grows on both sides in the mountain ranges, Thermal Waters (18.28) or the religious devotion to Our Lady of the Peña de Francia. All of these elements are narrated as cross-border assets. Other specific borderland issues, such as smuggling, also get particular attention. Smuggling is framed as a survival strategy in times of shortage. Interestingly, the activity is graded as the 'first cross-border cooperation developed by the popular classes' (12.33).

In terms of cultural heritage, the film draws a common cross-border scaled landscape composed of a mixture of art and history, and which embraces buildings, sites, traditions and individuals. Pre-Roman, Roman, Muslim and Jewish remains, castles, bridges, palaces, towers, heraldic shields, historical gardens, a university or a museum of sacred art are displayed as BIN-SAL built heritage: as 'places of interest' (30.30) located on both sides of the border. The video narrative also refers to traditions. Specifically, the film underlines an amateur bullfight celebrated annually in Sabugal (Portugal) (30.08), denominated borderline capeias (*capeias raianas*). AHD reproduces the scalarities of narration by underlining UNESCO World Heritage Sites located in BIN-SAL: the Old City of Salamanca (23.00) and the Prehistoric Rock Art Sites in the Côa Valley (Portugal) and Siega Verde (Spain) – an open-air transborder archaeological zone listed as UNESCO World Heritage Site (25.00).

Once again, BIN-SAL United Heritage features the national AHD by specifically addressing fifteen Historical Sites (*Conjuntos Históricos*) located on the Spanish side, and seven Historical Villages (*Aldeias Históricas*) in Portugal. The Historical Sites are part of the heritage designation system of Historical Spanish Heritage Law passed in 1985, which affected sites such as La Alberca, Ciudad Rodrigo or San Felices de los Gallegos, defined on the DVD as a place that, in an undefined past time, 'belonged to the Portuguese

Crown' (35.30), stressing the pre-state territorial ambiguities. On the Portuguese side, the Historical Villages are sites that have been affected by a heritagization programme started in 1991 by the national government and, from 1994 onwards, partially financed by EU Structural Funds. One of the Historical Villages, Almeida[1] (Portugal), is considered a 'bulwark, confronted to the military fortress of Concepción' (31.12).

The documentary continues with a reference to traditional knowledge and trades, describing heritage as an 'economic asset' (44.30). BIN-SAL autochthonous elements – namely air, water and soil – are designated as the basis of the 'sustainable quality' (44.52) of agro food and artisan products in a sort of 'comestible heritage' (45.00). Finally, popular culture – defined as oral literature, traditional dance and folk music – is labelled as 'an extended, unknown and very much in danger heritage' (46.57).

The video closes with a space-time reference to the past and the future of BIN-SAL: while depicting a scene of an unnamed battle, the narration frames the present time as 'the moment to forget mutual invasions in the two sides of the Iberian borderline, in an effort to walk closely along the path of cooperation' (47.30). The documentary ends by concluding that 'our joint heritage, sometimes as antique as thousands of years, is a solid and trusted proposal for the future. United, we have a lot to show to the world' (47.50).

Discussion

At the Portuguese-Spanish border, the BIN-SAL territory illustrates the process of EU-funded regional heritage making based on mobilizing different spatial identities to illustrate a cross-border landscape. Eco-raya and BIN-SAL United Heritage underline the diversity of scalar politics. The border gets contested, reassured, eaten, forgotten, celebrated, listened to or disrupted in discursive constructions spatially framed – or, in other words, in scalar narratives of heritagization.

Previous research has stressed food as cultural heritage (Brulotte and Di Giovine 2014; Povey 2011), emphasizing the meaning of regional food as a tourist attraction in heritagization and place-making processes (Hall, Mitchell and Sharples 2003; Hjalager and Corigliano 2000; Kneafsey 2000). Around Eco-raya we find cross-border food and gastronomy as a regional cross-border heritagization performance. Framed as an expression of local identity, the Eco-raya trademark and events are to be seen, experienced and consumed, branding the borderland by creating images of quality for cross-border products involving consumers, local producers and other actors. The events give content to a binational icon and border projection, reinforcing a sense of place and mapping the regional through Eco-raya trademark and events. Local food, wine, rural municipalities and folk music qualify the performance of heritagization of a cross-border territory. This mobilization of local resources frames a regional and comestible border, a space in the making that keeps the particularities of the two communities but that also puts forward fusion events and products. In 2015, Eco-raya did not happen. Moreover, the last edition of the fair, Eco-raya 2016, was not EU funded. But the entities that comprise BIN-SAL fully funded the event on this occasion. In fact, seven new municipalities of the Beira Interior (Portugal) have joined the BIN-SAL Working Community through an agreement signed in October 2016. In a personal communication dated 21 January 2017, Spanish local authorities confirmed that the new territory has applied again for EU funding to support the fair, confirming that Eco-raya remains as a conviviality and culinary exchange event, performed at multiple scales as an opportunity for community-appreciated heritage making. The BIN-SAL definition of heritage as a material and symbolic resource sets out a discursive horizon for the area, which is important not only for scholarly reviews but also for local populations, authorities, stakeholders and other actors involved in the EU programmes and initiatives.

In the case of BIN-SAL United Heritage, a multi-scalar politics of representation marks the heritagization of the region. The documentary itemizes a collection of objects, sites, memories, traditions and living beings to conform to the description of the transnational area. In this description, different scales frame the meaning of border heritage(s), underlining how border heritage may involve paradoxical scalar narrations of the same space. On the one hand, BIN-SAL natural heritage is monumentalized at the national scale. Presented as a system to preserve and conserve, nature is framed as a nationally scaled communal good. At the same time, UNESCO and EU listing systems are mentioned to qualify the heritagization of the local landscape.

Parallel scaled narratives also work when the local landscape is heritagized in the story through a reading of its value through the lens of the national scale. In other words, border heritage place making is also mediated by an eloquent connection with statehood stories, related to invasions, wars and state-building conflicts between both countries. In specific cases, associations with Spanish or Portuguese Crowns in undefined times are evoked to draw meaningful narratives for some local spots. Defensive systems – Almeida and Concepción fortresses – are narrated as local landmarks in the modern nation building, amplifying the symbolic character of military fortresses and the border conflicts as a normalized expression of national stories: it makes sense for walled and fortified cities to be at the border. But, at the same time, borderland narratives underline connections between both sides of the border, qualifying capeias, endemic flowers, prehistoric art or smuggling as particularities of the borderland landscape. Transnational narratives reinforce a cross-border spatiality of heritagization that addresses the particularities of the area and, specifically, the territorial logic of the states. Particularly, in the case of smuggling, the qualification of border historical transgression illustrates how local spatial identities become mobilized for local heritagization processes. Setting smuggling as the first cross-border cooperation by popular classes reframes border as a space of collaboration and situates that cooperation in a pre-EU moment.

Conclusions

The EU cross-border cooperation programmes unveil an opportunity to discuss the sociopolitical significance of EU geographies of governance. Cross-border regions promoted as spaces of development get institutionally labelled as scales for place-making identities based on border heritagization. Memories, stories, traditions, events and affections take on cultural significance through border representations and performances, which are constantly being negotiated by different actors. In this context, the scale of border representations and performances become a highly political terrain (Prokkola and Lois 2016: 17), since institutionally funded heritage making may qualify multiple practices of 'differentially scaled' (MacKinnon 2011) borders. Concurrently, EU cross-border cooperation politics and policies seem to be an essential dimension to reflect on heritage in the European context. On the one hand, policies and politics mark a general framework, an institutional reference and a scale for cross-border region making. On the other hand, the practices of heritagization related to this framework show the paradoxical and representational syncretism related to border cultures. The exhibition of heritage as a reconciliation path to be followed in cross-border areas sets border heritage as a contested space of border meaning, where state and non-state scaled representations of the border coexist in border heritage politics.

Firstly, the construction of a culinary heritage in Eco-raya displays a fusion of scales that puts forward new directions in affirming cross-border paths' common experiences. EU cross-border cooperation programmes enable practices of heritagization through meaning-making activities that perform the border as a space for coexistence and binational fusion. Simultaneously, the EU definition of heritage as an economic and symbolic asset is also confirmed and practised: even if there is not EU funding to support Eco-raya celebration, local authorities and agencies are able to finance the fair.

Secondly, an approximation to the promotional material related to BIN-SAL heritage making highlights the representational syncretism of border communities. Issues such as the heritagization of smuggling subvert the official geographies of the borderland: the transgression of the border is commemorated, centring a scaled narrative from the margins of statehood. In short, the diversity of heritagization agencies qualify the different scales of representation of the border. Moreover, the mention of AHD underlines the mobilization of multiple borderland spatial identities and meaning making: global, European, national and regional listing systems are evoked to qualify borderland heritage and to make sense of local resources through the interaction of multiple scales.

Finally, examining specific cases of cross-border regional place making allows the diverse socio-spatial organizations prevailing in border areas to be exhibited. Scaled narratives displayed in border heritage enunciate borders as spaces for national commemorations but also as arenas of meaning-making negotiation of local narratives and performances as well. In that universe, border understandings oscillate from defensive and conflictive to a nexus between similar peoples, underlining paradoxical and puzzling narratives of the past. The border is heritagized as a place of conflict where local communities defend their belonging to statehoods. But also, memories and objects are scaled in a cross-border narrative of collaboration that may commemorate the cooperative transgression of the borderline. Therefore, the interaction between EU institutional politics and policies and the practices of a range of national, regional and local actors enables other power geometries of EU internal borders. Coming closer to the border spatial stories highlights the authorized narratives, voices and performances of the border but also reorders and contests them, by normalizing other voices, other narratives, other experiences and, significantly, other border spatialities. As previous research has underlined, if similar practices occur in different EU border areas (Prokkola and Lois 2016), the stories about life in border regions gain wider significance. This question turns the EU cross-border cooperation politics and policies into a scalar politics, since institutionally promoted cross-border scale making through heritage may reorder the politics of representation of borders, qualifying different spaces and times and opening different horizons to think about border regions and cross-border interaction and cooperation.

Acknowledgements

This work was supported by the Ministry of Economy and Competitiveness of Spain under Grant CSO2012-34677, and by the Autonomous Community of Madrid under Grant S2015-HUM3317. A partial previous version of this case study has been published in Prokkola and Lois (2016).

María Lois (PhD, PoliSci) is a Lecturer at the Department of Political History, Theories and Geography, Universidad Complutense of Madrid (UCM), Spain. Lois specializes in political geography and geopolitics, particularly in heritage as spatial politics in the European and Latin American contexts. She is a member of the UCM Research Group Space and Power and also of Polarts (The Politics and the Arts), a Standing Research Group within the ECPR (European Consortium for Political Research). She also chairs the Research Committee 15 (Cultural and Political Geography) of the International Political Science Association (IPSA-AISP) and is co-editor of the journal *Geopolítica(s)*.

NOTE

1. For an analysis of Almeida border heritage through EU-funded Almeida History and Military Museum, see Lois and Cairo (2015).

REFERENCES

Aguilar, E. 2005. 'Patrimonio y globalización: el recurso de la cultura en las Políticas de Desarrollo Europeas', *Cuadernos de Antropología Social* 21: 51–69.
Bessière, J. 1998. 'Local Development and Heritage: Traditional Food and Cuisine as Tourist Attractions in Rural Areas', *Sociologia Ruralis* 38(1): 21–34.
BIN-SAL Patrimonio Unido. 2013. DVD recording. Salamanca: Comunidad de Trabajo BIN-SAL.
Brenner, N. 2001. 'The Limits to Scale? Methodological Reflections on Scalar Structuration', *Progress in Human Geography* 25(4): 591–614.
Brulotte, R. and M. Di Giovine (eds). 2014. *Edible Identities: Food as Cultural Heritage*. Farnham: Ashgate.
Caballero, A. and C. Cortés. 2013. 'Micro-producciones de base agrícola y desarrollo de la raya: Salamanca, Beira Interior Norte y Duero Superior', in Organismo Autónomo de Empleo y Desarrollo Rural (OAEDR) *La cooperación transfronteriza (POCTEP 2007–2013)*. Salamanca: Diputación de Salamanca, pp. 104–17.
EC (European Commission). 2017. 'Regional Policy'. Retrieved 15 April 2017 from http://ec.europa.eu/regional_policy/index.cfm/en/.
Graham, B., G.J. Ashworth and J.E. Tunbridge. 2000. *A Geography of Heritage*. London: Arnold.
Hall, C.M., R. Mitchell and L. Sharples. 2003. 'Consuming Places: The Role of Food, Wine and Tourism in Regional Development', in C.M. Hall, L. Sharples, R. Mitchell, N. Macionis and B. Cambourne (eds), *Food Tourism Around the World: Development, Management and Markets*. London: Butterworth Heinemann, pp. 25–58.
Harvey, D. 2015. 'Heritage and Scale: Settings, Boundaries and Relations', *International Journal of Heritage Studies* 21(6): 577–93.

Hjalager, A.-M. and M. Corigliano. 2000. 'Food for Tourists-Determinants of an Image', *International Journal of Tourism Research* 2(4): 281–93.
Jensen, O.B. and T. Richardson. 2004. *Making European Space: Mobility, Power and Territorial Identity*. London and New York: Routledge.
Kirshenblatt-Gimblett, B. 1998. *Destination Culture: Tourism, Museums and Heritage*. Berkeley: University of California Press.
Kneafsey, M. 2000. 'Tourism, Place Identities and Social Relations in the European Rural Periphery', *European Urban and Regional Studies* 7(1): 35–50.
Knippenberg, H. 2004. 'The Maas-Rhine Euroregion: A Laboratory for European Integration?', *Geopolitics* 9(3): 608–626.
Lähdesmäki, T. 2014. 'The EU's Explicit and Implicit Heritage Politics', *European Societies* 16(3): 401–21.
Lambregts, B. et al. 2008. 'Effective Governance for Competitive Regions in Europe: The Difficult Case of Randstad', *GeoJournal* 72: 45–57.
Lois, M. 2013. 'Re-significando la frontera: el caso de la Eurociudad Chaves-Verín', *Boletín de la Asociación de Geógrafos Españoles* 61: 309–27.
Lois, M. and H. Cairo. 2015. 'Heritage-ized Places and Spatial Stories: B/Ordering Practices at the Spanish-Portuguese *Raya/Raia*', *Territory, Politics, Governance* 3(3): 321–43.
MacKinnon, D. 2011. 'Reconstructing Scale: Towards a New Scalar Politics', *Progress in Human Geography* 35(1): 21–36.
Marston, S. 2000. 'The Social Construction of Scale', *Progress in Human Geography* 24(2): 219–42.
Murphy, A.B. 2008. 'Rethinking Multilevel Governance in a Changing European Union: Why Metageography and Territoriality Matter', *GeoJournal* 72(1): 7–18.
OADR-AMCB [Organismo Autónomo de Empleo y Desarrollo Rural and Associação de Municípios da Cova da Beira]. 2010. *II feria Eco-raya: Catálogo Sectorial*. Salamanca: Diputación de Salamanca.
Povey, G. 2011. 'Gastronomy and Tourism', in P. Robinson, S. Heitmann and P. Dieke (eds), *Research Themes for Tourism*. Oxfordshire: CABI International, pp. 233–48.
Prokkola, E.-K. 2007. 'Cross-border Regionalization and Tourism Development at the Swedish-Finnish Border: "Destination Arctic Circle"', *Scandinavian Journal of Hospitality and Tourism* 7(2): 120–38.
Prokkola, E.-K. and M. Lois. 2016. 'Scalar Politics of Border Heritage: An Examination of the EU's Northern and Southern Border Areas', *Scandinavian Journal of Hospitality and Tourism* 16(1): 14–35.
Ray, C. 1999. 'Towards a Meta-Framework of Endogenous Development: Repertoires, Paths, Democracy and Rights', *Sociologia Ruralis* 39(4): 521–37.
Rose, G. 2007. *Visual Methodologies: An Introduction to the Interpretation of Visual Materials*. Sage: London.
Smith, L. 2006. *Uses of Heritage*. Oxford: Routledge.
Smith, N. 1984. *Uneven Development*. New York: Routledge.
Taylor, P.J. 1982. 'A Materialist Framework for Political Geography', *Transactions of the Institute of British Geographers* 7(1): 15–34.
Van der Wusten, H. and V. Mamadouh. 2008. 'Geographies of Governance in the European Union: An Introduction', *GeoJournal* 72(1): 1–5.

 CHAPTER SIX

Broadening the Scope of Heritage
The Concept of Cultural Environment and Scalar Relations in Finnish Cultural Environment Policy
Satu Kähkönen and Tuuli Lähdesmäki

There has been a growing trend of strengthening the role of cultural heritage values in environmental discussions, policies and management plans in Europe. These discussions, policies and plans have traditionally been dominated by ecological and economic perspectives, but recently more holistic approaches have been developed by international, national and regional actors in order to respond to the scope and complexity of heritage management and environmental issues. At the European level, attempts at a more holistic approach to the environment and its cultural heritage values have been put forward in several conventions and policy strategies, such as the Council of Europe Framework Convention on the Value of Cultural Heritage for Society (commonly referred to as the Faro Convention, 2005) and the European Commission's heritage policy 'Towards an integrated approach to cultural heritage for Europe' (2014). The policy discourse of these European actors emphasizes 'an enlarged and cross-disciplinary concept of cultural heritage' and 'the value and potential of cultural heritage wisely used as a resource for sustainable development and quality of life in a constantly evolving society', as the Faro Convention puts it (CofE 2005: 1). A key idea in these holistic approaches is to encourage the collaboration of diverse stakeholders to promote 'sustainable growth and employment' and 'innovative forms of community-oriented management' that are perceived to improve the economic and social potential of areas – particularly in rural and remote regions (EC 2014: 6).

In Europe, the integrated approach to heritage has been followed and applied in national and regional policies and management plans, in which environmental aspects and cultural heritage values are often connected to broader questions of sustainability, development, biodiversity, livelihood and well-being of regions. Differences in academic, administrative and institutional settings have, however, brought about many different but parallel conceptualizations of cultural heritage values in a broader environmental and societal context and introduced various policy models, initiatives and collaborative activities to deal with these values. Since the adoption of the European Landscape Convention in 2000, the concept of landscape has often been promoted as a useful holistic frame to organize cooperation and to understand, protect and promote natural and cultural heritage. For example, UNESCO launched its Urban Historic Landscape (HUL) approach in 2011.

In the Nordic countries, an expanded and cross-disciplinary context of heritage has been discussed and rationalized with the concept of cultural environment. The idea of cultural environment was selected as an administrative concept in Nordic countries in the late 1980s and the beginning of the 1990s. The concept's selection was influenced by the topical discussions of sustainable development, and it was seen as a neutral and fitting concept to help to promote integrating built heritage protection into the other administrative sectors, especially strengthening preservationist points of view in land use planning. This conceptual innovation has particularly established its position in Swedish and Finnish heritage policy and management discourses. In Finland, the focus of the concept has mainly been on regions, but its regional emphasis is in various ways connected to international environment and heritage policy discourses.

Cultural environment is a conceptual innovation that merges and penetrates several scalar categories. The concept broadens the focus of the concept of heritage by drawing together cultural heritage values, environment and their capacity to function as an economic, social and cultural resource for the region. Cultural environment policies are typically structured as top-down but with a strong emphasis on engaging bottom-up views and actions in the preparation and implementation of the policies. These policies are based on broad inter-sectoral collaboration by experts from different policy sectors. In the cultural environment policies the interests, key themes and vocabulary of the regional, national, European and international heritage and environmental discourses intersect.

This chapter discusses the emergence of the concept of cultural environment and explores how cultural environment has become an issue in heritage policy and what role scale plays in this policy. The chapter focuses on a genealogy of the concept in the Nordic countries in general, and particularly in Finland, from the point of view of politics of scale. First, we examine the semantic meanings of the concept and how it broadens the notion of heritage into a cross-disciplinary and inter-sectorial category. Secondly, we explore cultural environment administration and the interaction and power relations in its scalar structure. Our discussion focuses particularly on the relationality of 'the regional' and its connections to the other scales – the local, national and European/EU – in the cultural environment policy discourse and administration. We claim that cultural environment is a conceptual tool for negotiating broader meanings of the region and 'the regional', such as competitiveness of the region, and, thus, it has a crucial role in the politics of scale in current heritage policy discourse.

Our research material consists of heritage legislation and governmental heritage policy documents from Finland, Sweden, Norway and Denmark and cultural environment programmes produced in different Finnish regions between 1995 and 2013. Between these years, altogether nineteen Finnish regional cultural environment programmes were created. The material was examined by the method of close reading (Brummet 2010) with a focus on textual analysis of the semantic contexts, meanings and uses of the concept of cultural environment. The analysis focused particularly on scalar relations that the concept and its use entail in the research material.

The chapter proceeds from the discussion of the emergence and development of the concept of cultural environment to exploration of the concept's semantics in Nordic heritage legislation and policy discourse. This discussion is deepened by close reading of the contents of regional cultural environment programmes produced in Finland. We end with a discussion of scalar relations in Finnish cultural environment policy and conclusions on the politics of scale included in the concept.

From Cultural Landscape to Cultural Environment

The roots of the concept of cultural environment can be traced to the discourse on cultural landscape. These two concepts have many points of resemblance in administrative use and in many ways they overlap. However, in contrast to cultural environment, the concept of cultural landscape has a long tradition in academic use. Cultural landscape (*Kulturlandschaft*) is one of the classical concepts of geography, first used by German geographers such as Carl Ritter in 1832, Carl Vogel in 1851, Joseph Wimmer in 1882 and Friedrich Ratzel in 1893 (Potthoff 2013). The use of the concept in nineteenth-century German academic discussion includes different notions of the concept, ranging from perceiving cultural landscapes as developed from natural landscapes – and, thus, opposing nature and culture – to an understanding of cultural landscape as agricultural or park landscape (Potthoff 2013). In nineteenth-century German discussion in general, the concept of cultural landscape refers to a landscape modified by human influence. In the early twentieth century, the concept found its way to English-speaking academia as well as to geographers and ethnologists in the Nordic countries. From the 1960s onwards, other disciplines increasingly adopted the concept, and it entered the terminology of environmental management, becoming a part of agricultural politics, nature protection and cultural heritage management (Jones 2003; Jones and Daugstad 1997).

In the 1990s, several international actors adopted the concept of cultural landscape as a conservation category (Jones 2003: 21). UNESCO's World Heritage Committee agreed in 1992 on revised operational guidelines specifying that cultural landscapes could be protected in accordance with the 1972 World Heritage Convention (UNESCO 1992). In 1996, the operational guidelines were expanded to describe how cultural landscapes fall into three main categories: 'clearly defined landscapes designed and created intentionally by man'; 'organically evolved landscapes'; and 'associative cultural landscapes' that include 'powerful religious, artistic or cultural associations of the natural element rather than material cultural evidence' (UNESCO 1996: 11). In 1995, the Committee of Ministers of the Council of Europe adopted a Recommendation on the Integrated Conservation of Cultural Landscape Areas as Part of Landscape Policies (CofE 1995). In this recommendation, a cultural landscape area is defined as:

> specific topographically delimited parts of the landscape, formed by various combinations of human and natural agencies, which illustrate the evolution of human society, its settlement and character in time and space and which have acquired socially and culturally recognised values at various territorial levels, because of the presence of physical remains reflecting past land use and activities, skills or distinctive traditions, or depiction in literary and artistic works, or the fact that historic events took place there. (CofE 1995: 2)

Despite the differences, administrative use of the concept of cultural landscape can be seen as a useful immediate point of reference when analysing the emergence of the concept of cultural environment. In fact, the concept of cultural environment has been sometimes used as a synonym for cultural landscape. The concept of cultural environment was introduced in European policy discourse by the Council of Europe in 1996 in its Fourth European Conference of Ministers responsible for Cultural Heritage. The Helsinki Declaration on the Political Dimension of Cultural Heritage Conservation in Europe stated: 'Contact with the cultural heritage allows individuals to locate themselves in their own historical, social and cultural environment. This applies to the cultural heritage in its widest sense, including the cultural landscape, the movable and the intangible heritage, as well as the architectural and archaeological heritage' (sited in Pickard 2005: 81). The concept is also referred to – but not further explained or defined – in article eight of the

Faro Convention (CofE 2005) that deals with 'environment, heritage and quality of life'.

The appearance, adoption and varying use of the concept of cultural landscape, as well as the conceptual innovation of cultural environment, reflect particular ideological and political agendas and power interests. Examination of the concept of cultural environment and cultural environment programmes reveals the challenges in finding new means for governing cultural heritage in a situation where heritage is no longer seen as buildings and sites in need of preservation nor as landscapes whose values are expected to be recognized and fostered, but rather as dynamic resources enhancing a sustainable future in diverse social and societal sectors. Besides the broader understanding of heritage, the concept of cultural environment reflects the emphasis of recent heritage policy discourses on broader participation and deeper involvement of communities and civil society in the diverse processes of heritagization. With the new concept, policymakers have sought to respond to the current pressure to decentralize control over defining and managing heritage.

Scalar Semantics of the Concept of Cultural Environment in the Nordic Countries

Before the concept of cultural environment was introduced in European heritage policy discourse, it emerged in Nordic heritage administration and legislation. Sweden, Norway, Denmark and Finland adopted the concept of cultural environment into their heritage and environmental policies around the turn of the 1990s. Although all four countries have used the concept in their administration vocabulary, its meaning, usage or administrative role is not uniform.

In Sweden, the concept (*kulturmiljö*) was added to heritage legislation in 1988, when previously separate laws on archaeological and built heritage and some special provisions for older cultural heritage were merged into a single law (Kulturminneslag 1988). The concept was brought up in an introductory chapter of the law as an overarching concept, stating that protection and care of the cultural environment is a national concern and that responsibility for the cultural environment belongs to everyone (Kulturminneslag 1988: 1 §). In Norway, the concept of cultural environment (*kulturmiljø*) was added to the cultural heritage law in 1992 but in a more limited sense. It was defined as 'areas where cultural heritage is a part of a large entity or context' (Kulturminneloven 1992: 2 §, translation SK).

In Denmark and Finland, the concept was not first introduced in a legislative context. In Denmark, the concept was launched as a part of environmental policy by the Ministry of the Environment in 1994 (Kristiansen 2003). However, its role and use in heritage discussions has declined (Guldberg 2002, 2007). In Finland, the concept of cultural environment (*kulttuuriympäristö*) was taken into active use in environmental and cultural heritage administration in the mid 1990s, when the first cultural environment programmes were launched as tools for cooperation between heritage actors, various administrative sectors and other stakeholders to enhance integration of heritage values into regional and municipal development and planning practices. In the Finnish environment and heritage administration, the concept of cultural environment was selected as the core of the programmes in order to combine the strategic discussion and management of built heritage, cultural landscape and archaeological heritage under the same conceptual frame.

Today in Finland and Sweden the concept of cultural environment is one of the key concepts in national and regional heritage administration. In Sweden, the Cultural Memory Law (Kulturminneslag 1988) was renamed as the Cultural Environment Law (*Kulturmiljölag*) in 2014. At the end of the same year, the Finnish government launched its first national Cultural Environment Strategy. This strategy starts by defining the concept as follows:

> In this strategy, cultural environment refers to a whole formed by human activity, an interaction between humans and the natural environment that includes different kinds of elements of different ages – the everyday human environment. Some parts of it have been defined as targets for protection or otherwise particularly important objects of value. The cultural environment also includes the intangible. (Cultural Environment Strategy 2014–2020 2014: 8)

In Finland, the concept of cultural environment has recently replaced the concept of built heritage in its diverse previous uses (Kähkönen 2015). For example, the European Heritage Days – the annually organized and locally led joint initiative between the Council of Europe and the EU – was called in Finnish 'European Built Heritage Days' (*Euroopan rakennusperintöpäivät*) until 2014, when the name was changed to 'European Cultural Environment Days' (*Euroopan kulttuuriympäristöpäivät*). Similarly, the web portal Rakennusperintö.fi – a portal on built heritage in Finland sustained by the Ministry of the Environment, the Ministry of Education and Culture and the Finnish Heritage Agency – changed its name in 2014 to Kulttuuriympäristömme.fi – 'our cultural environment'. 'Cultural environment' is today a core concept in both heritage administration and communication of the Finnish Heritage Agency. According to it, '[t]he cultural environment consists of relics, the cultivated environment, scenery and traditional biotopes' (Museovirasto 2015), and it uses the concept to draw together preservation, conservation, development, management and legislation in this broad field.

The use of the concept of cultural environment in Nordic legislative and governmental discourse gives its administration a national dimension. The cultural environment is nationally governed through legislation and governmental strategies, although its more specific management is downscaled (see Lähdesmäki, Zhu and Thomas and Zhu in this volume) to regional and local actors. In addition, the semantics of the concept in the administrative discourse downscales its meaning: the discourse emphasizes the proximity of cultural environments to their inhabitants and promotes subsidiarity in their protection and care. The administrative discourse on cultural environment is about politics of scale in action: it seeks to bring heritage as a broad spatial and environmental entity closer to people – both discursively and in administrative practices. Thus, the concept functions as a downscaling tool.

Finland offers an interesting case for closer analysis of politics of scale in cultural environment administration as the national-level policy discourse is put into practice in regional cultural environment programmes produced in different parts of the country. In these programmes the concept is regionalized and concretized while it is affixed to certain physical locations.

The Finnish regional cultural environment programmes commonly start by discussing and defining the concept. The definitions commonly consist of two parts: firstly, a cultural environment is defined as an environment created or influenced by human activity. Secondly, a cultural environment is stated as being comprised of a built heritage, cultural landscapes and archaeological sites. The first part of the definition resembles geography's classical definition of cultural landscape (*Kulturlandschaft*): landscape as areas modified by man, as opposed to natural landscape. The second part brings to the fore tangible heritage categories commonly referred to in traditional heritage discourses. In the broadest sense, the cultural environment is seen in the programmes as covering all environments where one can perceive the actions or effects of humans. This broad understanding of the concept includes all kinds of living environments, such as cities, towns, villages, environments related to livelihoods (agricultural and industrial) and recreational environments (summer settlements, gardens and nature reserves). The programmes commonly point out that the cultural environment is not separated from the everyday living environment. At the same time, the programmes refer to the cultural environment as a primarily endangered environment – as areas or sites with cultural historical values needing care and protection. However, the programmes avoid the word 'protection'. The risks that they suggest threaten the cultural environment include lack of resources, knowhow and appreciation; the end of their original use; climate change; new needs for environments; and a zeal for reform.

The programmes commonly perceive the cultural environment as a spatial unit that has particular cultural historical meanings and a recognized value based upon it. The programmes are about negotiation on what these cultural historical values are and which parts of the environment are perceived as needing special attention or care. In most of the programmes, the focus is on environments whose cultural historical values have already been recognized by previous heritage actors. However, the programmes' contents have been complemented as inventories, and research on new areas has been implemented. For example, modern architecture and suburban areas and their cultural values have been added to recent cultural environment programmes.

Although the concept of cultural environment is used to approach heritage as a cross-disciplinary field, the semantic context of the concept draws from attempts to broaden the policy discussion on built heritage. Through the concept, the programmes seek to expand preservation of the built heritage from separate architectural monuments to broader spatial units and, thus, strengthen the preservationist point of view in planning of land use and construction in both urban and rural areas. Although the concept is explained as covering cultural landscapes, the notion of landscape itself in the programmes mainly refers to a traditional agricultural landscape and, thus, locates the idea of a landscape into rural areas. Although the cultural environment programmes seek to bring together built heritage and cultural landscapes in regional heritage policies and administration plans, the distinction between these two categories still determines the contents of the programmes (Kähkönen 2015).

Networked Nature of Scale and Multidirectional Power Relations in Regional Cultural Environment Programmes

The Finnish regional cultural environment programmes do not only reflect and concretize national-level administration discourse. The programmes include and circulate various international heritage policy discourses whose timely themes, focuses and vocabulary (seek to) make the programmes convincing – and appealing. The programmes manifest the networked nature of scale in heritage policy. In them, various scalar discourses are linked, producing a networked and multi-scalar interaction of discourses.

Moreover, the programmes manifest multidirectional power relations. Heritage discourses and their new concepts do not only move top-down from international to national and from national to regional and local levels but may first emerge, for example, at the national level, as the discussion in the previous section indicates. Neither do heritage policy actors form a top-down hierarchy of power relations. In the case of Finnish cultural environment programmes, regional-level actors do not only implement the policies created at the national level but also develop it by interpreting and concretizing the policy discourse and its core concepts from the regional point of view while putting the policy into practice. Indeed, regional- and local-level actors use their performative power by defining what the concept of cultural environment means in practice and how its care should be managed. The adaption of international heritage policy discourses to regional programmes is a part of this performative power practised by regional actors.

The close reading of Finnish regional cultural environment programmes brought out how their rhetoric is influenced by various international heritage and environmental agreements and strategies and their current policy discourses. Next, we discuss five of these discourses that are most commonly repeated in our research material. The core theme in recent international heritage and environmental policy discourses is to emphasize *cultural heritage as a resource*, as heritage is framed, for example, in the Faro Convention and the European Commission's heritage policy 'Towards an integrated approach to cultural heritage for Europe'. In Finnish regional cultural environment programmes, heritage is also commonly explained as a valuable resource for local and regional communities and for society at large. Heritage is understood as cultural and social capital that enables economic and social well-being in the region.

One of the key goals in Finnish regional cultural environment programmes is to recognize and bring forward the uniqueness of regional or local cultural heritage and promote them as supporters of regional and local identities. This discourse that focuses on *promoting 'the regional'* reflects the broader regional emphasis of EU policy discourses. In European politics, the idea of 'Europe of the Regions' was brought to the fore in the 1980s and early 1990s as a response to emerging European integration (Elias 2008). The EU's new regional emphasis and regional funding instruments opened up new possibilities to elaborate regions in Europe in economic, social and cultural terms and to rethink their identities. In the early cultural environment programmes, the concept of cultural environment was mainly used in a singular form, such as 'the cultural environment of Central Finland'. In these programmes, the (regional or local) environment with its natural characteristics and its heritage sites is seen as a unifying element, forming a base for a shared identity. Thus, the programmes function as tools in regional identity building. In recent years, the plural use of the concept has increased: the concept of cultural environment is used in plural when the desire is to emphasize the importance of the diversity of cultural environments, such as distinctly different features between rural and urban/ modern cultural environments.

The so-called participatory turn (Giaccardi 2012; Roued-Cunliffe and Copeland 2017) has had a strong impact on international heritage and environment management and policy discourses. This turn has transformed heritage into an area of collaborative action and engagement of diverse stakeholders. At the European level, *the participatory emphasis* is brought to the fore, for example, in the Faro Convention and in the Council of the European Union's notices titled 'Council conclusions on participatory governance of cultural heritage'. The Faro Convention includes a conceptual innovation of a 'heritage community' that is expected to be included in the preservation and management of heritage (EofC 2005). The Council conclusions include a list of concrete suggestions on how participatory governance of cultural heritage could take place at the local and regional levels (CofEU 2014).

The Finnish cultural environment programmes emphasize participation and collaboration, though this emphasis is often narrowly understood as collaboration between different administrative sectors. The main goal in the early programmes was to develop collaborative methods for built heritage protection; make it more effective by forming new built heritage working groups or extending already existing ones; distribute responsibilities and concrete work between different actors in the region; and develop collaboration and interaction between regional administrations and municipalities. One important goal was to integrate cultural environment values into regional land use planning and social and economic decision making. The programmes have sought to encourage the inhabitants of a municipality, village committees and landowners to voluntarily care for heritage areas or sites. In some Finnish municipalities, participation in the preparation of cultural environment programmes has been wide-ranging, including, for example, representatives from zoning, nature protection, building supervision, agriculture, schools, day-care centres, travel agencies, local societies and museums. However, the possibilities of participating in the heritage site selection and valuation processes have been limited. Inventories and valuations of the programmes have been commonly conducted by heritage and environment experts.

The notion of *sustainable development* has been present in the Finnish cultural environment programmes from the beginning. The roots of the current discourse of sustainability and its governance can be traced back to the UN Conference on the Human Environment in Stockholm in 1972 (Rouhinen 2014). The term 'sustainable development' was enhanced by the World Commission on Environment and Development (WCED) that was set up in 1983 to unite countries in pursuing sustainable development together. The Commission's report, titled 'Our Common Future', introduced and defined the term (UN 1987). Finland adopted the idea of sustainable development within the political framework early. Finland used the political guidelines of both the Stockholm Conference and the World Commission on Environment and Development to design and institutionalize national environmental and sustainable development policies at the end of the 1980s (Rouhinen

2014). Since then, the cultural aspect has been integrated into the discussion on sustainable development, especially in the context of regional development and planning. In this discussion, cultural sustainability is commonly understood as development that respects and promotes the cultural conceptions of the people involved.

Environmental education is a core idea enhanced by international environment and heritage policy actors. For example, the LIFE Programme – the EU's funding instrument for the environment – was broadened in 2007 with a strand focusing on environmental education, pedagogical interests, awareness-raising campaigns and knowledge-sharing projects. Respectively, the Finnish regional cultural environment programmes underline the educational aspects of caring for and promoting the cultural environment. In the programmes, environmental education is understood in the sense of raising the awareness of civil servants, elected officials, consultants and the citizens about the cultural historical values of the environment. The aim of the education, via the informing and offering of expert services to the municipalities and their inhabitants, is to improve the level of zoning by taking cultural historical values into consideration. Especially in the early programmes, it was often stated that one of the barriers for development of heritage care is the negative attitudes towards protection. In the earliest programmes, the education was, however, mainly directed towards regional and local officials. Later programmes have sought to communicate more directly with the local inhabitants and to pass on to them cultural historical knowledge of locally valuable, characteristic cultural environments.

Scalar Relations in Finnish Cultural Environment Policy

The analysis of the administrative context of the emergence of the cultural environment policy in Finland indicates how the policy is based on close interdependence and interaction of administrative structures – and their changes – at the different scalar levels. The start of the creation of Finnish regional cultural environmental programmes relied on policy reforms at two scalar levels: regional policy reform that had started already in the 1980s and policy reforms at the beginning of the 1990s related to Finland's preparation for accession to the EU. In the administrative and legislative changes made in the 1980s and 1990s, responsibility for regional development was transferred from the national to the regional and local levels. At the same time, the programme work became one of the instrumental tools in regional planning. The law on regional development from 1993 emphasized independent development of regions. In 1994, Finland was divided into twenty regions and they were given their current significance as regional administrative units.

In 1995, Finland joined the EU, and the EU's regional target programmes became a key to complete regional programmes in Finland (Sotarauta and Karppi 2009; Vartiainen 1998). The 1997 reform strengthened further the role of the regions: since the reform, the regions have been governed by regional councils, which serve as forums of cooperation for the municipalities of a region. Regional councils are central actors in promoting the region's interests. The main tasks of the regional councils laid down by law are regional development and regional land use planning. The councils are also largely responsible for the EU's Structural Fund programmes and their implementation – funding through which the EU seeks to support and revive the economy, livelihoods and development of remote or less-developed regions or regions suffering from declined industries or other economic difficulties.

Regional Environmental Centres, established in 1995 as a part of the regional policy reform, have had a core role in coordinating the cultural environment programme processes in Finland. The Act on Environmental Administration from 1995 defines the tasks of the Regional Environmental Centres as follows: 'The Regional Environment Centre is responsible in its territory for the tasks concerning environmental protection, land use, nature protection, care of the cultural environment, building control and use and management of the water resources prescribed and laid down on it' (Laki ympäristöhallinnosta 1995: 4 §, translation SK). In the law, promotion of the management of the cultural environment and preservation of the cultural heritage is mentioned as one of the highlighted tasks of the centres. In 2010, the Regional Environmental Centres were dispended and their tasks were transferred to the newly founded Centres for Economic Development, Transport and the Environment (ELY).

There are major differences between the Finnish regions in terms of resources for preparing cultural environment programmes and investing in cultural environment policies and management. Since 2000, the regional cultural environment programmes have often been prepared in projects funded by the EU's structural and social funds. In addition, EU funding has been used to create new or update existing inventories of cultural environments in the regions and to arrange educational or participatory activities for local people, such as courses on traditional craft skills.

Conclusions

The regional cultural environment programmes have a scalar political goal. Their purpose is to increase the understanding of heritage values in the environmental context and to strengthen the importance of heritage perspectives in broader environmental discussions, policies and management plans.

The cultural environment programmes are promoted and used as tools to extend cooperation between heritage actors, various administrative sectors and other stakeholders. Their aim is to improve integration of cultural heritage into development and planning practices and thereby ensure its preservation and sustainable use. As a conceptual innovation, cultural environment is, thus, used to broaden the traditional scope of heritage. As a policy, it means downscaling the management of heritage. The discourse on cultural environment itself is multi-scalar: it relies on interdependence of various timely heritage discourses at different scalar levels. Its downscaled policy reflects policy goals and structures at 'higher' levels.

The Finnish regional cultural environment programmes are an example of a policy in which the aims of the regional and EU levels merge. The regional cultural environment programmes have often been prepared as a part of broader regional projects funded by the EU. Both policy levels share the same interest in regions and their holistic development and identity building. At the regional level, the fundamental motivation behind the regional policies is to increase the competitiveness of the regions. The EU funding enables the regions to implement various development projects. For the EU, the support for regional development is a tool in its integration politics: viable regions are expected to increase the coherence of the union. In addition, the focus on 'the regional' draws attention away from 'the national', which is a scalar level often considered as problematic by the EU in its attempts to increase the feeling of belonging to the union and creating a European identity (Lähdesmäki 2014; Lähdesmäki and Mäkinen in this volume).

Due to its wide-ranging, transforming and context-specific meanings, the concept of cultural environment easily turns into a tool for politics of scale. Although the management of cultural environments is commonly structured on the basis of territorial administrative units, concrete spatial borders between cultural environments are impossible to draw, as the concept as such is flexible and relational. Cultural environment is, thus, characterized by an ambiguity of meanings. This quality increases its usability, for example, in identity politics, image building, place promotion and city branding.

Acknowledgements

Lähdesmäki's work in this study was supported by the Academy of Finland under Grant SA274295 (EUCHE).

Satu Kähkönen (PhD) is a Postdoctoral Researcher at the Department of Music, Art and Culture Studies, University of Jyväskylä, Finland. Her research focuses on the current trends in Nordic heritage and environmental administration.

Tuuli Lähdesmäki (PhD, DSocSc) is an Academy Research Fellow and Adjunct Professor at the Department of Music, Art and Culture Studies, University of Jyväskylä (JYU), Finland. Lähdesmäki specializes in heritage, culture and identity politics, particularly in the European context. She currently leads the research projects 'European Cultural Heritage in the Making: Politics, Affects and Agency' (EUCHE), funded by the Academy of Finland, and 'Legitimation of European Cultural Heritage and the Dynamics of Identity Politics in the EU' (EUROHERIT), funded by the European Research Council. She is the Co-PI in JYU's research profiling area 'Crises Redefined: Historical Continuity and Societal Change' (CRISES).

REFERENCES

Brummet, B. 2010. *Techniques of Close Reading*. London: Sage.
CofE (Council of Europe). 1995. Recommendation No. R (95) 9 of the Committee of Ministers to Member States on the Integrated Conservation of Cultural Landscape Areas as Part of Landscape Policies, 11 September 1995. Strasbourg.
———. 2000. European Landscape Convention. European Treaty Series – No. 176. 20 October 2000. Florence.
———. 2005. Framework Convention on the Value of Cultural Heritage for Society, Faro, 27 October 2005. Strasbourg.
CofEU (Council of the European Union). 2014. 'Council Conclusions on Participatory Governance of Cultural Heritage', *Official Journal of the European Union* C 463: 1–3.
Cultural Environment Strategy 2014–2020. 2014. Finnish Government Resolution 20 March 2014. Helsinki.
EC (European Commission). 2014. Towards an Integrated Approach to Cultural Heritage for Europe. Communication from the Commission to the European Parliament, the Council, the European Economic and Social Committee and the Committee of the Regions, COM(2014) 477 final, 22 July 2014. Brussels.
Elias, A. 2008. 'Introduction: Whatever Happened to the Europe of the Regions? Revisiting the Regional Dimension of European Politics', *Regional & Federal Studies* 18(5): 483–92.
Giaccardi, E. (ed.). 2012. *Heritage and Social Media: Understanding Heritage in a Participatory Culture*. London: Routledge.
Guldberg, M. 2002. 'The Cultural Environment – The Danish Case', *Ethnologia Scandinavica* 32: 100–14.
———. 2007. 'Fra kulturmiljø til kulturarv: Museerne og det kulturhistoriske arbejde', in M. Hahn-Pedersen (ed.), *Sjæk'len 2006*. Esbjerk: Årbog for Fiskeri- og Søfartsmuseet, pp. 96–117.

Jones, M. 2003. 'The Concept of Cultural Landscape: Discourse and Narratives', in H. Palang and G. Fry (eds), *Landscape Interfaces: Cultural Heritage in Changing Landscapes*. Dordrecht: Kluwer Academic Publisher, pp. 21–51.
Jones, M. and K. Daugstad. 1997. 'Usages of the "Cultural Landscape" Concept in Norwegian and Nordic Landscape Administration', *Landscape Research* 22(3): 267–81.
Kristiansen, K. 2003. 'Forskning, forvaltning og politik – kulturmiljøbegrebets historie som eksempel', in N. Carlberg and S. Møller Christensen (eds), *Kulturmiljø: mellem forskning og politisk praksis*. Copenhagen: Museum Tusculanums Forlag.
Kähkönen, S. 2015. 'Kulttuuriympäristöohjelmien kulttuuriympäristö', *TAHITI – Taidehistoria tieteenä* 4. Retrieved 4 January 2017 from http://tahiti.fi/04-2015/tieteelliset-artikkelit/kulttuuriymparistoohjelmien-kulttuuriymparisto/.
Kulturmiljölag. 1988. The Swedish Parliament. Stockholm. Retrieved 4 January 2017 from http://www.riksdagen.se/sv/dokument-lagar/dokument/svensk-forfattningssamling/kulturmiljolag-1988950_sfs-1988-950.
Kulturminneloven. 1992. The Norwegian Parliament. Oslo. Retrieved 4 January 2017 from https://lovdata.no/dokument/NL/lov/1978-06-09-50.
Lähdesmäki, T. 2014. 'The EU's Explicit and Implicit Heritage Politics', *European Societies* 16(3): 401–21.
Laki ympäristöhallinnosta. 1995. The Finnish Parliament. Helsinki. Retrieved 4 January 2017 from http://www.finlex.fi/fi/laki/alkup/1995/19950055.
Museovirasto. 2015. Cultural Environment, Website of the Finnish Heritage Agency. Helsinki. Retrieved 4 January 2017 from http://www.nba.fi/en/cultural_environment.
Pickard, R. 2005. *European Cultural Heritage: A Review of Policies and Practice*. Strasbourg: Council of Europe Publishing.
Potthoff, K. 2013. 'The Use of "Cultural Landscape" in 19th Century German Geographical Literature', *Norwegian Journal of Geography* 67(1): 49–54.
Roued-Cunliffe, H. and A. Copeland (eds). 2017. *Participatory Heritage*. London: Facet.
Rouhinen, S. 2014. *Matkalla mallimaaksi? Kestävän kehityksen juurtuminen Suomessa*. Kuopio: University of Eastern Finland.
Sotarauta M. and I. Karppi. 2009. 'Aluekehittäminen ja alueellisen muutoksen hallinta', in I. Karppi and L-M. Sinervo (eds), *Governance: Uuden hallintatavan jäsentyminen*. Tampere: Hallintotieteiden keskus, pp. 138–55.
UN (United Nations World Commission on Environment and Development). 1987. 'Our Common Future/Brundtland Report', A/42/427, 4 August 1987. New York.
UNESCO. 1992. Operational Guidelines for the Implementation of the World Heritage Convention, WHC 2, 27 March 1992. Paris.
———. 1996. Operational Guidelines for the Implementation of the World Heritage Convention, WHC/2, February 1996. Paris.
———. 2011. Recommendation on the Historic Urban Landscape adopted by the General Conference at its 36th session 10 November 2011. Paris.
Vartiainen, P. 1998. *Suomalaisen aluepolitiikan kehitysvaiheita*. Helsinki: Sisäasiainministeriön aluekehitysosaston julkaisu 6.

PART III

SCALE IN HERITAGE PRACTICES

CHAPTER SEVEN

Locals, Incomers, Tourists and Gold Diggers
Space, Politics and the 'Dark Heritage' Legacy of the Second World War in Finnish Lapland

Suzie Thomas

In this chapter I draw on the multidisciplinary research project 'Lapland's Dark Heritage', which explores the ways in which people engage with and understand the material legacy of the German presence in Finnish Lapland from the time of the Second World War (WWII). I attempt to conceptualize the notion of politics of scale through the ways in which it relates to this so-called 'dark' heritage, at local, regional, national and international scales, with the scale itself approached in varying ways. The research starting point has been the history of Lapland in WWII, including the so-called 'Lapland War' (1944–45), framed as a contested (and dark) heritage of sorts, with tensions appearing between the public and private spheres, and differently scaled notions of heritage meaning making. Here, one can find 'silenced' and 'forgotten' stories (e.g. Thomas and Koskinen-Koivisto 2016 for discussion of the Lapland War's coverage in Finnish museums), as well as subaltern, alternative approaches to material heritage (e.g. Herva et al. 2016). These varying perspectives have influenced approaches to the research, and in turn the project itself has influenced heritage practices and debates both locally and nationally, in addition to international impacts through academic discourse, and even social media.

According to Jürgen Habermas' 1964 encyclopaedia piece (in Habermas, Lennox and Lennox 1974), the public sphere is 'a realm of our social life in which something approaching public opinion can be formed'. This is different to the private sphere, which is not accessible to all citizens but instead remains exclusively available only to some. The boundaries between private and public spheres within constructions of 'heritage' as a notion and a concern are not always simple to define and delineate. This is true also in the context of scale – with different scalar levels interacting with the private and public in different ways. Heritage professionals' work – museum curators, archaeologists, conservators and others – is often funded through the public purse and espouses to create and share knowledge and resources for 'the public good'. It is a well-trodden path only briefly revisited here, to remind however of the exclusivity of these fields regarding where the power sits, which heritages are valued and told and how access to both knowledge and material culture can be strictly controlled. Similarly, the private and personal perspectives that have been encountered in Lapland are in one sense exclusive (situated within very individual interpretations and perspectives, or in some cases finding synergies within closed special interest groups, for example history hobbyists – see Koskinen-Koivisto and Thomas 2017 for some suggested typologies). Simultaneously, however, they are also based upon public, unrestricted access to places within the cultural and historic environment (although in some cases special knowledge may be needed in order to know how to find these places).

Within the many disciplinary fields clustering around cultural heritage studies, researchers recognize the fluidity of cultural heritage, falling within both private and public spheres. In folklore studies, for example, scholars have acknowledged the role of academic folklorists in transforming what might have once been 'private sphere' practices into discourses in the public sphere (e.g. Bendix and Hasan-Rokem 2012). In archaeology we also see the gaze of 'the academy' falling perhaps belatedly upon topics and periods that long before were already attracting private sphere, non-professional and 'alternative' interest. Concepts such as Smith's 'Authorized Heritage Discourse' (e.g. Smith 2006) and its parallels with discussions of 'officially sanctioned memory' (e.g. Moshenska 2006: 58) remind us that the professional-sanctioned (and sometimes state-influenced, according to Marston 2004 and others) versions of the past and of cultural identity may not necessarily reflect – or even intersect with – the experiences of individuals and groups that encounter that cultural heritage on a localized, daily basis. This has an impact therefore also at the scalar level, with local, regional, national and global understandings of heritage more or less likely in different cases to relate to public or private sphere realms of knowledge and familiarity.

The Notion of 'Dark' Heritage

Terms closely connected to 'dark heritage' include 'difficult heritage', 'contested heritage' and 'dark tourism'. 'Difficult heritage' can relate to aspects of the past that may be difficult or painful to reconcile. It may be characterized as 'concerned with histories and pasts that do not easily fit with self-identities of the groups of whose pasts or histories they are part' (MacDonald 2008: 9). Thus, it can open up challenges to self-image or even social conflicts and controversies. Researchers have also used the idea of 'contested heritage' to acknowledge the differing perspectives that can affect different understandings or interpretations of the same phenomenon. Some events may even be contested to the extent that some deny that they ever happened. Pam Smith (2007) discussed this in relation to the contested heritage of the massacre of Aboriginal people at Mistake Creek in Australia. While the event is commemorated by memorial plaques and remembered with great sadness by the local Aboriginal community, there have been suggestions by some (predominantly white) historians that the atrocity never took place (Smith 2007). This case of course also relates to power and the privileging of some forms of 'evidence' over others for interpretation of the past. The idea of 'dark tourism' appears to have originated as a means of recognizing the process of touristically visiting heritage sites connected with atrocity 'for remembrance, education or entertainment' (Foley and Lennon 1996: 195).

There are clearly overlaps between difficult, contested and dark heritage. Dark heritage must arguably have an element of physical conflict, destruction, forced internment or other kind of atrocity, which may include but also go beyond other, less physically violent or event-related controversies. Therefore, 'dark' heritage is always 'contested' and 'difficult'; but 'difficult' and 'contested' heritage is not always necessarily 'dark', as such types of heritage may relate to controversies or disagreements that are not necessarily connected to violence or violation of some kind. 'Dark heritage' terminologically goes further than 'dark tourism' to recognize that 'dark' heritage has more than just touristic aspects. It can even present problems for public sphere, official heritage interpretations if it has the potential to suggest or support alternative stances to the state-sanctioned version. As Laura McAtackney noted in her study of Long Kesh (also known as the Maze) prison in Northern Ireland: 'The knowledge that dark heritage sites can have a variety of meanings for the various publics that wish to consume them can result in contested and politically loaded sites being overly controlled and interpreted through state interventions' (McAtackney 2014: 229). The 'darkness' of the heritage also depends on the perspective of the viewer, with some finding particular events and periods more traumatic than others, depending on their own perspectives and experiences, including possibly family or other personal associations, and the individual's temporal and geographical proximity to the historical period and location with which the dark heritage is primarily connected.

Brief Historical Context: Finland and Lapland in WWII

Providing a brief historical overview gives context and also helps to illustrate why there is such an abundance of WWII German military material culture in Finnish Lapland. After the 1939–40 three-month 'Winter War' against the Soviet Union, Finland came to cooperate as a 'co-belligerent' with Germany. Between 1941 and 1945, 200,000 or more German troops were stationed in Finland, mostly in the northern regions. Although part of Hitler's Operation Barbarossa against the Soviet Union, the northern front was soon stationary, and German troops based in Finnish Lapland were involved in other activities, developing many different military sites across the region, from Prisoner-of-War camps of different sizes through to garrisons and supply depots (Thomas, Seitsonen and Herva 2016).

From 1941–1944 relationships between the Germans and the local population – Finns and the indigenous Sámi – appear to have been relatively harmonious (Seitsonen and Koskinen-Koivisto 2018). Things, however, began to change in the summer of 1944 when the Soviet Union forced Finland into a ceasefire treaty. As well as losing physical territory – notably from the north, parts of Salla and the area around Petsamo, now known as Pechenga and part of the Russian Federation (Figure 7.1) – the treaty stipulated that the Germans should leave Finland within two weeks. This unrealistic schedule meant that the time it took for Germans to evacuate from Finland into occupied Norway led to increased Soviet pressure on Finland. The Finns therefore turned against their former *Waffenbrüder* (brothers in arms), with the Germans in turn resorting to 'scorched earth' tactics in what became known as the Lapland War (September 1944–April 1945). The enormous scale of destruction included in its wake the German military sites and infrastructures that had been established as well as those settlements that were easy to access from roads (the most remote settlements were spared somewhat).

As Veli-Pekka Lehtola noted, 'many Sámi people in northern Finland had to leave straight from the peatland on an evacuation journey' (Lehtola 2015: 126). The speed at which the evacuation of the whole region started and the 'rupture' (ibid.), particularly in traditional Sámi ways of life, triggered by both the Lapland War and subsequent reconstruction of the dilapidated province into the 1950s, have had profound effects on the way in which notions of place and particularly built heritage have been understood. The Lapland wilderness also has thousands of former German military sites that are now ruins or, as is often the case, 'scars' on the forest floor with little left standing above ground. Due to the volume of seeded landmines as the Germans retreated and despite de-mining efforts shortly after WWII, unexploded ordnance can still also sometimes be found, making the landscape at times a dangerous place.

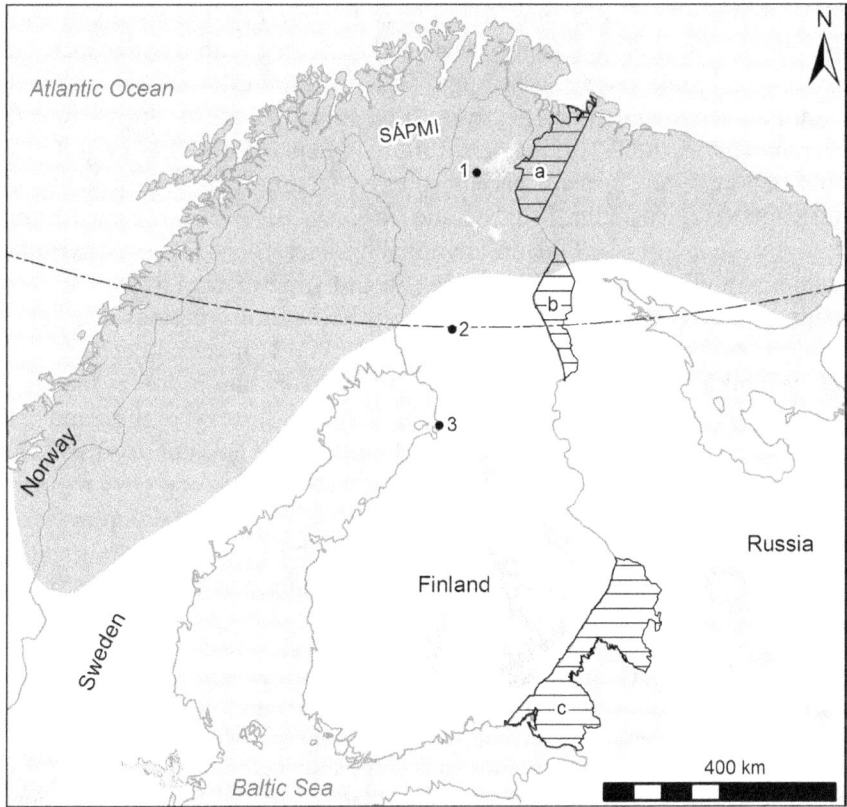

Figure 7.1 Map of Finland and surrounding area showing: 1. Inari; 2. Rovaniemi; 3. Oulu. Areas of Finland ceded to the Soviet Union: a. Petsamo; b. Salla-Kuusamo; c. Karelia. © Oula Seitsonen 2017. Published with permission.

Scaling the Dark Heritage

The presence of military material culture in the wilderness has always been well known *within* Finnish Lapland. Local people have interacted with the materiel in different ways for many years – ranging from forming the setting for children's playtime adventures through to hobbyist historical research and artefact collection. At the same time, this materiel attracted little broader interest and gained virtually no 'official' (public sphere) attention until relatively recently. It is possible to consider the material culture left by WWII in the context of the different ways of considering 'scale', as outlined in the Introduction to this volume.

Within the first definition, of '*scale as a hierarchy*', it is possible to apply the 'nesting doll' concept of scale and heritage to the German materiel present in Finnish Lapland by appraising it from local, regional, national, continental and global perspectives. The Lapland's Dark Heritage research has shown that the WWII material culture in Lapland itself has a significant meaning as 'local', perhaps private sphere (personal) history for many informants (e.g. Koskinen-Koivisto and Thomas 2017: 126). A crowdsourcing venture in 2014 by Finland's national broadcasting company *Yleisradio* demonstrated the nationwide interest in and appetite for history and heritage connected to WWII and other twentieth-century periods of conflict (Seitsonen 2017). Yet in terms of Lapland's WWII material heritage's regional and national significance, its status arguably diminishes as the scale expands outwards, as compared to other 'conflict history' of the same era. Löfström (2011) has also noted that Finnish national identity has been strongly attached to history and particularly conflict history. On a national scale, this history is expressed, recalled and understood on different levels from the personal, private and familiar through to public sphere popular culture. He explains how for Finnish understanding of a national historical narrative:

> Particularly, the years 1939–1944, with two successive wars against the Soviet Union and one against Nazi-Germany, were a formative collective experience that would be summoned up and recalled in numerous films and novels and, to some extent, in family tradition also decades afterwards. Still at the turn of the Millennium, the story about the 'battle of national survival' was the key narrative of Finnish history among the adolescents and an important element of their historical identity. (Löfström 2011: 98)

Despite its position as one of three wars that form Finland's WWII experience, scholars have noted that within this national, arguably state-sanctioned and public sphere imagery, Lapland's wartime experience is often marginalized, compared to the experiences of the Winter and so-called Continuation Wars (e.g. Herva 2014; Kivimäki 2012; Lehtola 2015). These two 'heroic' wars were against the Soviet Union rather than Nazi Germany, itself an awkward issue: 'there is the embarrassment that Finns sided with Nazis who also ended up, as it is remembered in Finland, "burning down Lapland"' (Herva 2014: 300). Furthermore, there is also the feeling, at least among some of the Lapland residents, that their wartime experiences are still neglected as less significant politically than the more southern regions: 'the marginalization of Lapland in the war narratives resonates with a much longer and broader tendency in Finland to regard the north of the country as remote, peripheral and generally less important than the southern "heartlands"' (Herva et al. 2016: 276).

The image of 'evacuee' in Finland is also connected strongly with the Karelians, who had to migrate from the ceded territories in the south (Figure 8.1), and 'Karelianism' itself has been central to Finnish national identity since the early nineteenth century (Mikula 2015: 759). Much less often considered are the people of Lapland, who lost their homes (although see Paksuniemi, Turunen and Keskitalo 2015 for a recent study of Lapland's child evacuees). In terms of continental and global scales of heritage, Lapland shares a commonality with the numerous forms of cultural heritage – from family histories through to places exhibiting evidence of former conflict and to sites of official memorialization – in its connection to the global phenomenon of WWII. However, this common connection does not make for material heritage of WWII becoming global heritage in its own right, and there are tensions – discussed elsewhere (e.g. Hazen 2008) – between the global and the local significance of heritage, which to date have had little impact on the still largely unmanaged conflict heritage of Finnish Lapland. Moshenska's identification of different 'scales' of memory – individual memory, group narratives and social memorialization (Moshenska 2006: 58) – is also relevant in this context.

It is possible to apply the notion of *'scale as an instrument of power'* to the WWII material heritage in Finnish Lapland by scrutinizing the ways in which it is prioritized (or not) in relation to other types of heritage and also by appraising its treatment by different social actors, authorized and otherwise. This particular history is potentially downplayed and thus downscaled by public sphere institutions such as museums (Thomas and Koskinen-Koivisto 2016) while at the same time until recently only enjoying legislative protection primarily through its military status (coming under the ownership of the Finnish Defence Forces) rather than for any heritage considerations. In practice, however, this status is also downplayed, and sites have been vulnerable to looting and other losses of material (Herva et al. 2016: 271; Seitsonen and Herva 2011: 178). There are also scaled issues of power concerning the treatment of Laplanders' identity and issues (including the impact of WWII on them), certainly nationally as colonially 'othered', influencing the outsiders' perception of Lapland and its residents as both exotic and marginal at the same time (e.g. Herva 2014: 298, 315).

Arguably, then, Lapland's 'dark heritage' also has a particular exotic draw – both locally and for actors from further afield. Several interviewees who have engaged with this heritage (especially those originally from elsewhere) commented on the 'magical' experience of being in Lapland (see also Herva 2014). The phenomenological sensation of the 'unspoilt' wilderness, combined with the notion of Lapland as a peripheral, mysterious and even frightening zone on the edge of Europe, creates a sense of excitement for those that consume it as heritage, especially in touristic consumption. Within this framework, it is also possible to consider the Nazis – based on their image in popular fiction (think Indiana Jones' perennial 'bad guys' for example) – as similarly fitting into a fantastical and imagination-laden version of Lapland for those encountering and enjoying this material heritage. Such transformations in status and reimaginings of this heritage also help us to view it in the context of *'scale as a process'* – one that changes and provides different spaces for varied encounters and interactions, as the examples below suggest.

The notion of Lapland as an unspoilt space, a place to experience a 'true' wilderness, also inspired the activities of one local environmental organization in the mid 2000s. *Pidä Lappi siistinä* (Keep Lapland Tidy) organized teams of volunteers from 2005 until around 2007 to clear away the 'war junk'. Seemingly driven by the wish to 'restore' the wilderness to a 'pristine' condition, as well as to remove the potential safety hazards posed by rusting barbed wire, unexploded ordnance and other material, some in the media began to accuse the organizers of profiting from selling the collected material as scrap metal and even sometimes (allegedly) as collectors' items to memorabilia collectors (Thomas, Seitsonen and Herva 2016: 339). At the same time, while the sites had no protection through the status of official cultural heritage, the clearing activities did move some heritage professionals to criticize openly the way in which these wartime sites were being dismantled and destroyed without scientific documentation. As Vesa-Pekka Herva has noted (Herva 2014: 303–4), local communities also complained that *their* heritage and history was being destroyed, perhaps another reference to scaled power or, in this case, scaled powerlessness on the most local level in the face of decisions being made about the historic environment.

It is noteworthy that since then not only have the clearing activities of *Pidä Lappi siistinä* ceased but state-authorized surveys of WWII sites have increased, and the Finnish Heritage Agency– Finland's national cultural heritage authority – has even extended its categories to include the vague typology of 'other cultural heritage site' (Enqvist 2014: 113; Seitsonen 2017). This broad classification nonetheless shows the potential within Finnish cultural heritage management at last to bring WWII sites to national level, state (public sphere) recognition as worthy of protection. Furthermore, in 2010–2015 Metsähallitus (the Finnish Forestry Commission) surveyed and mapped war historical sites on its land, and archaeological research into WWII heritage is underway at Siida, the Finnish Sámi Museum. The timing, in the mid 2000s, of this apparent 'dawning' of a professional and academic interest in sites connected to the twentieth century incidentally corresponds with similar developments in other parts of Europe – such as the First World War's Western Front regions. There, interest in the conflict sites transitioned from the non-professional and arguably private sphere of history hobbyists and amateur researchers to the more public (and yet in other ways exclusive) sphere of professional archaeology and museology (Van Hollebeeke, Stichelbaut and Bourgeois 2014). Similar to this dawning of scholarly interest in not only the history but also the material culture of the First and Second World Wars seen elsewhere, the research in Finnish Lapland – through the very existence of this research project and also others (e.g. Sääskilahti 2016) and the active dissemination of findings – is networking this heritage (previously mostly of interest to a few local and private actors) into a global academic discourse. The project has, in effect, 'upscaled' the heritage in terms of those networks of scholarly actors that are aware of and discussing it. This has brought with it the researcher team's own networks – with colleagues from overseas accompanying field excavations and dissemination through international conferences and publications. A public excavation in August 2016 in Inari also triggered a debate in the national press as to whether there should be more attention paid to the touristic potential of the WWII heritage (Suoninen 2016). Furthermore, live updates from the excavation via social media channels such as Twitter, Facebook and Instagram garnered followers and interactions from around the world. There has been other regional networking as the research team has made connections, potentially also for future related research avenues, with heritage and museum professionals across Finland and transnationally in neighbouring countries.

The project has also uncovered and analysed more private sphere local networks involving different community actors and the military materiel. The politicization of heritage is no less visible in Lapland than elsewhere. Even the 'war junk' – at one time officially neglected and removed – can become contested at international, national, local and personal levels and across networks. We have encountered challenges to our own presence as researchers, with some Sámi residents in the village of Vuotso the summer of 2015 asking why the team, as non-Sámi, are researching *their* heritage, in effect taking ownership of the decaying 1940s German military materiel. Questions put forward about where excavated material and archives will be deposited (originally our intention was to consider archives in Oulu and Rovaniemi) quickly made the research team realize that the archives must also be offered to Siida, located in Inari, in order to acknowledge not only the geographical location context of our research but also its specific meaning to Sámi communities. This sense of ownership is perhaps for some due simply to the geographic location of many of our case studies in *Sápmi* – the traditional lands of the Sámi people. It may also reflect the impact – at the time – of the German presence in Lapland and, perhaps even more than this, the normalization of remnants of the war in the landscape and hence everyday lives of people living and going about their business.

Similarly, the research team, and I in particular, have been interested in the activities of artefact collectors in the region – some of whom amass their (good condition) collections directly from their network of contacts among local survivors and their families, while others collect (less well preserved) material directly from the wilderness. Almost all of the collectors interviewed have a particular interest in German (Nazi) material and also material connected to the Finnish SS. Due to the research aims of our project, we actively sought out collectors interested in WWII militaria in Lapland or of Lapland rather than general militaria collectors, which naturally also skewed the viewpoints of our interview sample as a whole. We interviewed four collectors among our many informants, all of whom were based in Lapland, and all of whom were introduced to us through antiques dealers with whom we had already been acquainted through our research. Eva Kingsepp has researched in depth the so-called 'Nazi fans', people who collect (often secretively, for fear of being misunderstood) Nazi memorabilia. She concludes that the fascination with Nazi memorabilia most often has nothing to do with any identification with Nazi ideology but is far more situated in the role of Nazi Germany in popular culture; a fantasy version of the Nazis (Kingsepp 2006). It is less clear, however, that this kind of 'Nazi fan' is what we are encountering in Finnish Lapland.

The research has uncovered yet another lens through which to view collectors in Lapland, one which is deeply tied to notions of place and territory, but also to family. Most of the collectors have a relative who was involved in the military in WWII (for example as a Finnish SS officer or even as a German soldier – the offspring of German men and Finnish women in Lapland during this period has been discussed elsewhere – e.g. Väyrynen 2014: 223–225). Furthermore, many informants have explained in interviews and conversations that – for them – the period is not a 'dark heritage' (as our project's title would suggest), but it is interesting to them because it is *local* history. It is situated in *their* landscapes and townscapes, *their* local environment. By collecting the material and caring for it privately in their homes – and in some cases in 'home museums' (or 'vernacular museums' – see also Mikula 2015 for discussion of these in connection to Karelia), many also want to make sure this material heritage stays where it 'belongs'. Hence this concept of 'belonging' – often connected to identity and conceived of as scalar or even 'multi-scalar' (see Lähdesmäki et al. 2016) – can relate as much to objects and materiality as it can to people.

Closing Reflections

In this chapter I presented just some of the different ways, privately and publicly, in which engagement with the 'dark heritage' of Lapland's WWII experiences may take place and how this may relate to practice – both of heritage professionals and of hobbyists and other community actors. This is a period of change, with the Lapland War enjoying a recent limelight moment in popular culture (for example, forming the backdrop for a feature film based on a bestselling novel – *Kätilö* (Kettu 2011) – in 2015) and with cultural heritage managers, the media and other decision makers and influencers beginning to pay attention to the physical remains of this period as a 'national', albeit locally (and nationally) contested, heritage. Despite the impact of recent research, and of the media and other interest that it has generated, the issues connected to the north of the country and the communities therein are still felt by many to be sidelined at a national scale. Some of this feeling no doubt also has to do with the perceived peripheralization of indigenous issues generally.

Furthermore, studies of WWII in general are in a crucial and transitional period, with many of those who remember the period first hand coming to the end of their lifespans. This will undoubtedly have a profound impact on the nature of research and the approaches that are possible in the future as, for example, memory studies and interviews with remaining survivors become less possible. Public and private spheres appear to be porous, with aspects of the heritage also transitioning between – or coexisting within – the two. Combining this back and forth, or perhaps more accurately coexistence, between the public and the private, with the different scales of heritage perceptions and the politics that are associated, presents an even more complex and fluid picture. It also seems likely that our own actions as researchers have an impact on the ways in which this particular region and period is perceived and thus understood at local, national and international levels. We may find that certain aspects of the heritage discourses transition from private to public spheres of interest, as we ourselves draw attention to the region and its WWII legacy.

Acknowledgements

This chapter stems from the research project 'Lapland's Dark Heritage: Understanding the Cultural Legacy of Northern Finland's WWII German Materialities within Interdisciplinary Perspectives', which is funded by the Academy of Finland, decision number 275497.

Suzie Thomas (BA, MA, PhD) is Professor of Cultural Heritage Studies at the University of Helsinki, Finland. She is interested in non-professional and so-called alternative engagements with cultural heritage, 'dark' heritage and heritage crime. She worked as a Postdoctoral Researcher on the Academy of Finland Project 'Lapland's Dark Heritage: Understanding the Cultural

Legacy of Northern Finland's WWII German Materialities within Interdisciplinary Perspectives' (decision number 275497) and is now Principle Investigator of Academy of Finland Consortium Project 'SuALT: Collaborative Research Infrastructure for Archaeological Finds and Public Engagement through Linked Open Data' (decision numbers: 310854, 310859 and 310860). She teaches masters-level courses in Cultural Heritage Studies and Museum Studies.

REFERENCES

Bendix, R. and G. Hasan-Rokem. 2012. 'Introduction', in R. Bendix and G. Hasan-Rokem (eds), *A Companion to Folklore*. John Wiley & Sons, pp. 1–6.

Enqvist, J. 2014. 'The New Heritage: A Missing Link between Finnish Archaeology and Contemporary Society?', *Fennoscandia Archaeologica* XXXI: 101–23.

Foley, M. and Lennon, J.J. 1996. 'Editorial: Heart of Darkness', *International Journal of Heritage Studies* 2(4): 195–97.

Habermas, J., S. Lennox and F. Lennox. 1974. 'The Public Sphere: An Encyclopedia Article (1964)', *New German Critique* 3: 49–55.

Hazen, H. 2008. '"Of Outstanding Universal Value": The Challenge of Scale in Applying the World Heritage Convention at National Parks in the US', *Geoforum* 39(1): 252–64.

Herva, V.-P. 2014. 'Haunting Heritage in an Enchanted Land: Magic, Materiality and Second World War German Material Heritage in Finnish Lapland', *Journal of Contemporary Archaeology* 1(2): 297–321.

Herva, V.-P., E. Koskinen-Koivisto, O. Seitsonen and S. Thomas. 2016. '"I Have Better Stuff at Home": Alternative Archaeologies and Private Collecting of World War II Artefacts in Finnish Lapland', *World Archaeology* 48(2): 267–81.

Kettu, K. 2011. *Kätilö*. Helsinki: WSOY.

Kingsepp, E. 2006. '"Nazi fans" but not Neo-Nazis: The Cultural Community of "WWII Fanatics"', *Critical* Studies 28(1): 223–40.

Kivimäki, V. 2012. 'Between Defeat and Victory: Finnish Memory Culture of the Second World War', *Scandinavian Journal of History* 37(4): 482–504.

Koskinen-Koivisto, E. and S. Thomas. 2017. 'Lapland's Dark Heritage: Responses to the Legacy of World War II', in H. Silverman, E. Waterton and S. Watson (eds), *Heritage in Action: Making the Past in the Present*. New York: Springer, pp. 121–33.

Lähdesmäki, T. et al. 2016. 'Fluidity and Flexibility of "Belonging": Uses of the Concept in Contemporary Research', *Acta Sociologica* 59(3): 233–47.

Lehtola, V.-P. 2015. 'Second World War as a Trigger for Transcultural Changes among Sámi People in Finland', *Acta Borealia* 32(2): 125–47.

Löfström, J. 2011. 'Historical Apologies as Acts of Symbolic Inclusion – and Exclusion? Reflections on Institutional Apologies as Politics of Cultural Citizenship', *Citizenship Studies* 15(1): 93–108.

MacDonald, S. 2008. 'Difficult Heritage: Unsettling History', in M.-P. Jungblut (ed.), *Museums and Universal Heritage: History in the Area of Conflict between Interpretation and Manipulation*. Paris: International Committee for Museums and Collections of Archaeology and History, pp. 8–15.

Marston, S. 2004. 'Space, Culture, State: Uneven Developments in Political Geography', *Political Geography* 23(1): 1–16.

McAtackney, L. 2014. *An Archaeology of the Troubles: The Dark Heritage of Long Kesh/Maze Prison*. Oxford: Oxford University Press.

Mikula, M. 2015. 'Vernacular Museum: Communal Bonding and Ritual Memory Transfer among Displaced Communities', *International Journal of Heritage Studies* 21(8): 757–72.

Moshenska, G. 2006. 'Scales of Memory in the Archaeology of the Second World War', *Papers from the Institute of Archaeology* 17: 58–68.

Paksuniemi, M., T.A. Turunen and P. Keskitalo. 2015. 'Coping with Separation in Childhood – Finnish War Children's Recollections about Swedish Foster Families', *Procedia – Social and Behavioral Sciences* 185: 67–75.

Sääskilahti, N. (2016). 'Konfliktinjälkeiset kulttuuriympäristöt, muisti ja materiaalisuus', *Tahiti* 1/2016. Retrieved 20 April from http://tahiti.fi/01-2016/tieteelliset-artikke lit/konfliktinjalkeiset-kulttuuriymparistot-muisti-ja-materiaalisuus.

Seitsonen, O. 2017. 'Crowdsourcing Cultural Heritage: Public Participation and Conflict Legacy in Finland', *Journal of Community Archaeology and Heritage* 4(2): 115–30.

Seitsonen, O. and V.-P. Herva. 2011. 'Forgotten in the Wilderness: WWII PoW Camps in Finnish Lapland', in A. Myers and G. Moshenska (eds), *Archaeologies of Internment*. New York: Springer, pp. 171–90.

Seitsonen, O. and E. Koskinen-Koivisto. 2018. '"Where the F… is Vuotso?" Material Memories of Second World War Forced Movement and Destruction in a Sámi Reindeer Herding Community in Finnish Lapland', *International Journal of Heritage Studies* 24(4): 421–41.

Smith, L. 2006. *Uses of Heritage*. London and New York: Routledge.

Smith, P. 2007. 'Frontier Conflict: Ways of Remembering Contested Landscapes', *Journal of Australian Studies* 31(91): 9–23.

Suoninen, I.-E. 2016. 'Toisen maailmansodan sotajäänteet osaksi matkailuelinkeinoa Inarissa?' *Yle*, 10 August 2016. Retrieved 24 January from http://yle.fi/uutiset/osasto/sapmi/toisen_maailmansodan_sotajaanteet_osaksi_matkailuelinkeinoa_ina rissa/9082602.

Thomas, S. and E. Koskinen-Koivisto. 2016. '"Ghosts in the Background" and "the Price of War": Representations of the Lapland War in Finnish Museums', *Nordisk Museologi* (2): 60–77.

Thomas, S., O. Seitsonen and V.-P. Herva. 2016. 'Nazi Memorabilia, Dark Heritage and Treasure Hunting as "Alternative" Tourism: Understanding the Fascination with the Material Remains of World War II in Northern Finland', *Journal of Field Archaeology* 41(3): 331–43.

Van Hollebeeke, Y., B. Stichelbaut and J. Bourgeois. 2014. 'From Landscape of War to Archaeological Report: Ten Years of Professional World War I Archaeology in Flanders (Belgium)', *European Journal of Archaeology* 17(4): 702–19.

Väyrynen, T. 2014. 'Muted National Memory: When the Hitler's Brides Speak the Truth', *International Feminist Journal of Politics* 16(2): 218–35.

CHAPTER EIGHT

Becoming Mediterranean
The Intangible Cultural Heritage of Klapa Singing in Identity-Building and Nation-Branding Discourses
Eni Buljubašić and Tuuli Lähdesmäki

In critical heritage studies, heritage is approached as a complex phenomenon located at the intersection of diverse contemporary – and often competing – strivings of politics, community building projects, tourism and the globalized economy at large. One of the key questions in critical heritage studies is, 'What does heritage do?' – that is, how does heritage impact cultural meanings and people, and how does it produce action (Harrison 2013). This chapter explores the Croatian intangible cultural heritage of klapa singing, listed in UNESCO's Representative List of the Intangible Cultural Heritage of Humanity in 2012, and its transformation into a new cultural expression conceptualized as neoklapa. Following the key question of critical heritage studies, the chapter focuses on the multilayered effects of meaning-making discourses entangled with heritagization of klapa singing in contemporary Croatian society. In these meaning-making discourses, scalar relations and politics of scale have central roles.

Klapa singing is a traditional singing style that was formed in the mid nineteenth century in the southern regions of Croatia. It is traditionally *a cappella* multipart homophonic singing performed by men. Also dubbed Dalmatian klapa singing, it is most closely linked to the region of Dalmatia. In the UNESCO listing, klapa is defined as 'multipart singing of Dalmatia, southern Croatia' and as 'a marker of identity for the people of Dalmatia' (UNESCO 2012: 31). Similarly, the national heritage authorities bring forth the regional origin of klapa singing. According to the website of the Croatian Ministry of Culture (2017), 'Klapa singing is a multipart singing phenomenon of the urban Dalmatia. . . . The main aim of the singers is to achieve the best possible blend of voices. Topics of klapa songs usually deal with love, familiar life situations and the environment in which they live. Love, though, is the predominant theme.'

In ethnomusicological literature, klapa singing is often distinguished into three modes: traditional klapa, festival klapa (from the 1960s onwards and with a focus on performance and presentation) and contemporary, modern klapa marked by popularization and formal experimentation (Ćaleta 2003). The widening context of performance and the popularity of klapa singing are also explored. In today's Croatia, klapa singing can be readily placed into a category of popular music or popular heritage music. Klapa concerts fill football stadiums; klapa groups perform at political campaigns and special events, such as weddings and conference launches; and new, 'modern' forms of klapa music are widely circulated in the media. There has been talk of a boom in klapa singing since the early twenty-first century (Primorac 2008), with a number of existing klapas growing from a few dozen in the early 1960s to over 400 in today's Croatia (Ćaleta and Bošković 2011). The widening context and popularity of klapa has also been called 'the klapa movement' in the media as well as in academic discourse (ibid.). Buljubašić (2017) has used the concept of neoklapa to theorize the interdiscursive cultural expressions of contemporary klapa that are intertwined with the popularization, heritagization and political utilization of klapa's different musical forms.

Although the origin of klapa singing is commonly located in Dalmatia, the meaning-making discourses of klapa as an intangible cultural heritage entail also other geographical affiliations. These discourses participate in the creation of complex spatial positions, divisions and hierarchies. The key aim of our chapter is to explore how meaning-making discourses and affordances of klapa are used to promote identities and feelings of belonging to different scalarly organized communities and how certain layers of meanings of klapa are activated in certain discourses at different scalar levels (see Lähdesmäki, Yujie and Thomas, this volume). Our examination focuses particularly on identity-building and branding discourses that utilize klapa's heritage value and the politics of scale that these discourses entail. Our study emphasizes neoklapa as a multi-scalar heritage phenomenon whose meanings function at several scalar levels at the same time and in which the dynamics between these levels turn it into an instrument of power and a tool for scalar rearticulations and repositions.

The discourses around klapa's heritage value stem from the dualistic representation of the Dalmatian identity as divided into the littoral – perceived as Mediterranean – and the hinterland – perceived as Dinaric or Balkan. The dynamics of this dualism impact the identity and branding discourses of klapa at the different scalar levels, as it enables positioning and repositioning of Croatia in relation to connotations and imaginaries of European subregions – and, thus, enables the relocation of Croatia in Europe and the EU. The focus of our chapter is particularly on the articulations of 'the Mediterranean' and how and why these articulations are used for identity building and branding practices. Through qualitative reading of diverse texts that discuss the meanings, origin and communal connections of klapa, the chapter seeks to understand the transforming and contesting affiliations and affordances of klapa singing as an intangible cultural heritage.

Setting the Scene: The Mediterranean Turn and Rearticulations of Identity

Klapa singing and the region of Dalmatia (as the 'cradle' of klapa singing) are closely associated with a Mediterranean identity in Croatia. According to Croatian ethnomusicologist Ćaleta (1999: 193), the 'Southern Adriatic – Dalmatia – seems to be regarded as the most Mediterranean symbol among the Croats', while klapa singing is 'the most representative of the Mediterranean as far as the Croats are concerned'. On a symbolic level, thus, a close link between klapa, Dalmatia and the Mediterranean has been established (see Povrzanović 1989).

The Croatian national identity has often been perceived as a hybrid of Central European, Mediterranean and Balkan cultural traits (Luketić 2013; Pettan 1997). Historically, just as in some of its neighbouring countries, Croatian cultural and symbolic identification has been described with the metaphors of 'crossroads' and 'bridge' between East and West or 'bulwark' of Western culture and religion(s) (Žanić 2003). However, recent studies of political, cultural and tourism discourses (Luketić 2013; Rivera 2008; Škrbić-Alempijević 2014) have shown that the Croatian national identity is increasingly articulated as Central European and Mediterranean, both of which are often represented as uniformly Western and seen as positive sites of identification. Simultaneously, the perception of the Balkans is plagued by negative associations and stereotypes that portray the Balkans as Europe's internal Other or as primitive, backward, coarse, etc. (Bakić-Hayden 1995; Todorova 2009). Following the previous hegemony of the East-West divide (Wolff 1994), the Balkans in Croatian symbolic geography have in the wartime 1990s taken up the role of the demonized external Others (eastern neighbours) and, increasingly so after the 1990s, the internal Others (Jansen 2002; Obad 2011).

Events such as the break-up of Yugoslavia, the Homeland War, the transition to a capitalist economy and the development of democratic processes in the 1990s, followed by the accession to the EU in 2013, have required –

and have been co-constructed by – a number of discursive shifts. During the 1990s, the need for a unitary national narrative was commonly channelled to an emphasis on the Central European – i.e., continental, Pannonic identity of Croatia (Čapo Žmegač 1999; Pettan 1997). Simultaneously, and at an increasing rate to the end of the decade, Croatia's 'Mediterraneanness' was being rediscovered and reclaimed (Škrbić-Alempijević 2014). In an article entitled 'Why do we need the Mediterranean?' Škrbić-Alempijević (2014: 27) analyses contemporary Croatian academic, political and tourism discourses, concluding that 'the Mediterranean' is a signifier of Croatia's political and economic goals (to be achieved) within the EU. The author speaks of the 'Mediterranean turn' inasmuch as a Mediterranean identity is being 'revealed'

> as a niche with the help of which Croatia is attempting to position itself on the global tourism market; as an indicator that Croatian culture belongs to the 'high cultures' and is by analogy associated with its neighbours on the northern coast of the Mediterranean, while no reference is made to the south; as an epithet describing the everyday social life, lifestyle and world view of the local population. (Škrbić-Alempijević 2014: 47, translation EB)

The 'Mediterranean turn' in contemporary Croatia can be seen as a set of discursive claims – speech acts in Austin's (1982) terms – indicative of what Herzfeld (2005) has dubbed 'practical Mediterraneanism'. Not synonymous with the elusive geographical 'Mediterranean', this symbolic construct of the Mediterranean is rather a 'civilizational ideal', albeit kept alive by its 'stereotypical permutations' (Herzfeld 2005: 48). A 'practical' claim for a Mediterranean identity, it follows, is thus a claim for/of Europeanness. As a cultural form carrying strong (positive) Mediterranean connotations, heritagized and popularized (neo)klapa possesses suitable affordances to become the representable heritage of not only a region (Dalmatia) but also a nation (Croatia).

Before the Homeland War, tourism discourse representing Croatia revolved around the local distinctiveness and cultural hybridity of Croat, Slavic, European and Ottoman influences, while after the war the emphasis was laid on similarities between Croatia and Western Europe (Rivera 2008: 620–21). Today, branding and tourism discourses are the dominant fields where the Croatian Mediterranean identity is articulated. The implicit and explicit politicization of klapa's heritage value is inseparable from its discursive framing as a Mediterranean cultural form, and from the meanings – including romanticism, nostalgia and idealization – constructed within. This politicization of klapa's heritage value manifests the politics of scale in heritage: it brings forth the transformation of klapa's scalar meanings.

Klapa's Scalar Affordances and Symbolic Meanings

Candau and Mazzucchi Ferreira use the notion of an 'affordance of cultural heritage' to explore and explain how certain cultural objects and expressions become declared as official cultural heritage. According to them, all cultural objects and expressions can be potentially declared as heritage, but the probability that an object or expression is considered as such depends on its element of affordance that induces heritagization actions (Candau and Mazzucchi Ferreira 2015: 25). The affordance of klapa singing as heritage may be categorized as falling roughly into two groups, one being more 'material' and the other more 'symbolic', even though in practice these affordances form a continuum rather than a dichotomy.

The 'materiality' of klapa singing that creates a 'best possible blend of voices', where multiple voices come together in harmony, may function on an audible level as a metaphor for communal unity, whether fostering local, regional or national cohesion. The word *klapa* in Dalmatian dialect denotes a group of friends and still nowadays continues to carry the connotations of friendship and comradeship (see Bohlman 2004). This connotation refers to the idea of traditional klapa singing during work or in a tavern. As a marker of the local identity, traditional (and festival) klapas have usually borne the name of the town they originated from, or the town's symbol, or workplace names, such as factories, companies or universities (Povrzanović 1991: 114). Nowadays, in tune with the discourse of (restorative) nostalgia (Boym 2001), klapas are named after archaic words and objects. The metaphoric meaning of unity, harmony and friendship in (neo)klapa is taken a scalar move upwards – from local and micro-level unities to a national/macro-level unity. This upscaling (see Lähdesmäki, Zhu and Thomas and Zhu, this volume) of the communal meaning of klapa reflects the geographical widening of klapa activities outside Dalmatia, as klapas are increasingly being formed in the other regions of Croatia not traditionally connected to klapa singing (Ćaleta and Bošković 2011). Upscaling of klapa's heritage value from a symbol of a region to a national symbol can be found particularly in the lyrics of klapa songs. In traditional klapas, local and regional identities are marked by singing about 'my place' or 'my hometown', expressing a tight bond to the geographical and cultural space (Povrzanović 1991: 114). In addition to this, in contemporary neoklapa songs, the communal meanings of klapa are extended to the national scale, whether by infusion with patriotic discourse or by explicit apostrophization/thematization of Croatia. In other words, heritagized and popularized neoklapa has moved beyond the borders of the region to become an all-Croatian symbol.

Another important 'material' attribute of klapa is its calm and composed performative stance. Klapa singers traditionally form a (semi)circle in which movement of the singers is restricted. Alternatively, klapa singers may exhibit their 'Dalmatian/Mediterranean temperament', such as sentimentality and passion, with their kinaesthetic hand and facial gestures. This is related to the Mediterranean/Western attributes of klapa (as it is ethnomusicologically and culturally defined) and can be connected to the political rearticulation of identities pertaining to the Mediterranean turn.

The symbolic meanings related to the klapa heritage entail various scalar divisions and polarities. According to Povrzanović (1991: 106, translation EB), '"[b]eing a Dalmatian" is often "proven" by a person's dedication to the klapas and the stereotypical imagery their lyrics invoke: the sun and sea, wine and song, the hard but simple way "our ancestors used to live", handsome and cheerful people, and macho men'. Already in the post-WWII period, Dalmatia and its Mediterranean ambiance were commonly established in Croatian symbolic imaginary as the 'Other' to the continental national centre in Zagreb (Žanić 2012; cf. Čapo Žmegač 1999). In this imaginary, Dalmatia with its cultural practices, such as klapa, music festivals and regional dialect, has since the 1960s carried the meanings of 'summery Arcadia' in comparison with the continental centre (Žanić 2012).

Heritage is an important aspect of the Mediterranean and Dalmatian identity, regardless of klapa. Croatian conceptualization of a 'Mediterranean heritage' relies heavily on Greco-Roman monuments and sacral Medieval and Renaissance architecture (Harrison 2013: 147; Škrbić-Alempijević 2014: 35). Close connections between the notions of heritage and Mediterraneanism are also found in Croatian poetry and literary criticism (Knežević 2013) and other discourses pertaining to the arts. Heritage discourse is an important part of Croatian 'practical Mediterraneanism'. Heritage discourse and 'the Mediterranean turn' have cross-fertilized several attributes of klapa, such as its Mediterraneanism, urbanism, refinement, cultural cultivation and western aesthetics, and converged them with the Dalmatian regional identity (see Primorac 2008: 82). These attributes construct their counterparts with the following dynamics: littoral-hinterland; urban-rural; cultured-primitive; sophisticated-rough; Mediterranean-Dinaric/Balkan; and Western-Eastern. Whilst in Mediterranean studies some of these pairs are considered as common traits of Mediterranean societies, they also include a hierarchy of values (Herzfeld 2005: 54–56) that holds the pairs' former attributes as superior.

Similar binary relations that are found on a regional level also impact at the national level, where they more palpably fall into the East-West dichotomy and its power relations (Pettan 1997). In this dichotomy, West stands for positive qualities, such as democracy, civilization and a free market economy, while East represents negative qualities of disorder, corruption, primitivism and backwardness. In the Croatian case, East also equals communism, Yugoslavia, the Balkans and Serbia (Luketić 2013). Particularly, 'the Balkans' and 'the Mediterranean' function in contemporary Croatia as two poles of cultural, political, economic and societal duality (Škrbić-Alempijević 2014: 44). As Luketić (2013: 186, translation EB) claims, 'in the last two decades, Croatian official politics – but also media, print, science, culture – all have strongly fought to get the state outside of the Balkans in every way, geographically-, identity- and mentality-wise, to symbolically connect it to Europe, i.e. to Central Europe or the Mediterranean'. In this context, and considering the importance of tourism for the Croatian economy, which is predominantly based in the maritime regions, Pettan (1997) predicted already two decades ago the further Mediterranization of Croatia: 'As a result, parallel with the growth of tourism along the coast, one can predict further "Mediterranization" of Croatia. This "Mediterranization" will certainly emphasise Western values, at the expense of Croatia's Eastern cultural traits, here synonymous with the Dinaric heritage.'

In general, popular music tends to be the platform for marking political affiliations in ex-Yugoslav states (Baker 2011; Mijatović 2012). Klapa is not the only heritage music practice in Croatia that participates in the scalar positioning of meanings. Therefore, we briefly discuss klapa's relation to tamburitza music and ojkanje singing. Ojkanje, a type of singing typical of the Dalmatian hinterland, might be posed as klapa's intraregional (Dalmatian) counterpart. It is ojkanje that Pettan above refers to as a Dinaric heritage that is pushed back in national representations, being regarded as synonymous with unrefinement, rurality and the Balkans. Prica (2011: 40) has called this archaic, untempered singing style the national 'stubborn otherness', which 'stays away from full national heritage affirmation, positioning itself simultaneously as a recognised folklore element, but also as the fundamental symbolic code of formation of "ganga territory" [non-European / Balkan] of Croatia's belonging to Europe' (Prica 2011: 42–43, translation EB). Although designated as a UNESCO heritage in need of urgent safeguarding in 2010, ojkanje's support base and popularity are not as wide and institutionally organized as those of klapa. Thus, it might be concluded that in the present sociopolitical context of Croatia, the closer the symbolic meaning of heritage is to the desired image of the nation, the more 'visible', institutionally supported and used for nation building and branding it becomes.

While the relationship between ojkanje and klapa is characterized by a symbolic binary, the relationship between klapa and tamburitza music instead reflects a contest between two major regions/cities/sociolects – i.e. the Croatian North (tamburitza) and Mediterranean South (klapa). Tamburitza – folk songs played with a tambura, traditionally rooted in the northern regions of Croatia – has, in terms of media and symbolic presence, been superseded by klapa singing since the 2000s. The cultural myth of tamburitza, prevalent in the 1990s, 'used the motive of Croatia as the bulwark of Europe,

Christianity, democracy and/or the west' in addition to the tambura being regarded as a 'sacred national instrument' and a symbol of 'genuine Croatianness' by the first Croatian president F. Tuđman (Baker 2011: 73). Therefore, in the 1990s tamburitza music was instigated as the 'all-Croatian' musical symbol. While both klapa and tamburitza are primarily considered to be regional symbols, it is their involvement in political discourse that upscales this symbolism to a national level, for different purposes at different times.

Which Mediterranean? Heritage, Tourism, Nation Building and Branding

Although a Mediterranean identity is today seen in a positive light in Croatia, this has not always been the case. As anthropologist Rihtman-Auguštin (1999: 112) argues, Dalmatia was previously seen as not more than a 'suspicious periphery' from the state's northern 'upper regions', especially for its 'particular connection with other nations and cultures across the sea and/or its independence from the neighbouring hinterland'. Therefore, a Mediterranean identity was seen as unsuitable for nation building due to the alleged lack of fidelity towards the imagined national core (see Frykman 1999: 284). Čapo Žmegač (1999) confirms this conclusion on the status of the Mediterranean, claiming that neither Yugoslav nor Croatian political elites based their nation-building politics on a Mediterranean identity: 'the new state [Croatia] has an ambivalent relationship both with local cultural distinctions and with the founding of a national identity on the Mediterranean' (Čapo Žmegač 1999: 46). However, the attitude towards the Mediterranean has changed since the late 1990s.

Harrison (2013: 146–47) has discussed the connection between heritage and the nation state by applying Bauman's theorization of different phases of culture in the modern period. Within this theoretical frame, modernity is characterized as assuming a core role for heritage in the nation-building project, while late modernity is perceived as seeking to detach heritage from the nation-state project and instead turn it into a commodified object of experience economy. However, in some cases 'the state resists the dissolution of the link between nation building and heritage and tries to reassert control of heritage as part of the development of a "national story"', as Harrison (2013: 147) notes. In this context, Harrison briefly discusses the heritage discourse of the newly independent Croatian state as aimed at creating a 'monocultural national heritage' by strongly emphasizing Renaissance, Medieval and Roman monumental heritages (see Škrbić-Alempijević 2014: 31). The heritage Harrison discusses in his Croatian example can indeed be perceived as 'Mediterranean'.

The emphasis of heritage in national ideology is especially common in newly established states that are striving to acquire legitimacy (Mitchell 2001 in Rivera 2008). As a post-socialist country, the rearticulations of the Croatian national identity have taken place in a sociopolitical context laden with nation-branding strategies. As a 'new' country in Europe, Croatia has 'embraced the mania for self-branding with the enthusiasm of the newcomer' (Volčič 2008: 395). Nation-branding and tourism discourse are crucial sites of Croatian 'practical Mediterraneanism'. Indeed, the long-standing (2002–2015) slogan of the Croatian National Tourist Board has been: 'Croatia: The Mediterranean as it once was'. The discourse of this campaign represented Croatia as a mixture of European familiarity (to Western countries) and nostalgic exoticism (Rivera 2008). The latter was mainly achieved by rooting the Croatian identity in the Mediterranean past ('as it once was'), imagined as unspoilt, authentic, beautiful and historic. The Mediterranean cultural heritage plays a key part in current Croatian attempts at nation branding (Škrbić-Alempijević 2014: 29–31), as this heritage carries connotations of Europeanness, urbanity and refinement. In this context, heritage discourse is incorporated as an aide in the branding/tourism discourse of Croatia's 'practical Mediterraneanism' as 'Europeanism'. However, framing the nation and its identity with historicity, nostalgia and authenticity by emphasizing the Mediterraneanness might also be interpreted as 'backwardness', being stuck in the previous East-West division and attempting to 'change sides' within this division. The idea of the Mediterranean construed in Croatian branding/tourism discourses is simplified, homogenous and whitewashed, represented with a stereotypical imaginary of the 'warm South', rich in cultural heritage and classical history (Domšić 2013; Rivera 2008). The pitfalls of the postcard-like 'Mediterranean as it once was' are perhaps, from the nation-branding/building discourse perspective, a lesser concern than the symbolical detachment of the country from the Balkans.

Nation-branding and tourism discourses are 'located at the intersection of the economy, culture and politics' (Kaneva 2012: 5) and, thus, do not only affect foreign audiences but the citizens of the nation as well. If 'nation branding influences conceptions of a country both at home and abroad' (Clancy 2011: 282), it is all the more relevant when the state itself sanctions particular national narratives. Mediterranization of Croatia is such an example, and neoklapa discourse forms an important part of it. Indeed, neoklapa has recently represented Croatia in international events, sanctioned by the state. In 2013, the National Television Board selected a (neo)klapa song to represent Croatia at the Eurovision Song Contest in Malmö, Sweden. According to the Croatian Eurovision delegation manager, the UNESCO label given to klapa highly influenced this decision (HRT 2013). A one-time klapa comprising members of different klapa groups represented Croatia with a video made by the Croatian National Tourist Board, entitled 'Where is Klapa s Mora from?' and representing Mediterranean Croatia. After the unsuccessful result in the Eurovision Song Contest, the director of the Entertainment Unit of the Croatian National Television declared that the chosen klapa song nevertheless achieved its true mission of branding Croatia as a tourist destination by promoting its authentic heritage (Paić 2013). The following year (2014) a klapa song was selected as the official song of the Croatian football team in the Brazil World Cup.

Conclusions

In the 1990s, Croatian nationalist discourse was matched with the popularity of tamburitza music, which 'served as the leading musical symbol of the national or state community during the twentieth century, a position acquired by a combination of political uses of their music, professionalization and mediatization' (Ceribašić and Ćaleta 2010: 340). The discursive upscaling shift towards klapa as an 'all-Croatian' musical symbol and its inherent Mediterranean imaginary can be explained through the context of social, economic and political changes in early twenty-first-century Croatia. The intertwined promotion of the klapa heritage and the neoklapa movement are manifestations of the 'Mediterranean turn' in Croatia's recent identity-building and nation-branding discourses.

In the neoklapa discourse, 'old' cultural tropes related to the ideas of heritage and identity are rearticulated, reasserted and transformed. Many of the characteristics of neoklapa, such as nostalgia, romantization, pathos, idealization of the 'golden age' of forefathers/grandparents and the traditional/conservative community, characterized klapa already in the early 1990s (Povrzanović 1991: 108) – that is, before the heritagization and popularization of klapa in the 'klapa movement'. The Mediterranean turn and official heritagization of klapa have, however, invigorated these aspects and changed/rearranged their scalar meanings, bringing together 'idealization' and the nation-building and branding discourses.

The heritagization of klapa singing is intertwined with articulations and rearticulations of identities at different scalar levels. At the most intimate level, the heritage discourses of klapa reinforce an essentialist notion of identity in which klapa is connected to the individual's inherited, authentic and innate cultural roots transmitted from generation to generation. This kind of testimony of klapa's meanings can be found, for example, in the letters of support written by some of the key figures of current klapa organizations and attached to the nomination form for the UNESCO Representative List of the Intangible Cultural Heritage of Humanity. At the local level, there are particularities in the klapa singing styles of different towns and parts of Dalmatia and along the coast (Ćaleta and Bošković 2011). These different 'substyles' are fairly invisible in neoklapa as a popular music genre. On the regional level, the neoklapa discourse circulates the binary of littoral versus hinterland and symbolic meanings related to this division. The cultural dualities it entails are utilized at the national level in nation-building, branding and tourism discourses. At the subnational level, also, the neoklapa discourse includes a 'contest' between regions. In these discourses, the klapa heritage and neoklapa are used to articulate Croatia as a Mediterranean country.

The articulation of Croatia's Mediterraneanness through klapa is also about the politics of scale at the supranational level. It is about politics that seeks to rearrange the boundaries of European symbolical geography by utilizing the imaginaries related to different European subregions. These kinds of efforts construct and establish certain connotations and meanings of these subregions. The Mediterranean is, however, a fluid, transforming and symbolically complex ideational-spatial entity in today's Europe. It is a Janus-faced 'cradle of civilization' that is also increasingly perceived in Central and Northern European media discourses as a 'subaltern' space of political unrest and economic and refugee crises. However, the 'practical Mediterraneanism' in Croatia enables selection and promotion of those symbolic meanings that are seen as most useful for national identity building and branding practices.

The rearticulation of the Croatian identity through the klapa heritage brings forth the dynamics of scale in action. It indicates how politics of scale in heritage is not only about the formation of one scale or the interaction of several scales, such as the local, regional, national and supranational. Politics of scale is also about the transformation of scales. The recent promotion of the klapa heritage and the emergence of the neoklapa movement have, by shifting the focus of heritage from one scale to another, enabled a 'new scaling' of klapa and the Croatian identity.

Acknowledgements

Lähdesmäki's work in this study was supported by the Academy of Finland under Grant SA274295 (EUCHE).

Eni Buljubašić is a Postdoctoral Researcher and Teaching Assistant at the Faculty of Humanities and Social Sciences, University of Split (UNIST), Croatia. Her interdisciplinary dissertation (July 2017) focuses on 'neoklapa' as a heritage turned popular music phenomenon, investigating regional/ national identity representations in the context of Croatia's Mediterranean identity rearticulations. Eni has published in journals and edited volumes on the subjects of stylistics, literature, intangible heritage and popular culture. She is a research member on the project 'Adriatic Tale: Interdisciplinary Research of Adriatic Narratives' (UNIST) funded by Croatian Science Foundation and is currently pursuing her interests in ecocriticism and environmental humanities.

Tuuli Lähdesmäki (PhD, DSocSc) is an Academy Research Fellow and Adjunct Professor at the Department of Music, Art and Culture Studies, University of Jyväskylä (JYU), Finland. Lähdesmäki specializes in heritage, culture and identity politics, particularly in the European context. She currently leads the research projects 'European Cultural Heritage in the Making: Politics, Affects and Agency' (EUCHE), funded by the Academy of Finland, and 'Legitimation of European Cultural Heritage and the Dynamics of Identity Politics in the EU' (EUROHERIT), funded by the European Research Council. She is the Co-PI in JYU's research profiling area 'Crises Redefined: Historical Continuity and Societal Change' (CRISES).

REFERENCES

Austin, J. 1982. *How to Do Things with Words: The Williams James Lectures Delivered at Harvard University in 1955.* J.O. Urmson and M. Sbisà (eds). Oxford: Oxford University Press.

Baker, C. 2011. *Zvuci granice: Rat i nacionalizam u Hrvatskoj posle 1991.* [Sounds of the Borderland: War and Nationalism in Croatia since 1991]. Belgrade: XX vek.

Bakić-Hayden, M. 1995. 'Nesting Orientalisms: The Case of Former Yugoslavia', *Slavic Review* 54(4): 917–31.

Bohlman, P. 2004. *The Music of European Nationalism: Cultural Identity and Modern History.* Santa Barbara, CA: ABC-Clio.

Boym, S. 2001. *The Future of Nostalgia.* New York: Basic.

Buljubašić, E. 2017. 'The Discourse and Style of Neo-Traditional Klapa Singing (Neoklapa): Aspects of Interdiscusivity of Mediterraneanism, Heritage and Popular Culture', PhD dissertation. Split: University of Split.

Ćaleta, J. 1999. 'The Ethnomusicological Approach to the Concept of the Mediterranean in Music in Croatia', *Narodna umjetnost* 36(1): 183–95.

———. 2003. 'Klapsko pjevanje i ča val – mediteranske dimenzije popularne glazbe u Hrvatskoj' [Klapa Singing and ča-val – the Mediterranean Dimension of Popular Music in Croatia]. *Bašćinski glasi* 8(1): 225–48.

Ćaleta, J. and J. Bošković. 2011. *Mediteranski pjev: O klapama i klapskom pjevanju* [Mediterranean Song: About Klapas and Klapa Singing]. Zagreb: Večernji list.

Candau, J. and M.L. Mazzucchi Ferreira. 2015. 'Mémoire et patrimoine: des récits et des affordances du patrimoine' [Memory and Cultural Heritage: Narratives and Patrimonial Affordances]. *Educar em Revista* 58: 21–36.

Čapo Žmegač, J. 1999. 'Ethnology, Mediterranean Studies and Political Reticence in Croatia: From Mediterranean Constructs to Nation-Building', *Narodna umjetnost* 36(1): 33–52.

Ceribašić, N. and J. Ćaleta. 2010. 'Sound Review: Croatian Traditional Music Recordings: The 1990s and 2000s', *Journal of American Folklore* 123(489): 331–45.

Clancy, M. 2011. 'Re-presenting Ireland: Tourism, Branding and National Identity in Ireland', *Journal of International Relations and Development* 14(3): 281–308.

Croatian Ministry of Culture. 2017. 'Klapa Multipart Singing of Dalmatia, Southern Croatia', Website of Croatian Ministry of Culture. Retrieved 4 April 2017 from http://www.min-kulture.hr/default.aspx?id=8336.

Domšić, L. 2013. 'Touristic Photography and the Construction of Place Identity: Visual Image of Croatia', in V. Marascu-Klein, F.-V. Panaitescu and M. Panaitescu (eds), *Advances in Environment, Ecosystems and Sustainable Tourism*. Brasov: WSEAS Press, pp. 277–82.

Frykman, J. 1999. 'Culturization of the Mediterranean Space', *Narodna umjetnost* 36(1): 283–87.

Harrison, R. 2013. *Heritage: Critical Approaches*. New York: Routledge.

Herzfeld, M. 2005. 'Practical Mediterraneanism: Excuses for Everything, from Epistemology to Eating', in W. Harris (ed.), *Rethinking the Mediterranean*. Oxford: Oxford University Press, pp. 45–63.

HRT. 2013. 'Klapa s mora zapjevala "Mižerju"', 27 February 2013. Retrieved 4 April 2017 from http://zabava.hrt.hr/203031/klapa-s-mora-zapjevala-mizerju.

Jansen, S. 2002. 'Svakodnevni orijentalizam: Doživljaj "Balkana"/ "Evrope" u Beogradu i Zagrebu' [Everyday Orientalism: Experiences of 'Balkan'/'Europe' in Belgrade and Zagreb], *Filozofija i društvo* 18: 33–72.

Kaneva, N. 2012. 'Nation Branding in Post-Communist Europe: Identities, Markets and Democracy', in N. Kaneva (ed.), *Branding Post-Communist Nations: Marketizing National Identities in "New Europe"*. New York: Routledge, pp. 3–22.

Knežević, S. 2013. *Mediteranski tekst hrvatskoga pjesništva: Postmodernističke poetike* [Mediterranean Text of Croatian Poetry: Postmodernist Poetics]. Zagreb: Ljevak.

Luketić, K. 2013. *Balkan: od geografije do fantazije* [Balkans: From Geography to Fantasy]. Zagreb: Algoritam.

Mijatović, B. 2012. 'The Musical (Re)Branding of Serbia: Srbija Sounds Global, Guča, and EXIT', in N. Kaneva (ed.), *Branding Post-Communist Nations: Marketizing National Identities in the "New Europe"*. New York: Routledge, pp. 213–35.

Mitchell, T. 2001. 'Making the Nation: The Politics of Heritage in Egypt', in N. AlSayyad (ed.), *Consuming Tradition, Manufacturing Heritage: Global Norms and Urban Forms in the Age of Tourism*. London: Routledge, pp. 212–39.

Obad, O. 2011. 'Balkan Lights: O promjenama u predodžbama o Zapadu i Balkanu u Hrvatskoj' [Balkan Lights: On Changes in the Perception of West and the Balkans in Croatia], in I. Prica and T. Škokić (eds), *Horror, porno, ennui: Kulturne prakse postsocijalizma*. Zagreb: IEF, pp. 9–29.

Paić, V. 2013. 'Velimir Đuretić za Index: Zaboli me za neulazak u finale, Eurosong je jedna velika pizdarija i šaka jada', IndexHR. 15 May 2015. Retrieved 4 April 2017 from http://www.index.hr/black/clanak/velimir-djuretic-za-index-zaboli-me-za-neula zak-u-finale-eurosong-je-jedna-velika-pizdarija-i-saka-jada/677915.aspx?mobile =false.

Pettan, S. 1997. 'The Croats and the Question of their Mediterranean Musical Identity', *Ethnomusicology online* 3. Retrieved 4 April 2017 from http://www.umbc.edu/eol/3/pettan/index.html.

Povrzanović, M. 1989. 'Dalmatinsko klapsko pjevanje, promjene konteksta' [Dalmatian Klapa Singing, Changes of Context], *Etnološka tribina* 12: 89–98.

———. 1991. 'Regionalni, lokalni i individualni identitet: primjer klapskog pjevanja' [Regional Local and Individual Identity: The Example of Klapa Singing], in D. Rihtman-Auguštin (ed.), *Simboli identiteta*. Zagreb: Hrvatsko etnološko društvo, pp. 105–20.

Prica, I. 2011. 'Ganga teritorij hrvatske europske pripadnosti' [Ganga-Territory of the Croatian European Identity], in I. Prica and T. Škokić (eds), *Horror, Porno, Ennui: Kulturne prakse postsocijalizma*. Zagreb: IEF, pp. 31–50.

Primorac, J. 2008. 'Klapsko pjevanje i tradicijska vokalna glazba u Hrvatskoj' [Klapa Singing and Traditional Vocal Music in Croatia], in A. Muraj and Z. Vitez (eds), *Predstavljanje tradicijske kulture na sceni i u medijima*. Zagreb: Hrvatsko etnološko društvo, pp. 77–87.

Rihtman-Auguštin, D. 1999. 'A Croatian Controversy: Mediterranean – Danube – Balkans', *Narodna umjetnost* 36(1): 103–19.

Rivera, L.A. 2008. 'Managing "Spoiled" National Identity: War, Tourism, and Memory in Croatia', *American Sociological Review* 73: 613–34.

Škrbić-Alempijević, N. 2014. 'Zašto trebamo Mediteran? Pozivanje na sredozemni imaginarij u suvremenoj Hrvatskoj' [Why Do We Need the Mediterranean? Defining the Mediterranean Imaginary in Contemporary Croatia], in M. Belaj, Z. Čiča, A. Matkovič, T. Porenta and N. Škrbić-Alempijević (eds), *Ponovno iscrtavanje granica: transformacije identiteta i redefiniranje kulturnih regija u novim političkim okolnostima*. Zagreb and Ljubljana: Hrvatsko etnološko društvo; Slovensko etnološko društvo, pp. 27–48.

Todorova, M. 2009. *Imagining the Balkans,* updated edition. Oxford: Oxford University Press.

UNESCO. 2012. Convention for the Safeguarding of the Intangible Cultural Heritage. ITH/12/7.COM/11. Paris, 26 October 2012. Paris: UNESCO.

Volčič, Z. 2008. 'Former Yugoslavia on the World Wide Web: Commercialization and Branding of Nation-States', *The International Communication Gazette* 70(5): 395–413.

Wolff, L. 1994. *Inventing Eastern Europe: The Map of Civilization on the Mind of the Enlightenment*. Redwood City, CA: Stanford University Press.

Žanić, I. 2003. 'Simbolični identitet Hrvatske u trokutu "raskrižje" – "predziđe" – "most"' [Symbolic Identity of Croatia in the Triangle of "Crossroads" – "Bulwark" – "Bridge"], in H. Kamberović (ed.), *Historijski mitovi na Balkanu*. Sarajevo: Institut za istoriju, pp. 161–202.

———. 2012. 'Kako govori more? Jezična konstrukcija Dalmacije u hrvatskoj zabavnoj glazbi' [What Is the Dialect of the Sea? The Linguistic Construction of Dalmatia in Croatian Popular Music], in L. Pon, V. Karabalić and S. Cimer (eds), *Aktualna istraživanja u primijenjenoj lingvistici*. Osijek: HDPL, pp. 185–97.

CHAPTER NINE

Tuning in to Radio Heritage in Newfoundland

Michael Windover and Hilary Grant

In the last minutes of 31 March 1949, Newfoundland, Britain's oldest colony, became the Dominion of Canada's tenth province. This historic event was celebrated the next day with the kind of dignity and gravitas one would expect, with key players including Canadian Prime Minister Louis St. Laurent (1882–1973) and leader of the pro-Confederation movement and subsequent premier Joey Smallwood (1900–1991) fashioning themselves as modern-day Fathers of Confederation (Figure 9.1). But something was different about the experience of this event. The streets of St. John's, Gander, and other Newfoundland towns were quiet. There were no parades. In fact, given the closeness of the vote in favour of joining Canada, local authorities decided it best to avoid large public gatherings. Instead, the swearing in of the Lieutenant-Governor of Newfoundland in St. John's and the celebratory addresses made on Parliament Hill, over 2,500 kilometres away in Ottawa, were broadcast into Newfoundlanders' homes by the Canadian Broadcasting Corporation (CBC), who that same day had taken over from the Broadcasting Corporation of Newfoundland (Webb 2008: 203).

This event underlines the importance of mass media in the political projects of mid-century Canada and Newfoundland. It also provides a useful entry point into a consideration of how radio, as a spatial medium, structures heritage. In *A Geography of Heritage*, Graham, Ashworth and Tunbridge (2000: 2, 4) conceive of heritage as an inherently spatial phenomenon, an emplaced use of the past for present purposes. They describe heritage as a medium of representation, with heritage artefacts – and we would not limit 'artefact' to material remains – conceptualized as mechanisms through

Figure 9.1 Prime Minister Louis St. Laurent speaking at welcoming ceremonies, 1 April 1949. Library and Archives Canada, Ottawa, ON, Canada. National Film Board of Canada Still Photography Division, C–050808. Public domain image.

which meaning is produced and reproduced (2000: 2). Yet while Graham, Ashworth and Tunbridge (2000: 25) implicitly reference the work of Canadian media theorist Marshall McLuhan, claiming 'the medium is the message', they do not analyse how different media affect heritage experience. In response to Harvey's call for a closer consideration of the dynamics of heritage and scale in the context of power relations (2015: 577), we draw from the emergent field of media geography to develop a conception of heritage experience as framed by media forms. Similar to Ashworth, Graham and Tunbridge (2000: 257), we do not claim that place is sidelined by the time-space compression afforded through new media technology. Instead, this chapter unravels complexities of scalar place identity created through media experience. We concur with Harvey's contention that 'notions of scale, territory and boundedness have a profound effect on the heritage process' (2015: 577). With geographers Anssi Paasi's (2009) and Harvey's (2015) work in mind, we look at the time-space effects of radio, physically and culturally creating spatial and temporal boundaries, while allowing for a space of transgression.

As a seemingly invisible and 'borderless' (perhaps 'bordering') technology (Windover 2011), radio has myriad scalar and political consequences shaped by and shaping heritage experience. It is a key player in the formation of imagined communities on a variety of scales, from the local to the national, with both folklorists and historians highlighting the community-building function of Newfoundland radio (Narváez 1983; Webb 1997, 2008). We conceive of radio 'publics' as assembled entities of listeners and broadcasters, as well as non-human actants, such as radio infrastructure (Windover 2015), and contend that heritage is produced within these publics. Harrison (2013: 216), also drawing on Latour, argues that 'the production of heritage emerges from the relationship between people, "things" and their environments as part of a dialogue or collaborative process of keeping the past alive in the present'. Publics form around what Bruno Latour calls 'matters of concern' (Latour 2005), such as the broadcast event marking Newfoundland's entry into the Confederation.

Given its changing political situation within North America and the British Empire, Newfoundland provides a particularly rich example of the role of media in the dynamic interrelationships of scales. The occasion of Newfoundland's entry into Canada almost exaggerates various interpenetrating geographic scales: a colony is being transferred from the world's largest empire to the world's second largest country, yet this geographically immense event is experienced primarily in the intimate setting of the home. Because of its unique spatial qualities – its ability to collapse geographic distance in an intimate manner (Kuffert 2009) – radio provides an illuminating example of the role of media in how heritage is experienced in modernity.

Our study of radio in Newfoundland underlines the contradictions of modernity. On one hand, radio was absolutely modern, associated with the fleeting and ephemeral. On the other hand, the medium was often employed and even framed in a conservative manner to reinforce certain sociopolitical ideals. Its employment in the events around Newfoundland's entry into Canada offers but one example of this duality – participating in the celebrations by way of radio is modern and technologically advanced, yet the content of the broadcast and its context betray a more historically oriented and conservative agenda. Of course, radio would not have been considered a heritage artefact during the time of Confederation, but it was important in reorienting people's relationship with the past. Our study thus breaks with heritage studies' partiality towards contemporary case studies (Harvey 2001) and provides a rich case outside the authorized heritage discourse (Smith 2006) for considering heritage practice and its intersection with understandings of space and place.

Radio Space: The Medium is the Message

Perhaps because of the importance media plays in the experience of national space in Canada, key figures in Canadian media theory, such as Harold Innis (1894–1952) and Marshall McLuhan (1911–1980), emphasized space in their work (Cavell 2002). Innis's early work examined the history of Canada's political economy through a consideration of staples, key commodities such as fur, lumber or the cod so central to the Newfoundland economy. He argued that development followed a hinterland to heartland formula and that transportation networks were key drivers, not only of the economy but sociocultural production. The term 'communication' was undergoing a shift in meaning at the time of his writing, from 'means of transport' to 'communication of ideas', yet for Innis the two were interrelated, the former emphasizing the spatial dimension of the latter (Patterson 1990, 9–10). Innis's late work, published not long after Newfoundland's entry into Canada, focused even more directly on the relationship between media forms, sociocultural values and power (1964 [1951]). Media, he argued, are either time-biased or space-biased (Innis 1964 [1951]). Time-biased media, such as architecture or clay tablets, are durable, long lasting and are thus important factors in reasserting traditions and religious customs. Speech, given its spatial limitations, is also time-biased. Space-biased media such as paper are light but less durable and are associated with the conquering of space and 'present-mindedness'. From this perspective, a polity's heritage – its engagement with the past in the present – is deeply entwined in dominant media forms, and these forms have spatially structuring and political implications.

Innis's ideas on media influenced his younger colleague at the University of Toronto, Marshall McLuhan. To draw attention to the social, cultural and political effects of media rather than their content, McLuhan succinctly asserted that 'the medium is the message' (1994 [1964]). Particularly important for our case study is his analysis of electric and electronic media, which he envisioned as radically reorienting Western society's experience and production of space (1994 [1964]). Like Innis, McLuhan understood that media – whose effects were experienced as environments – affected users' relationship with the past. In his typically aphoristic manner, McLuhan described the radio as a 'tribal drum':

> It certainly contracts the world to village size, and creates insatiable village tastes for gossip, rumor, and personal malice. But while radio contracts the world to village dimensions, it hasn't the effect of homogenizing the village quarters. . . . Radio is not only a mighty awakener of memories, forces, and animosities, but a decentralizing, pluralistic force, as is really the case with all electric power and media. (McLuhan 1994 [1964]: 306)

McLuhan's analysis of radio helps to evoke the spatial politics of the medium. He emphasizes how it can both be global and local, how it can impact everyday life (e.g. weather reports, local talk shows) and how it can be a site of heritage production, as 'a mighty awakener of memories'.

McLuhan's and Innis's theorizations have influenced more recent work by media studies scholars interested in space and by geographers interested in media (Jansson and Falkheimer 2006; Pinkerton 2014: 55–56). For instance, media studies scholars André Jansson and Jesper Falkheimer (2006: 9) explain that since all communication 'occur[s] *in space*, and that all spaces are produced *through representation*', then 'theories of spatial production must also to a certain extent be understood as theories of communication and mediation'. They ask us to consider '*how communication produces space and how space produces communication*' (Jansson and Falkheimer 2006: 9; original italics). Geographer Paul C. Adams adopts a formulation for identifying four intersecting ways of thinking about media and human geography: media in space (space of infrastructure and flow), spaces in media (media topology), places in media (what he calls 'place images') and media in place (how media are/are not part of a place) (Adams 2009: 1–3). Whether approached from media studies, cultural studies or geography, media geography is an interdisciplinary field, as multifaceted as the spatial dynamism of media themselves. And its dynamism, we contend, resonates with Harvey's call to examine both the context of shifting spatio-temporal arenas (2015: 579) and how heritage is produced, practised, consumed, experienced, managed and deployed relationally within these arenas (2015: 577).

In what follows, we examine the spatial implications of radio in producing social space in the form of publics in the context of twentieth-century Newfoundland. From Adams's perspective, this includes space and place in media as well as media in space and place. An image of Newfoundland Ranger Ernest Clarke (Figure 9.2) helps to visualize this dynamic. Here we see the medium of radio in place – in this case, a domestic interior – and can imagine Clarke listening to a broadcast while looking at a book. The process of electromagnetic waves being sent from a microphone in a studio to a transmission station to the home receiver and finally into the room through the speaker illustrates radio in space, from a geographical perspective. The content of the broadcast might include discussion or 'images' of places or indeed might be a heterotopic intermingling of spaces (Windover 2017a). The image of Clarke represents one moment in the time-space of radio and allows us imaginatively to envision the radio space outside (yet implicated inside) the frame.

Clarke appears to be 'passively listening', but, bearing in mind media historian Kate Lacey's (2013) work on the politics of listening, we consider this scene much more active and politically charged than it first appears. By lis-

Figure 9.2 Newfoundland Ranger Sergeant Ernest Clarke (Regt. #57), between 1935 and 1950. The Rooms Provincial Archives, St. John's, NL, Canada. Newfoundland Ranger Force Association Fonds, item VA 127–52.2. Public domain image.

tening to the broadcast, even while doing something else, Clarke is joining a forum and becoming part of a radio public; in this case, a public framed by the Commission of Government's Broadcasting Corporation of Newfoundland (BCN). As a Ranger, Clarke would have been responsible for enforcing Commission rule in rural communities far removed from the capital of St. John's from where the broadcast likely emanates, let alone the metropole of the British Empire from where the power of the Commission stemmed. Participating in the radio public would allow him to position himself in relation to others within this complex scalar network. This positioning function of radio played, and continues to play, a key role in Newfoundland's political history.

The Voice of Newfoundland: From Dominion to Commission

Radio in Newfoundland was implicated by and implicated in changing scalar relationships as the island moved from an independent Dominion to a British colony in 1934, then to a province of Canada in 1949. In the 1920s and

1930s, the Dominion had no public radio broadcaster or regulatory body. Radio instead was left to private companies, volunteers and churches, who dedicated large amounts of air time to public service, particularly storm reports, life-saving information for the rural seafaring population (Webb 2008: 12, 14, 17, 20). Short of revenue, the Dominion government had collected a licence fee on radios, despite doing nothing to rectify sources of interference or otherwise improve the signal of the private stations (Webb 2008: 21). The British bureaucrats of the Commission of Government, which was appointed to 'reconstruct' Newfoundland both economically and morally to make Newfoundlanders more self-reliant and capable of self-rule (Keough 2011: 79; Webb 2008: 50), did little to change this (Webb 2008: 26–27). In keeping with the edifying mission of the British Broadcasting Corporation (BBC), in 1939 the Commission established BCN and took over the private station VONF, the Voice of Newfoundland (Klassen 2007: 207; Webb 2008: 1). With island-wide coverage by 1932, VONF was already an authoritative voice emanating from St. John's to the scattered coastal population (Webb 2008: 37–38). Transmission, however, was one way: the CBC and BBC did not rebroadcast Newfoundland programming (its imperially coloured inaugural broadcast and the BCN's coverage of the Royal Visit of 1939 being the only exceptions) (Webb 2008: 39–40, 55). William Fenton Galgay, General Manager from 1939 to 1966, bemoaned that Newfoundland was never included in the BBC's Christmas Day Programme. In response to his calls for geographic representativeness, the BBC informed him that quality, and only quality, was the deciding factor (Webb 2008: 39, 54, 205).

Newfoundlanders continued to listen to the same entertainment under the BCN as when the station was privately owned, with the Commission of Government paying surprisingly little attention to cultural concerns, including tuning in to American or Canadian content (Webb 2008: 31, 73, 74, 78). Newfoundlanders received local news and some local programming in addition to three hours a week of CBC programming and the complete seventy hours of the Empire Transcription Service (Webb 2008: 74, 82). Yet while popular commentators assume that this new mass medium replaced local Newfoundland culture, it is 'falsely dichotomous' to set an authentic folk culture against the North American entertainment industry (Webb 2008: 11). Rather, the experience of radio in Newfoundland resonates with McLuhan's later observations: the medium collapsed the space of empire but did not bring with it homogeneity in cultural content and in fact may have heightened regional cultural forms. Locally produced content drew heavily from local cultural traditions, and, in spite of its newness, or perhaps because of it, radio programming was understood through traditional categories. For example, most Newfoundlanders distinguished between songs and ditties – a song being that which was about a serious subject such as sea tragedies or other sombre historical events, and ditties less serious songs purely for entertainment (Webb 2008: 5, 76–77). Webb (2008: 75) argues that delineations between female and male, commercial and educational, and popular and elite programmes omnipresent in American broadcasting were less sharply drawn in Newfoundland. This reminds us that, while radio allowed for a potentially cosmopolitan experience, it also could reassert local inflections of cultural practice.

An Electronic Forum: Radio as Multidirectional

Newfoundland radio is markedly participatory and multidirectional. It is usually explained in deference to Newfoundland's storytelling culture and oral traditions (Narváez 1986; Webb 2008, 1997). Talk radio, which captures almost 30 per cent of the province's radio audience (Marland and Kerby 2010: 1000), for example, electronically extends Newfoundland's popular and oral culture, using the medium to share information and unite communities and families over land and sea (Marland and Kerby 2010: 1001). The best-known and politically consequential example is *The Barrelman*. Dedicated to ridding Newfoundlanders of their inferiority complex, the one-man show created and hosted by future Premier Joey Smallwood endeavoured to 'make Newfoundland better known to Newfoundlanders'. *The Barrelman* aired 6:45 to 7 PM, six nights a week, eleven months a year, from October 1937 to December 1943, and continued to be rebroadcast on private station VOCM (the Voice of the Common Man) until 1956 (Narváez 1983: 61; Webb 1997: 169, 2008: 205).

In contrast to the Commission, Smallwood openly wanted to use radio to foster culture, unifying Newfoundlanders. He argued that 'Radio ... was invented by God especially for Newfoundland' (Klassen 2007: 208). The electronic medium enabled 'all the people of Newfoundland to get together', creating a networked global village across the island, or 'neighbours – all one big Newfoundland family'. It formed a unique, Newfoundland public, for the first time giving the country 'a Voice: a voice that speaks the good old Newfoundland language, one that must make us clearly conscious of our common national heritage, conscious of all that we have in common ... – a common language, a common history, a common tradition, and a common destiny' (as quoted in Webb 1997: 181).

Smallwood used radio to help shape the idea of Newfoundlanders as a people with a shared historical background – 'a background of struggle against the forces of nature, against oppression and injustice and intolerance and bigotry' (Webb 1997: 175), with the first recorded public usage of the slur 'Newfy' being broadcast on *The Barrelman* 10 March 1938 (Narváez 1983: 72). He sought to 'do the American job' of self-glorification, helping Newfoundlanders see the value in their own culture instead of seeing everything as better 'upalong' in Nova Scotia, Ontario and Boston (Narváez 1983: 65–66). By presenting geographic and economic facts, historical information and folklore, Smallwood fostered a Newfoundland identity based on the hardiness and resilience of the island's citizens (Narváez 1983: 61; Webb 1997: 173–75).

Smallwood cultivated the appearance of *The Barrelman* as democratic and community-created and, in turn, created a more tightly scaled sense of community (Webb 1997: 183). His frequent appeals to listeners for content were very successful – in 1938 he reported 1,500 letters having been received from 200 communities in a four-month period. Half of these, Smallwood reported, held a 'story or anecdote' (Narváez 1983: 70). Though such stories were not labelled folklore, they fell within a long tradition of storytelling on the island, particularly that of telling tall tales or cuffers. Traditionally, male fishers, loggers, hunters and soldiers, far away from their homes, told tall tales, disallowing the possibility of their audience fact-checking their stories, creating humour through a mix of outrageous content and dramatic oration. Weaving a good cuffer traditionally commanded high esteem and respect (Narváez 1983: 75–77; Webb 1997: 172). Rather than simply translating Newfoundlanders' oral culture to radio, Smallwood used radio to spark a mass popular culture and nationalism based on extant Newfoundland traditions and practices (Webb 2008: 70), 'allowing listeners to cuffer along with him in a new kind of social space' (Webb 1997: 172).

Through this process, Smallwood was uneasily shaping Newfoundlanders' relationship with the past within a complicated constellation of scalar relations. *The Barrelman*'s historic moralistic content became a space of transgression, an arena for subaltern political debate. The unelected Commission would not allow political discussions on the air, and since radio was transmitted directly into people's homes, care was taken to ensure programming was inoffensive (Webb 1997: 180). Smallwood refused to answer contemporary political questions received from listeners on air; instead, he would read historical questions and quotations that paralleled current struggles and that listeners would have undoubtedly understood as veiled criticisms of the Commission, according to Webb (1997: 178–80). In the face of a non-democratic government, Newfoundlanders across the island engaged in a discourse on cultural heritage as a surrogate for political discourse through the new medium radio (Webb 1997: 167–68).

We Are Not a Nation: The Confederation Debate

Following the Second World War, British Prime Minister Attlee announced that a National Convention would give Newfoundlanders the opportunity to request a return to responsible government or another form of government. Lifting its ban on political discussion, the BCN broadcast nearly the whole of the debates over VONF, totalling 256 hours and 45 minutes (Webb 2008: 168). The debates surrounded whether to shift Newfoundland's scalar position, maintaining its place as Britain's oldest colony or aligning itself with North America (Webb 2008: 170). Smallwood, the well-seasoned broadcaster, espoused the material benefits that would flow from being part of the Canadian welfare state. He reminded people of the hard times of the Great Depression and the risks of returning to 'fishocracy', exploitation at the hands of elite fish merchants. The confederates tied Confederation to renewing Newfoundland's connection to the empire, while the Responsible Government League made a nationalistic appeal: 'Don't sell your country' (Webb 2008: 162–65).

In contrast, Smallwood declared during the debates that 'We [Newfoundland] are not a nation' (as quoted in Webb 1997: 186). His Newfoundland nationalism was not based on what he called the 'artificial and superficial' structures and symbols of statehood but rather on the spirit of the population (Webb 1997: 186). The almost neighbourly listening publics he engaged with (and helped create through his broadcasts) likely informed his conception of Newfoundland nationalism: a public could exist comfortably within – indeed benefit from – a larger state, just as a regional broadcasting of the CBC could speak to local concerns through national infrastructure (Windover 2015, 2017b). In the July 1948 referendum to join Canada, the motion passed with 51 per cent of the vote, which split along a wealthy urban and poor rural divide; voters in St. John's and the rest of the Avalon Peninsula had voted 67.2 per cent in favour of returning to responsible government, against 32.7 per cent for union with Canada (Keough 2011: 79; Webb 2008: 202).

While VONF had to be absorbed into the CBC network, Smallwood reassured Newfoundlanders that there would be no attempts to Canadianize Newfoundland radio: 'Broadcasting in Newfoundland has acquired a peculiarly personal and intimate character not ordinarily found elsewhere on a large scale', Smallwood explained to the Newfoundland delegation to Ottawa. 'It has also become a very important medium of expression of Newfoundland culture and atmosphere. It would, therefore, be extremely hazardous to interfere drastically … to "Canadianise" the Island' (Webb 2008: 193). It would not, delegate Gordon Winter suggested, be wise to replace the 'Ode to Newfoundland' with 'O Canada' or 'The Maple Leaf Forever' as the opening music of the broadcast day during the first few weeks of Newfoundland being a province (Webb 2008: 193). There was an implicit understanding that broadcasting would not be unidirectional; Newfoundland would develop programming to show itself to Canada and the world (Webb 2008: 199). Smallwood reassured the public that 'They [the Canadians] are quite happy for us to remain Newfoundlanders. We will have our own programmes, our own local news, our own Newfoundland broadcasting' (Webb 2008: 190).

A Medium of Modernization: Newfoundland and the CBC

However, during the Confederation broadcast 1 April, Newfoundlanders were met with an unfamiliar voice. Despite the Terms of Union ensuring the retention of the VO call sign, the inaugural broadcast's introduction, 'This is CBN, St. John's, Newfoundland', was followed by the radio transmission of the scratch of the pen signing the union papers (Webb 2008: 203), and with that Newfoundland's voice was subsumed into a new national scale (Figure 9.3). Radio was a modernizing force, bringing with it new infrastructure to shore up existing routines and listening patterns while engendering new relationships and power dynamics. Indeed, Premier Smallwood planned to haul Newfoundland 'kicking and screaming into the twentieth century' (Crocker 2000: 88).

A distinct part of this modernizing drive was felt temporally, with radio offering a unique spatio-temporal structure. Drawing on Ernst Bloch's concept of non-synchronicity, Crocker (2000: 85) explains that, after Confederation, 'what had been largely experienced as a spatial juxtaposition of two incongruous worlds became a temporal relation between present and future'. The signs of modernity and the temporal structures of progress brought by new technologies such as radio revealed what ought to be rather than what could be, such that integration with Canada was not defined by newness but by a sense of catching up with a predetermined future, the modern present already established and experienced in the metropole (Crocker 2000: 85). Smallwood himself explained, 'The newer conceptions of what life can be, of what life should be, have widened our horizons, and deepened our knowledge of the great gulf that separates what we have and are from what we feel we should have and be' (as quoted in Crocker 2000: 85).

This meant great upheaval for Newfoundland. Those along the coasts became subject to resettlement in the face of widespread industrialization and centralization programmes. The CBC built four relay stations planned, but unrealized by the Commission, and opened a transmission station in Grand

Figure 9.3 Mr Joseph Smallwood signing the agreement that admitted Newfoundland into Confederation, Hon. A.J. Walsh, chairman of the Newfoundland delegation, is at the right, 11 December 1948.
Library and Archives Canada, Ottawa, ON, Canada. National Film Board of Canada Still Photography Division, PA–128080. Public domain image.

Falls, improving radio coverage on the island (Webb 2008: 196). This reminds us of the significant place non-human actants play in the production of national space (i.e. Canadian investment to bring Newfoundlanders into a larger Canadian national public).

With the CBC takeover and investment, the perspective of news shifted from London-based to Toronto (Webb 2008: 201), with Newfoundland stations peripheral to the CBC's Ontario centre (Webb 2008: 208). After Confederation, Canadian English became the standard, Newfoundland English mocked as signalling a lower class and lack of education (Collins 2012: 6). Newfoundland dialects already had a political valence prior to Confederation – General Manager Galgay, for example, disliked the non-standard and colloquial nature of Newfoundland's dialects and tried to standardize the English of the BCN's broadcasters (Webb 2008: 218–19) – but shaming by Canadians led to widespread linguistic suppression in post-Confederation Newfoundland (Collins 2012: 7). Yet despite its informal style (broadcasting personal messages similar to *The Barrelman*), the *Gerald S Doyle News Broadcast,* which had been part of VONF's inaugural 1932 broadcast, continued to provide local news in post-Confederation Newfoundland. This must have provided continuity for listeners, and it saved a place for a distinctly Newfoundland voice on the local CBC stations up until its final broadcast in 1965 (Webb 2008: 85–86, 201, 218–19).

In reaction to the changes of Confederation and the Canadian Federal Government's later closure of the cod fishery grew a Newfoundland 'spirit of salvage anthropology', or what Gerald Pocius (1991) has more generally termed 'nativism' – the attempt to isolate and preserve a pure, distinct Newfoundland culture (Keough 2011: 79–80). Newfoundland Irish-English soon re-emerged as a positive cultural maker, in part in reaction to what was deemed inauthentic Newfoundland speech performed within media (Collins 2012: 3). Just as VONF has been the space of a subaltern political discourse in the 1930s, CBN became a place to criticize the ultimately disappointing modernization schemes of the 1950s (Webb 2008: 209). In the 1970s, with folk culture increasingly seen as under threat, Newfoundland folk music that had never been broadcast on the likes of VONF was played frequently on Newfoundland radio (Webb 2008: 79, 209), and music about or produced in Newfoundland is played on almost every Newfoundland radio station today. Radio remains an important medium for renegotiating hegemony and preserving cultural expression (Keough 2011: 79–80, 93), with programmes like the CBC's Fisheries Broadcast continuing to share 'the stories of people in Newfoundland and Labrador' (Canadian Broadcasting Corporation 2018).

Conclusion

The history of radio in Newfoundland in the second quarter of the twentieth century highlights the electronic medium's role in creating sociopolitical spaces on a variety of overlapping scales. Radio was a powerful instrument of modernization yet reinscribed certain socio-economic and political conditions. Our examination of its place in Newfoundland in this period reveals its unique spatio-temporal qualities. While at times Newfoundlanders felt historically out of step with seemingly more modern Britons or Canadians, the medium imbricated Newfoundland in larger political entities, and its intimacy amplified existing oral cultural traditions, serving to reinforce a distinct Newfoundland identity. Radio made Newfoundland a global village.

Like wallpaper (Berland 1990: 180), radio is usually a secondary medium, sitting in the background of everyday life and can, as a result, be easily overlooked. Yet, as our case study shows, it played (and continues to play) a powerful role in Newfoundlanders' negotiation of time and place within scalar politics. Our case study points to the potential of attending to the role of radio (or any medium) in framing heritage experience. With the advent of other dominant media (e.g. television and the internet) and changes to extant media forms (e.g. the move from FM to digital radio) these experiences are in flux. The time is ripe for further analysis.

Acknowledgements

We would like to acknowledge the support of the Office of the Vice President (Research and International) at Carleton University for this research.

Michael Windover (PhD) is Associate Professor in the School for Studies in Art and Culture at Carleton University in Ottawa, Canada where he teaches in the History and Theory of Architecture Program. He is also adjunct curator of design at the Canada Science and Technology Museum. An architecture and design historian with special interest in media spaces and twentieth-century popular modernisms, he is author of *Art Deco: A Mode of Mobility* (Presses de l'Université du Québec, 2012), co-author with Anne MacLennan of *Seeing, Selling, and Situating Radio in Canada, 1922-1956* (Dalhousie Architectural Press, 2017), and co-editor with Bridget Elliott of *The Routledge Research Companion to Art Deco* (forthcoming).

Hilary Grant is a PhD candidate in Carleton University's Cultural Mediations programme in the Institute for Comparative Studies in Literature, Art and Culture. She has over a decade of experience working in the non-profit and public heritage sector at the provincial, national and international level. Hailing from St. John's, Newfoundland, Hilary is Vice-President of the Society for the Study of Architecture and Canada. She has published in the *Journal of the Society for the Study of Architecture in Canada* and the *International Journal of Heritage Studies*.

REFERENCES

Adams, P. 2009. *Geographies of Media and Communication*. Malden, MA: Wiley-Blackwell.

Berland, J. 1990. 'Radio Space and Industrial Time: Music Formats, Local Narratives and Technological Mediation', *Popular Music* 9(2): 179–92.

Canadian Broadcasting Corporation. 2018. *The Broadcast with Jane Adey*. Retrieved 5 February 2018 from http://www.cbc.ca/listen/shows/the-broadcast.

Cavell, R. 2002. *McLuhan in Space: A Cultural Geography*. Toronto: University of Toronto Press.
Collins, M. 2012. 'They Do Be Anxious about Their Speech: Performance and Perceptions of Authenticity in Irish-Newfoundland English', *The English Languages: History, Diaspora, Culture* 3: 1–17.
Crocker, S. 2000. 'Hauled Kicking and Screaming into Modernity: Non- Synchronicity and Globalization in Post-War Newfoundland', *TOPIA* 3: 81–94.
Graham, B., G. Ashworth and J. Tunbridge. 2000. *A Geography of Heritage: Power, Culture and Economy*. New York: Oxford University Press.
Harrison, R. 2013. *Heritage: Critical Approaches*. New York: Routledge.
Harvey, D. 2001. 'Heritage Pasts and Heritage Presents: Temporality, Meaning and the Scope of Heritage Studies', *International Journal of Heritage Studies* 7(4): 319–38.
———. 2015. 'Heritage and Scale: Settings, Boundaries and Relations', *International Journal of Heritage Studies* 21(6): 577–93.
Innis, H. 1964 [1951]. *The Bias of Communication*. Introduction by Marshall McLuhan. Toronto: University of Toronto Press.
Jansson, A. and J. Falkheimer. 2006. 'Towards a Geography of Communication', in J. Falkheimer and A. Jansson (eds), *Geographies of Communication: The Spatial Turn in Media Studies*. Göteborg: Nordicom, pp. 7–23.
Keough, S.B. 2011. 'Promoting and Preserving Cultural Identity through Newfoundland Radio Music Broadcasts', *Aether: The Journal of Media Geography* 7: 75–96.
Klassen, J. 2007. '"I Am VOWR": Living Radio in Newfoundland', *Newfoundland and Labrador Studies* 22(1): 205–26.
Kuffert, L. 2009. '"What Do You Expect of This Friend?": Canadian Radio and the Intimacy of Broadcasting', *Media History* 15(3): 303–17.
Lacey, K. 2013. *Listening Publics: The Politics and Experience of Listening in the Media Age*. Cambridge: Polity.
Latour, B. 2005. 'From Realpolitik to *Ding*politik or How to Make Things Public', in B. Latour and P. Weibel (eds), *Making Things Public: Atmospheres of Democracy*. Cambridge, MA: exh. cat., ZKM/Center for Art and Media in Karlsruhe, pp. 4–31.
Marland, A. and M. Kerby. 2010. 'The Audience Is Listening: Talk Radio and Public Policy in Newfoundland and Labrador', *Media, Culture & Society* 32(6): 997–1016.
McLuhan, M. 1994 [1964]. *Understanding Media: The Extensions of Man*. Introduction by L. Lapham. Cambridge, MA and London: MIT Press.
Narváez, P. 1983. 'Joseph R. Smallwood, "The Barrelman": The Broadcaster as Folklorist', *Canadian Folklore Canadien* 5 (1–2): 60–78.
Paasi, A. 2009. 'The Resurgence of the "Region" and "Regional Identity": Theoretical Perspectives and Empirical Observations on Regional Dynamics in Europe', *Review of International Studies* 35(1): 121–46.
Patterson, G. 1990. *History and Communications: Harold Innis, Marshall McLuhan, the Interpretation of History*. Toronto: University of Toronto Press.
Pinkerton, A. 2014. 'Radio', in P.C. Adams, J. Craine and J. Dittmer (eds), *The Ashgate Research Companion to Media Geography*. Farnham, Surrey and Burlington, VT: Ashgate, pp. 53–67.
Pocius, G. 1991. *A Place to Belong: Community Order and Everyday Space in Calvert, Newfoundland*. Montreal: McGill-Queen's University Press.
Smith, L. 2006. *The Uses of Heritage*. Abingdon: Routledge.

Webb, J.A. 1997. 'Constructing Community and Consumers: Joseph R. Smallwood's *Barrelman* Radio Programme', *Journal of the Canadian Historical Association / Revue de la Société historique du Canada* 8(1): 165–86.
———. 2008. *The Voice of Newfoundland: A Social History of the Broadcasting Corporation of Newfoundland, 1939–1949*. Toronto: University of Toronto Press.
Windover, M. 2011. 'Transmitting Nation: "Bordering" and the Architecture of the CBC in the 1930s', *Journal of the Society for the Study of Architecture in Canada* 36(2): 5–12.
———. 2015. 'Designing Public Radio in Canada', *RACAR* 40(2): 42–56.
———. 2017a. 'Situating Radio: How Radio Changed Canadian Space', in M. Windover and A. MacLennan, *Seeing, Selling, and Situating Radio in Canada*. Halifax: Dalhousie Architectural Press, pp. 65–127.
———. 2017b. 'Placing Radio in Sackville, New Brunswick', *Buildings & Landscapes* 24(1): 46–66.

Afterword
The Politics of Scale for Intangible Cultural Heritage
Identification, Ownership and Representation

Kristin Kuutma

Heritage posits a value-laden configuration without a neutral ground of connotation. The concept of cultural heritage carries a powerful emotional charge and a value structure that implies scalar practices. It furthers a mode of cultural production with reformative social and economic significance. Cultural heritage is not a given but a social construct and cultural practice with reverberations on a global scale. The making of heritage emanates from appended valorization of symbolic and material resources (see Kirshenblatt-Gimblett 2006). Designation of cultural heritage renders a project of ideology with ambivalent temporal entanglements between a past moment and present concerns.

The concept of cultural heritage is today profoundly informed by the international discourse led by UNESCO, the global organization whose conventions play an instrumental role in producing such heritage. Reformative activities initiated and governed by this supranational body for arbitration and policy development set the stage for particular institutional structures, define the subject matter and orchestrate culture-orientated politics on a global scale. At the same time, the designated legal instruments and respective heritage industries have concurrently generated the conceptual and institutional polarization of cultural heritage into tangible and intangible, which is embedded in the rhetoric of scale that demarcates target spheres and areas of expertise. When many of the contributions in the present volume circle the tangible orbit, this concluding chapter[1] focuses particularly on the politics of scale operational in and by the institutional structures of *intangible cultural heritage* as established by UNESCO. The relevant international instrument, the Convention for the Safeguarding of the Intangible Cultural Heritage, was adopted in 2003.

The scalar principle permeates the social and political aspects of cultural heritage. Processes of heritage simultaneously function across a variety of scales and spaces. Like heritage, scale is not a given but presents a discursive construction of space where scale is negotiated and contested (see Herod and Wright 2002). Space signifies the range of politics and relations within which heritage is implicated and shaped (see Massey 2005). Taking note of scale, defined as the spatial configuration and extent of a set of practices, I propose to consider the heritage-scale relationship especially from the perspective of intangible cultural heritage and look at how local, regional, national or global scalar rhetoric functions, as suggested by David Harvey (2015).

In the UNESCO-framed intangible heritage context, scales are implemented as an organizational device in establishing operational structural hierarchies. In the following I am going to tie the processual concepts of heritage to relational understandings of interscalar politics in order to examine the politics of scale from three angles: identification, ownership and representation. It should be noted that many of the arguments presented here still apply to the cultural heritage sphere in general. However, the main theme of this book, the politics of scale, operates already from the very beginning due to the institutional division between the two major signifiers, the 1972 World Heritage Convention and the 2003 Convention. Obviously there is a difference in the temporal scale, but most importantly, the social and capital revenue drawn continue to elevate and recognize the former, 'the world heritage' designation. This hierarchy of significance trickles down the scales and complicates further the inbred tension between universality and particularity. The global provisions of UNESCO initiatives with salvation agendas address the universal level with an implicit goal of making an impact on the particular. As a cultural process, heritage curation is inherently particular and particularizing.

Politics of Scale in Identification: Terminology

The concept of intangible heritage assumed its signifying position in the UNESCO-initiated system of heritage regulation. Targeted programmes referring to intangible cultural heritage started in the 1990s, but the concept became operational and disseminated more widely only in the new century. The emergence of 'intangible cultural heritage' as an overarching designation created a new knowledge format with instrumental political implications and scalar practices. It legitimized the term 'intangible' to define cultural expressions and practices (storytelling, craftsmanship, rituals, lifestyles, etc.), with the aim to be universally inclusive in avoiding references to social stratum or inferiority that are perceived to be present in other terms such as 'folklore', 'traditional culture' or 'popular culture' that were previously used for identifying that sphere. Global cultural politics consider the latter too delimiting or prescriptive, which, however, may contradict vernacular practices and local interpretations. When we look at the vocabulary deployed, we can see how terminology signifies and reflects the geographies of power or politics of scale: terms categorize reality and become political tools (Herod and Wright 2002: 147). The emergence of 'intangible cultural heritage' as an overarching and instrumental designation has transferred from international policymaking to the academic sphere and public imaginaries as a powerful asset and an intervention (see Kuutma 2015).

The UNESCO 2003 Convention for the Safeguarding of the Intangible Cultural Heritage became fully operational in 2006, when the required number of states had ratified this international instrument[2] that defined its target sphere and presumed expertise in the context of its legal provisions and action programme. The 2003 Convention proclaims to safeguard living intangible cultural heritage, which denotes manifestations that are spontaneously transmitted from generation to generation, being liable to change but remaining an identity marker for particular communities. Thus intangible cultural heritage is characterized by being human borne, hence mobile and ephemeral, by being limited in duration and evolving, by frequent absence of link with specific location and by being often spread over large areas or dispersed (Smeets 2004: 146–48).

Hence special prescriptive terminology was worked out – the Convention emanated from an aspiration to establish global provisions for safeguarding intangible cultural heritage. However, policy and legal provisions denote in essence regulations that operate differently on different levels when substantive obligations and recommendations transfer to regional and national instruments. When the international scale denotes agreements on prescriptive regulations, the regional level assumes cooperation. The national level aspires to celebrate cohesive identity construction, whereas the local level in contrast seeks to be recognized. The scalar rhetoric (Harvey 2015: 590) of intangible cultural heritage prescribed by the Convention functions similarly to the World Heritage framework, but with a noticeable difference in the establishment of the politics of scale. First, legal and definitional challenges prove difficult to form legal protections while still allowing for living heritage to thrive (see Lixinski 2013). Second, the role of community is specifically foregrounded in the intangible heritage configuration. The safeguarding regulations and continued transmission is a delicate issue where it is hard to strike a balance between regularization as an enabler versus regularization as freezing the natural dynamics of cultural practices, of people's lifeworld.

The adoption of the 2003 Convention, as well as the term of intangible heritage, emanates nevertheless from an antithesis to the 1972 Convention and its target sphere, identified as the World Heritage, in an ambivalent way. The latter definitely operated as an example and was dominant in crafting legal and political provisions, but at the same time the new convention argued for an altered politics of scale. Its provisions foreground the role of communities and negate the scales of significance, as they are pronounced by the terms of 'universal value' or 'authenticity'. Although the official UNESCO discourse in the intangible heritage framework shuns such external evaluative categorization, it need not be the case on the ground. Local scales are associated with authenticity, while branding in tourist industry requires both singularity and authentic heritage (see, for example, Buljubasić and Lähdesmäki in this volume).

On the other hand, the Convention demands awareness-raising as part of safeguarding, which entails inventorying and listing (UNESCO lists (a)). The concurrent heritage designations are embedded in politics of scale, in hierarchies invoked and enabled in heritage processes. The acting regime (Falser 2015: 2) of the Convention employs particular scaling instruments for producing heritage: the Representative List of Intangible Cultural Heritage of Humanity and the List of Intangible Cultural Heritage in Need of Urgent Safeguarding. The practice of listing effectuates the notions of scale, territory and boundedness. On the geographic scale the heritage space is territorially defined as states where cultural expressions appear bounded and ranked. In the heritagization or heritage-making process, a cultural expression, a practice or an environment becomes singled out with particular social significance attributed to it, which builds upon the politics of inclusion and exclusion, of rootedness and rights of possession. Heritagization procreates and functions on the mechanism of political arbitration and social engineering (see Kuutma 2012). Mapping and identification of 'intangible heritage' as the formational premise of cultural politics signifies a sociocultural reform – shared experience and practices are transformed into political assets both on a local and global arena. This process inevitably involves codification of cultural expressions and practices into manageable symbols of representation and argumentation. However, like all terms in the discourse of culture, heritage is an abstraction, and what it signifies is subject to interpretation and evaluation that may fluctuate between positive and negative over time and space.

The process of heritage making implies a social construction that generates institutional positions and legitimizes certain experiences and identities. Politics of scale in heritage regimes denote politics of relations with various stakeholders who may have invested and conflicting interests from the perspective of property or management, which may concern both social and economic capital. Their competitive practices sustain the scalar structuration that emanates from the existence of authorized heritage discourse (AHD). Laurajane Smith, who has analysed the mechanism of social construction of heritage value, criticizes such discourse as predominantly Western and class-specific (see Smith 2006). But I would argue for the more universal sanctioning with authority that emerges in various scales. In the intangible heritage framework, AHD becomes established on a national scale often based on previous scholarly practices and imaginaries in cases where national identity has been built on ethnographic and folklore collections. That has been the experience in many post-Soviet Eastern European countries where AHD holds firmly on to the nation-building ideologies of the past century that focused on pre-industrial rural (peasant) culture. Today, institutionalized authorities and scholarship (e.g. governmental or international conservation agencies, museums, research institutes, NGOs) regulate identification, evaluation, selection, preservation, administration and representation of cultural heritage on the global scale. In the intangible heritage configuration, power hierarchies in AHD that are sanctioned by state authority valorize the scale of 'local' as a spatial and moralizing denominator for a particular purpose.

Politics of Scale in Ownership: Community and State

The politics of scale observable in the process of heritagization reveal conflicting individual, communal or state perspectives in the predicaments of appropriation, contested restitution or celebration. Claims of heritage depend tacitly on claims of ownership, while property relations are ultimately social and political. Ownership is a product of interests; the possession or appropriation of something is grounded in the perception of established social and political domains (Strathern 1999). Private ownership is related to the individual but depends on social relationship and cultural ramifications, complicating the implied homogeneity in this association that is embedded in a Western capitalist perception of ownership. Ownership reflects the nexus of specific relations, and yet it appears to be easier to understand rights over things than rights between people. Scalar structure appears in particular economies of distribution and sharing. It is determined by positions in status hierarchy, control and power. The agency of ownership concerning cultural expressions complicates individual or communal appropriation with capitalist interests when a cultural product or a site is transformed into a heritage commodity with significant economic and social implications.

The policy of scale implemented by the 2003 Convention foresees a particular gradation of social control where the community level is claimed to be paramount. However, defining the notion of community is problematic in universalist terms, as it has become more complex in a diverse and globalized world. Community refers to social cohesion based on mutuality, affiliation, proximity or propinquity, but it indicates by default also the inherent agenda of contestation and exclusion (Hoggett 1997). Communities may be linked by manifold social and cultural experiences; criteria for identification range from objective (ethnicity, language, etc.) to subjective ones (self-identification, solidarity, etc.); communities are segmented into those of culture, of location, of interests, etc. The denotation of community has broadened, but it brings with it layers of historical meaning and carries varied political significance in international settings where communities appear defined in scales. The matter of ascribing the quality of 'community' seems to depend on whether it happens within or if it is a prescriptive act by outsiders; whether it is an affiliation by choice or a result of an external organizational agenda, particularly in reference to state politics. The identification of community membership denotes profound social, political and economic impact on individuals and groups within the state.

Community participation – that is, mobilization around intangible cultural heritage – favours the emergence of a clearly bounded and targeted group, who would be easier to administer. And yet, communities are not homogeneous by nature. The scalar structure plays its role also internally, because the grass-roots level in the intangible heritage framework is multifarious with different social layers and strands involved. There exist also those who are the innovators and who contest the traditionalists; there occur others who negate the ascribed heritage label, or those who have been left out, or who have chosen to stay outside of the range of the intangible heritage denominator; there form hierarchies based on acknowledged expertise but also those reflecting power play, focusing on deprivation and domination. Attitudes towards heritage reflect in addition disjunctions of social practice and historical experience that involve the so-called dissonant heritage – it encompasses experiences of pain, suffering and destitution that also constitute a vital part of the human condition and generate communal identities.

Community enthusiasts or heritage promoters are not necessarily active practitioners themselves, which makes their agendas differ with respect to carrying on the meaning of a practice and worldview or reducing it to maintaining a façade. This results in bringing forth a simulacrum – that is, a representative performance, an imitation of oneself. The project of maintaining intangible heritage denotes interventions that complicate explicit or implicit hierarchies inside the communities involved, whereas lived expressive forms are reconfigured into codified symbols implemented in cultural policymaking and mediated on a national and international level through various agencies and organizations. It may also dislocate the previous status of community members by granting them new positions in reference to cultural expertise or local administrative office.

When we move further, however, to consider the triangle of community, culture and government, it appears that such functional arrangement effectuates potential tensions. In this framework the state is not simply external and impositional from the perspective of community: it could be argued that 'community' emerges from within the practices of government, who needs a bounded entity for the process of governance (see Bennett 1998). From the perspective of the state, the implementation of the framework of 'culture' stands out as a prominent preference: 'culture' is endorsed on the state level for its capacity to provide a relief in potential conflict situations; it serves the state as an alternative to politics that might complicate the state's authority. Cultural forms and activities are governmentally deployed as part of social management programmes. When heritage accentuates values for the communities, it signifies interests for the state, who promotes it with an expectation to accumulate symbolic and economic capital as well as presumably procure a political position, either internally, among geographic neighbours, or on the wider international scale.

An international convention relies on strategies of cultural engineering that are based on nation-state logics and global governance (see Hannerz 2006). The Convention calls forth the mobilization of inventorying – that is, to map and identify heritage, but voiced claims for heritage often appear simultaneously uplifting and profoundly problematic. The involvement of communities – who are signified by invoking the grass-roots perspective – is predestined to being weakened by the national validation process that is necessary for heritage authorization in the UNESCO system. UNESCO's institutional frame of reference recognizes only a 'state party'. To what extent a particular protecting or safeguarding mechanism would go beyond securing the interest of state parties in order to be capable of addressing localized needs and deliver culturally appropriate mechanism of safeguarding remains problematic.

Documentation for UNESCO-nomination purposes may have a disruptive impact that is related to making a judgement between singularity and commonality in elements of culture. Such identification of intangible cultural heritage highlights the exceptional, even if the opposite is what is aspired to. That is, the member state who proposes a nomination in the sphere of intangible cultural heritage may claim to celebrate a representational phenomenon in national culture, which is typical in the case of a widely disseminated practice. Nevertheless, what may have appeared a habitual element for a community becomes thus singled out ever after. Heritage nominations incorporate effects of moralizing and ennobling (see Bendix 2009). This process relies upon quality control and evaluation, which build on the late modern competitive practices of ranking and auditing.

The heritagization process denotes a constant reshuffling of social spaces where the process of scaling inscribes hierarchies and defines relations of power (see Lähdesmäki, Zhu and Thomas in this volume). Heritage functions as an instrument of control and a tool for scalar rearticulations and repositions. For example, under the circumstance of nation building or a newly independent state, the foremost agenda requires the promotion of a monocultural national heritage (see Harrison 2013). A unified representation aspires to demonstrate temporal continuity and spatial unity that serves the programme of nationalism. In this context, the symbolic capital of UNESCO acknowledgement plays an instrumental role in redefining the scalar significance of national identity. On the other hand, UNESCO programmes and nominations affect the regional – that is, subnational – level of identification with concurrent upscaling of regionalism.[3] But in the framework of an intangible heritage regime, contestation of hierarchies on a vertical scale does not necessarily serve an uplifting role for practice communities. The process of 'downscaling' towards community should be critically observed in juxtaposition with 'upscaling' towards the authorized heritage regime (cf. Harvey 2015). These operations in heritage politics may be much more complex, with positive but also negative reverberations for community positioning (see, for example, Herz 2015). Projects fostering both bottom-up and top-down as well as horizontal cooperation between various stakeholders (government, civil society and community representatives, academia, etc.) is an intricate task with unpredictable results. State authority catalyses risks regarding the determination of AHD, of over-politicization, possible abuse of power and implementation of control.

Politics of Scale in Representation: Inventorying and Listing

The UNESCO institutional imperative grants the practice of inventorying and listing a vital position in safeguarding intangible cultural heritage. It requires particular significance on the scale of gaining international recognition and fuelling cohesive national pride. The scalar structuration and politics find instrumental mediation through the two lists established by the 2003 Convention, the Representative List and the List of Urgent Safeguarding. Yet by default, the identification and the evaluation of cultural heritage are inevitably surrounded by contestation. Heritage regimes – i.e. the conditions that instigate this cultural and political phenomenon, as well as heritage mobilizations, create new arenas for competing political and economic interests that seek to appropriate viable heritage resources. Programmes for preservation and safeguarding pertain simultaneously to the politics of inclusion and exclusion: about who matters, who is counted in, who defines.

The operational guidelines of UNESCO conventions call for signatory states to prepare inventories in order to identify intangible heritage present in their state – inventorying imply activities on various scales. If entries for various heritage lists are sought, this entails the presentation of vast amounts of descriptive material. In sum, the states need to carry out documentation, which poses a problem from the vantage point concerned with the corollary effect in the reification of cultural dynamics, of ossifying the ever-changing phenomenon. At the same time, any documentation is a parallel act to the historically prevalent practices of collecting ethnographic artefacts in settings esteemed exotic, whereas those collection endeavours were and continue to be complexly – and often disturbingly – related to the issues of ownership.

Classification entails construction of models and categorization of cultural knowledge that tends to be historically contingent, whereas classificatory systems of thought appear to be culturally biased. Therefore, particular segmentations of social reality, assignment of categories and naming of diversities may not apply universally. The conflict becomes poignant when observed from another triangular perspective: that of indigenous groups, claims for collective or individual ownership and the state. For example, an indigenous group may not wish or allow their intellectual property or environmental knowledge to be registered, because once documented, its ownership may easily pass out of their hands. Inventorying reflects interests and ideologies that are often driven by external agendas; it is rarely taken up on the initiative of cultural communities themselves, but assumes a brokerage and mediation role (see Arantes 2009). The exercise of inventorying raises the problem of subjectivity and agency in relation to the state: who takes the initiative, who has the right to document and to preserve, who interacts with communities and how, who represents them. In the context of intangible heritage, the issue of 'representativeness' appears problematic in reference to scale: what is the scope of a cultural element identified and who is the subject represented. The practice of listing both establishes the scales as well as employs these scales. The practice and implementation of such politics of scale is contrastingly illustrated by, for example, the Oruro carnival in Bolivia, the compannonage practice in France, or the song and dance celebration in the Baltic countries (UNESCO lists (b)).

The state weighs in on the representational validation process on the constructive participation of various mediators who are instrumental for the government in the course of identifying and defining heritage. In the field of heritage policy, authority is accorded to expert knowledge and precedence given to professional interventions that create in turn particular communities of interest, involving stakeholders and stewardship. The discursive impact of the concept and perception of cultural heritage paves the way for a battleground of celebration and contestation among those entangled in the process of heritage production. Frictions appear based on cultural competence; debate and conflict arise between conservationists and innovators, while hierarchies of authority become structured and expand. To a certain extent, such expert-battles may reflect institutional agendas that do not resonate with locally grounded concerns.

The implied scalar categorization entails choices of inclusion that are based on representational agendas and preservation policies, which are usually defined by cultural custodians and relevant curatorial institutions. In their input to making public policies concerning preservation procedures, however, they may ignore the sphere of cultural communities. The politics of representation and decision making happen to favour particular social groups, whereas the ennobling cause of venerating heritage tends to overshadow social inequalities. An international organization like UNESCO depends on the institutionalization and maintenance of elite power and expert knowledge, while experts often derive from the ranks of economic elites. The construction of public policies in cultural preservation tends to be biased by hegemonic values and conceptions about national culture that serve elitist perspectives. UNESCO functions as a supranational institution where networks of globalized national(ist) elites gather to care for regional heritage formations, which concurrently fuel national pride and practices of identity construction.

Heritage making produces effects, and the concurrent rhetoric defines the field. Those effects range from branding to moral economies. The fundamental conceptualization of the notion of heritage comprises negative emotions and painful experience – its constitutive factors are destruction and loss. The idea of heritage care emerges as a central theme in conflict situations and in preservation agendas. The discordant nature of heritage preservation springs from the modernist obsession with loss and the unpredictability of future events. The ideology of safeguarding intangible heritage still relies on an identification process, which is often a result of modern scholarship (ethnographic studies or collections) and its knowledge production process. The preservationist programmes involved have often a noble cause of care for heritage on a global scale – but may, however, reveal a severe friction with local perception of priorities in representational symbols of cultural practice, or priorities concerning sustainable livelihoods among the locals. The concept of heritage assumes boundedness, which is often torn by digression: heritage can be dissonant and heritage may be contested. Cultural traditions and suppressed histories have become powerful assets in previously dominated regions or for oppressed and marginalized social strata. Thus it remains worthwhile to question who heritage empowers and what the sociocultural repercussions are in the heritagization process.

Effects of Representation

The social construction of scale in the framework of intangible heritage reflects struggles for power and control that correspond to the effects of representation. The 2003 Convention declares its domain of reference to encompass only such intangible cultural heritage that is deemed compatible with international human rights instruments. Thus from the perspective of human rights, heritage framework does not appear to be inclusive by default. Notably, issues concerning migration, minorities and indigenous groups in dominant or national frameworks complicate the field of intangible cultural heritage in a significant manner. And in general their rights (or existence) tend to be ignored when agendas of national representation are at stake.

In fact, there is a sharp clash in addressing the issue of ownership in post-industrial societies when juxtaposed with indigenous groups and their regulations. The agency of indigenous ownership is a common challenge compounding international legal instruments seeking to sufficiently maintain state sovereignties that attract signatories. According to Lucas Lixinski (2013), the focus on indigenous cultures and aboriginal peoples is obvious, as the majority of substantial legislative and legal protections of culture relate to these groups, despite the difficulties of providing legal protection for constantly evolving and self-defining living phenomena.

Another complicated yet hierarchical scaling factor in heritage politics appears to be the representation and acknowledgement of gender. The sphere of intangible cultural heritage concerns directly the issue of rights from the perspective of gender equality. Very often intangible cultural heritage is gender-specific, or actually has been in the past; sometimes this is exactly the reason why an element has preserved. Whether that is compatible with the modern world and advocating of gender equality needs careful reflection from the perspective of inclusiveness and regulations.

In addition, the management of intangible heritage correlates with economic concerns that reversibly relate to poverty and deprivation, when we think about cultural expressions and environments in marginal communities or less affluent, non-Western settings or countries. Heritage maintains a deep and complicated relationship with poverty. In a contradictory way, the modern world designates by the term 'intangible heritage' mostly cultural practices and expressions of relatively deprived groups who have often experienced social marginalization. The concept of cultural heritage was transferred to the non-European world as a form of colonial modernity, situated within a distinct discourse that was indebted to the modern, Western agendas of restoration, conservation and preservation. There it served 'a civilizing mission' – deemed thus by Falser (2015) – when employed to forge new identities based on shared cultural meanings and a sense of belonging in the national context. Consequently, economic advancement has usually incorporated a profound change in cultural practices, often with a notable demise in variety. Intangible cultural heritage is often inherently related to notions of exclusion, of segregation, of deprivation. The condition of poverty usually sustains a diverseness of intangible cultural heritage that tacitly undergirds the contradiction with development agendas that aspire economic, social and environmental empowerment. Also, a tradition by nature repudiates 'development' due to the inner conflict of the agenda to preserve against that of fostering a change or economic growth. As an instrumental factor in preservationist agenda there lurks a risk of losing the localized nature of heritage through commercial exploitation or international involvement. And yet, on the other hand, a signified intangible heritage may also comprise of elements and practices that are by default tangled with affluence – that is the case, for example, with (one-time) courtly customs and practices that have been thus designated and listed in several Asian countries (UNESCO lists (b)). Similar complexities become apparent in the context of branding cultural practices that relate to coveted revenue and privileged status.

A significant tool for scalar structuration from a national or elitist perspective in cultural-political representation is the notion of purity presumed for symbolic reference of cultural phenomena. By preservationists particularly, hybridity is regarded a negative feature from the perspective of heritage politics. However, in the context of cultural dynamics, where change is immanent, it would seem impossible to pin down and define the moment when 'a hybrid' begins (see Canclini 1995). The heritage engineering agenda appears to hang on to the notion of 'purity' in origin, particularly in its political implications, thus often ignoring the borrowing and lending between cultures, or fusions that generate new structures, subjectivities and practices. The notion of purity is intricately tied to contingencies and constraints of ownership, or arbitrary demarcation lines between overlapping phenomena.

Politics of heritage depend on an established politics of scale, not only in the process of arbitration but also in its management principles, which are inclined to favour clearly defined categories and tacit hierarchies. Heritage is a mode of cultural production that covets singularity: the ultimately complex notion gets transformed into a bounded and objectified entity that lends itself to a deceptive illusion of being easily managed, monitored or organized. However, the target sphere of intangible cultural heritage shuns being treated as a detached thing in itself, because designations configure meaning and policies affect people's living surroundings and lifeworlds in an intricate manner. Their effects become apparent in the larger social background. For example, people need roads to come together to dance; an engaged audience is a prerequisite at festivities of singing; food practices depend on agriculture, animal husbandry; weaving carpets requires mechanisms to sell them, or acquire yarn. In this framework, regulated commercial interests suggest societal benefit.

Heritagization concerns the complexity of human existence and community economy, involving all sectors with social, economic, political, medical etc., ramifications. Scaling processes have political and social consequences when interaction of size and level on spatial and cultural scale operates differently and denies clearly defined borders between domains or states. The complex nature of vibrant forms of human expression and mental capacities resists fixation, contends with external regulations and considers the living practices to be incessantly renegotiated.

Politics of Scale Reviewed

UNESCO is the standard-setting legal instrument on a supranational scale whose organizational logic instigates and orchestrates the relevant politics. The inherent structuration commissions hierarchies that define and transmit the politics of scale in the heritagization process. Policies developed for safeguarding intangible cultural heritage envision cooperation between different levels of governance with scalar effects. Administrative bureaucracy needs quantifiable and concrete results that can demonstrate accomplishment. The situation with intangible cultural heritage deems accomplishment as a concrete and bounded result to be elusive, however.

The claims for intangible heritage invoke politics of scale embedded in the framing of culture, its history and expression. These major interventions combine insider activism with interests from the outside involving political gain. Heritage emerges from the nexus of politics and power. It is a project of symbolic domination: heritage privileges and empowers foremost elitist narratives and often sustains dominant identities that reinforce support for particular state structures and related political ideologies.

Heritage politics are never neutral: they are all about choice where different and often oppositional interest groups concurrently select and promote particular activities and symbols. There appear frictions based on cultural competence, debates on protective ideals and hierarchies of authority. The general implementation of the Convention depends on the multi-scalar cooperation between engaged stakeholders from government bodies (central, provincial and local level), communities, NGOs/CSOs and cultural heritage institutions, academia and others.

The contrivances outlined command the politics of scale in the identification of practices into manageable categories, in the imposition of hierarchies or exploitation of positions, but also in the consolidation into collective bodies under the aegis of particular signifiers. There emerge normative pressures of institutionalized power relations but also practices that may contravene administrative authority or the framework that representation dictates. Therefore, it is reasonable to investigate how people act, create positions and find new potential in the designated cultural heritage interaction – with the aim of recognizing the empowering or latent moments for agency and dialogue. That would lend an opportunity to notice steps and situations when the politics of scale become obstructed or conversed.

Kristin Kuutma (PhD) is Professor of Cultural Research at the University of Tartu (UT), Estonia, and leads the UT programme of the Graduate School of Culture Studies and Arts. She has represented Estonian academics in the European Science Foundation humanities committee. She chairs the UNESCO national commission and has represented Estonia on the Intergovernmental Committee for the Safeguarding of Intangible Cultural Heritage. Kuutma has carried out extensive fieldwork on the UNESCO 2003 Convention policymaking and implementation on an international and local level. She holds currently an institutional research grant 'Cultural Heritage as a Socio-cultural Resource and Contested Field'. Her numerous publications in cultural history and anthropology focus on disciplinary histories, knowledge production, representation and critical heritage studies.

NOTES

1. This work was supported by the Estonian Ministry of Education and Research under the Institutional Research Grant IUT34–32.
2. By January 2018 the number of state parties to the Convention was 176.
3. Such reconceptualization of regionalism has been described by Buljubasić and Lähdesmäki in this volume.

REFERENCES

Arantes, A.A. 2009. 'Heritage as Culture: Limits, Uses and Implications of Intangible Cultural Heritage Inventories', in T. Kono (ed.), *Intangible Cultural Heritage and*

Intellectual Property: Communities, Cultural Diversity and Sustainable Development. Antwerp, Oxford and Portland: Intersentia, pp. 51–75.

Bendix, R. 2009. 'Heritage between Economy and Politics: An Assessment from the Perspective of Cultural Anthropology', in L. Smith and N. Akagawa (eds), *Intangible Heritage*. London and New York: Routledge, pp. 253–69.

Bennett, T. 1998. *Culture: A Reformer's Science*. London: Sage Publications.

Canclini, N.G. 1995. *Hybrid Cultures: Strategies for Entering and Leaving Postmodernity*. Minneapolis: University of Minnesota Press.

Falser, M. 2015. 'Cultural Heritage as Civilizing Mission: Methodological Considerations', in M. Falser (ed.), *Cultural Heritage as Civilizing Mission: From Decay to Recovery*. Cham, Heidelberg, New York, Dordrecht and London: Springer, pp. 1–32.

Hannerz, U. 2006. 'Cosmopolitanism', in J. Vincent and D. Nugent (eds), *A Companion to the Anthropology of Politics*. Oxford: Blackwell, pp. 69–85.

Harrison, R. 2013. *Heritage: Critical Approaches*. New York: Routledge.

Harvey, D. 2015. 'Heritage and Scale: Settings, Boundaries and Relations', *International Journal of Heritage Studies* 21(6): 577–93.

Herod, A. and M.W. Wright. 2002. 'Introduction: Rhetorics of Scale', in A. Herod and M.W. Wright (eds), *Geographies of Power: Placing Scale*, Malden, MA and Oxford: Wiley-Blackwell, pp. 147–53.

Herz, E. 2015. 'Bottoms, Genuine and Spurious', in N. Adell, R.F. Bendix, C. Bortolotto and M. Tauschek (eds), *Between Imagined Communities and Communities of Practice*. Göttingen: Universitätsverlag Göttingen, pp 25–58.

Hoggett, P. (ed.) 1997. *Contested Communities: Experiences, Struggles, Policies*. Bristol: Policy Press.

Kirshenblatt-Gimblett, B. 2006. 'World Heritage and Cultural Economics', in I. Karp and C. Kratz et al. (eds), *Museum Frictions: Public Cultures/Global Transformations*. Durham, NC: Duke University Press, pp. 161–202.

Kuutma, K. 2012. 'Between Arbitration and Engineering: Concepts and Contingencies in the Shaping of Heritage Regimes', in R.F. Bendix, A. Eggert and A. Peselmann (eds), *Heritage Regimes and the State*. Göttingen: Universitätsverlag Göttingen, pp. 21–36.

———. 2015. 'From Folklore to Intangible Heritage', in W. Logan, M. Nic Craith and U. Kockel (eds), *A Companion to Heritage Studies*. London: Wiley-Blackwell, pp. 41–53.

Lixinski, L. 2013. *Intangible Cultural Heritage in International Law*. Oxford: Oxford University Press.

Massey, D. 2005. *For Space*. London: Sage.

Smeets, R. 2004. 'Intangible Cultural Heritage and its Link to Tangible Cultural and Natural Heritage', in M. Yamamoto and M. Fujimoto (eds), *Utaki in Okinawa and Sacred Spaces in Asia*. Tokyo: The Japan Foundation, pp. 137–50.

Smith, L. 2006. *Uses of Heritage*. London: Routledge.

Strathern, M. 1999. *Property, Substance, and Effect: Anthropological Essays on Persons and Things*. London: Athlone Press.

UNESCO lists (a) = 'Purpose of the Lists of Intangible Cultural Heritage and of the Register of Good Safeguarding Practices'. Accessed 6 April 2017 from https://ich.unesco.org/en/purpose-of-the-lists-00807.

UNESCO lists (b) = 'Browse the Lists of Intangible Cultural Heritage and the Register of Good Safeguarding Practices'. Accessed 6 April 2017 from https://ich.unesco.org/en/lists.

Index

NOTE: Page references with an *f* are figures.

Abélès, Marc, 57
Act on Environmental Administration (1995), 106
actors, local-level, 45
Adams, P., 144
Adams, Paul C., 144
affections, 91
agency, 1, 160
aggregators, 50, 52, 59
Aldeias Históricas (Historical Villages), 88
alternative heritage, 10
Angkor Archaeological Park, 72
Angkor World Heritage Site (Cambodia), 65–80; case studies, 69–70; creation and existence of, 70–74; heritage as scale, 66–69; value of, 75–76
Angkor Zoning and Environmental Management Plan, 72–74
apostrophization/thematization of Croatia, 130
application program interfaces (APIs), 54
Archaeological Park Carnuntum (Austria), 40
archaeologists, 68
Archdiocesan Museum (Czech Republic), 40
archeology, 114
architects, 68
architecture: European Heritage Label (EHL), 38; Medieval, 131; Renaissance, 131

archives, 54
Ashworth, G., 5, 9, 21, 140, 141
Association of Municipalities of the Beira Interior Norte, 86
atrocities, tourism, 115
Australia, Mistake Creek, 115
authenticity, 67, 68, 159
authority, 168. *See also* hierarchies
Authorized Heritage Discourse (AHD), 9, 37, 39, 44, 88, 92, 160

Balkan cultural traits, 128, 132
The Barrelman, 147, 148, 152
Beijing Declaration (2007), 27
Bennett, Tony, 51, 52, 57
Bertacchini, E., 11
BIN-SAL, 82, 84
BIN-SAL (Beira Interior Norte-Salamanca), 84–89, 86–89
BIN-SAL United Heritage (DVD), 85
Bloch, Ernst, 150
borderline capeias *(capeias raianas),* 88
borders: BIN-SAL (Beira Interior Norte-Salamanca), 84–89; cross-border cooperation, 82–84; cross-border regionalization, 84; heritage, 81–94; heritagization, 82; identity, 89
Bortolotto, C., 10
branding, 129, 133–35, 136
Brenner, N., 7, 8, 22, 83
Broadcasting Corporation of Newfoundland (BCN), 145
brothers in arms *(Waffenbrüder),* 116
Buljubašić, Eni, 14

Burra Charter, 25
Butland, Rowena, 13

Cambodia, 13, 65–80
Campanula da Estrela, 88
Canada, 140. *See also* Newfoundland
Canadian Broadcasting Corporation (CBC), 140, 150, 151
capeias raianas (borderline capeias), 88
case studies: Angkor World Heritage Site (Cambodia), 69–70; BIN-SAL, 82 (*see also* BIN-SAL)
Castells, M., 7
categorization, 67, 165
Centres for Economic Development, Transport and the Environment (ELY), 106
Charter of Law of Abolition of the Death Penalty (Portugal), 42
China, 12; cultural heritage in, 21–35; downscaling, 25–27; heritage administrative system in, 24*f*; hierarchies in heritage governance, 23–25; National Tourism Administration, 27; Principles, 25, 28; scalar mobilization, 27–30; State Council *(guowuyuan)*, 24; upscaling and downscaling heritage, 30–32; World Heritage System in, 22
Chinese Academy of Arts, 26
Chinese Academy of Cultural Heritage, 26
Christianity, 133
chuantong wenhua (traditional culture), 23
Clarke, Ernest, 144, 145, 145*f*
classification, 164
colonialism, France, 69
Commission of Government, 146
Committee of Ministers of the Council of Europe, 98
community, 161
compatibility, 57
conflict history, 118
Conjuntos Históricos (Historical Sites), 88
connectivity, networks of, 7
conservation, laws, 25

contemporary modern klapa, 127
contestation, sociopolitical process of, 22
control, 160
Convention for the Safeguarding of the Intangible Cultural Heritage (UNESCO [2003]), 21, 23, 157
Coombe, Rosemary, 56
cooperation, 81–94; BIN-SAL (Beira Interior Norte-Salamanca), 84–89; cross-border, 82–84
craftsmanship, 158
creative reuse, 56
Critical Heritage Studies, 2, 3, 6, 9, 14, 15, 83
Croatia: apostrophization/thematization of, 130; klapa singing, 126–39; Mediterranean identity in, 128–29, 133–35; tourism, 129
Croatian National Television, 135
Croatian National Tourist Board, 134, 135
cross-border: cooperation, 82–84; governance, 82; policymaking, 81; products, 89, 90; regionalization, 84
Crown of Aragon (Spain), 40
cultural custodians, 165
Cultural Environment Law (*Kulturmiljölag* [2014]), 100
cultural environments, 95–109; concept of, 99–102; cultural landscapes to, 97–99; regional cultural environment programmes, 102–5; scalar relations (Finland), 105–6
cultural heritage, 114, 146; in China, 21–35; European Union (EU), 36, 37; intangible, 156–70; klapa singing, 126–39; management, 66; Mediterranean, 134; as a resource, 103
cultural hybridity, 129
cultural landscapes to cultural environments, 97–99
Cultural Memory Law (Kulturminneslag 1988), 100
cultures, 39, 158; concept of, 52; digital heritage, 50–62
curation, 56
curatorial institutions, 165

Dalmatian klapa singing, 126. *See also* klapa singing
Dalmatian/Mediterranean temperament, 131
dark heritage (of Finnish Lapland), 113–25; definitions of, 114–15; historical context, 116–17; scaling, 117–22
dark tourism, 114, 115
Darnton, Robert, 54
databases, 50, 53. *See also* digital heritage
Declaration of Qufu (2005), 27
degrees, 65
democracy, 131, 133
Denmark: cultural environments, 99; documentation, 97
development, sustainable, 104
difficult heritage, 114
digital aggregators, 50, 52
digital heritage, 13; Europeana and the DPLA, 53–59; governmentality and scale, 51–52; scale, 50–62
distribution, 160
diversity, social movements, 8
documentation, 70, 77, 97
downscaling, 6, 163; China, 25–27; heritage in China, 30–32
DPLA (Digital Public Library of America), 50, 51, 53–59
DPLA metadata application profile (DPLA MAP), 55

economies, 39
Eco-raya, 84, 85, 86f, 89, 91
Eder, K., 45
embeddedness of politics, 57
Empire Transcription Service, 146
employment, promotion of, 95
environments, management, 97, 98, 103
equality, gender, 166
ethnicity, 23
Europe, idea of, 46
Europeana and the DPLA, 53–59
European Built Heritage Days *(Euroopan rakennusperintöpäivät)*, 100
European Commission (EC), 36, 46, 53
European Community, 81

European Data Model (EDM), 55
European digital library, 53
The European District of Strasbourg (France), 40
European Heritage Label (EHL), 37, 38, 39, 43, 44
Europeanism, 134
European Landscape Convention (2000), 96
Europeanness, 52
European Parliament (EP), 36
European Semantic Elements (ESE), 55
European significance, meaning of, 38–44
European Union (EU): cross-border cooperation, 82–84; cultural heritage, 36, 37; funding, 107; meaning of European significance, 38–44; policies, 83; politics of scale, 44–46; promoting identity of, 46–47; significance of heritage, 36–49
Europe of the Regions, 103
Eurovision Song Contest (Malmo, Sweden), 134
evacuees in Finland, 119
exclusions, 9, 66–69
extents, 65

Falkheimer, Jesper, 144
Falser, M., 167
Faro Convention (2005), 95, 99, 104
Fathers of Confederation, 140, 142
Ferreira, Candau, 130
Ferreira, Mazzucchi, 130
festival klapa, 127
Finland: concept of cultural environments, 99–102; cultural landscapes to cultural environments, 97–99; documentation, 97; map of, 117f; politics of scale, 101; regional cultural environment programmes, 102–5; scalar relations, 105–6; scope of heritage, 95–109; tourism in, 119. *See also* Finnish Lapland
the Finnish Forestry Commission (Metsähallitus), 120
Finnish Heritage Agency, 100, 120

174 • *Index*

Finnish Lapland: dark heritage of, 113–25; definitions of dark heritage, 114–15; historical context, 116–17; scaling dark heritage, 117–22
Finnish Sámi Museum, 120
First World Peace Conference (1899), 41
First World War, 56
fishocracy, 149
folklore, 114, 132, 142, 148, 158
food, 85
Foucault, Michel, 51, 52, 56, 59
Fourth European Conference of Ministers (1996), 98
France, colonialism, 69
Franz Liszt Academy of Music (Hungary), 40
free speech, 58
friendship, 130
funding, European Union (EU), 107

Galgay, William Fenton, 146
gender equality, 166
generalizations, 57
General Library of the University of Coimbra (Portugal), 40
A Geography of Heritage (Graham, Ashworth, and Tunbridge), 21, 140
Getty Conservation Institute, 25
gold diggers, dark heritage (of Finnish Lapland), 113–25
Google Books Project, 53, 54, 58
governance, 39; cross-border, 82; hierarchies in heritage, 23–25
governmentality and scale, 51–52
Graham, B., 5, 21, 140, 141
Grant, Hilary, 14
Great Guild Hall (Estonia), 40
Greco-Roman monuments, 131
growth, promotion of, 95
guidelines (UNESCO), 164
guowuyuan (State Council), 24

Habermas, Jürgen, 113
Hambach Castle (Germany), 39
Harrison, R., 32, 133
Harvard University, 54

Harvey, D., 5, 32, 141, 144, 157
Harvey, David C., 52
HathiTrust, 54
The Heart of Ancient Athens (Greece), 40, 41
Helsinki Declaration, 98
heritage, 1–18, ix, x; administrative system in China, 24*f*; aggregators, 52, 59; alternative, 10; borders, 81–94; in China, 21–35; concept of, 2; constructions of, 114; cross-border cooperation, 82–84; cultural, 114; Dalmatian/Mediterranean temperament, 131; dark (*see* dark heritage [of Finnish Lapland]); definitions of, 11, 165; difficult, 114; digital, 13; downscaling, 25–27; European Union (EU), 36–49; hierarchies and, 5; hierarchies in governance, 23–25; impact of, 126; klapa singing, 126–39, 133–35; management, 103, 104; meaning of European significance, 38–44; networks, 7; policies, 15, 26*f*; politics of, 167, 168; and politics of scale, 8–11; production, 82; professionals, 68; promoting identity of European Union (EU), 46–47; radio heritage (in Newfoundland), 140–55; scalar mobilization, 27–30; as scale, 66–69; scope of, 95–109; value, 66–69
Heritage Bureau of Lijiang, 31
heritage-scale relationship, 4
heritagization, 126, 159, 163, 168
Herod, A., 8
Herva, Vesa-Pekka, 120
Herzfeld, M., 129
hierarchies, 4–5, 6, 23–25, 117–22, 160, 163, 165, 167
Historical Sites *(Conjuntos Históricos)*, 88
Historical Villages *(Aldeias Históricas)*, 88
The Historic Ensemble of the University of Tartu (Estonia), 40
Historic Gdańsk Shipyard (Poland), 39
Hitler, Adolf, 116
home, idea of, 31

Homeland War, 128, 129
human-environment relationships, 65
human influence on landscapes, 97, 98

ICC, 69, 70, 71, 72, 75, 76, 77
ICOMOS (International Council on Monuments and Sites), 7, 9, 25, 28
idealization, 129
identification, politics of scale, 157–60
identity: Balkan cultural traits, 132; borders, 89; Khmer Nation, 76; klapa singing, 126–39; Mediterranean identity in Croatia, 128–29, 133–35; promoting European Union (EU), 46–47; sense of, 66
Impact Assessment (EC), 46
The Imperial Palace (Austria), 40
inclusion, 66–69
incomers, dark heritage (of Finnish Lapland), 113–25
Innis, Harold, 143
institutions, 12–15
intangible cultural heritage: effects of representation, 166–68; identification, 157–60; inventorying, 163–66; listing, 163–66; ownership, 160–63; politics of scale for, 156–70; review of politics of scale, 168–69
Intangible Cultural Heritage (ICH), 24
INTERREG, 84
Interreg Spanish-Portugal Programme funds, 87
interurban networks, 7
intrinsicity, 68
inventorying, 159, 163–66

Jansson, André, 144

Kähkönen, Satu, 13
Kätilö (Kettu), 123
Kaunas of 1919–1940 (Lithuania), 43
Keep Lapland Tidy *(Pidä Lappi siistinä)*, 120
Kettu, Katja, 123
Khmer Nation, 76
Kingsepp, Eva, 122
Kirshenblatt-Gimblett, B., 2

klapa singing, 126–39; Mediterranean identity in Croatia, 128–29, 133–35; politics of scale, 129; scalar affordances, 130–33; symbolic meanings, 130–33; topics of klapa songs, 127
Krapina Museum (Croatia), 40
Kuutma, Kristin, 14

labour unions, 8
Lacey, Kate, 144
Lähdesmäki, Tuuli, 13, 14
landscapes, 71; cultural, 97–99; human influence on, 97, 98. *See also* managed landscapes
Lapland. *See* Finnish Lapland
Lapland War, 116
Latour, B., 7, 142
laws, conservation, 25
Lefebvre, H., 6
legitimacy of heritage managers, 68
Lehtola, Veli-Pekka, 116
levels, 65
libraries, 54, 58
LIFE Programme, 105
lifestyles, 158
Lijiang, China, 22, 23, 25, 27–30, 31
Lisbon Strategy, 83
listing, 159, 163–66
List of Intangible Cultural Heritage in Need of Urgent Safeguarding, 159
List of Urgent Safeguarding, 163
List of World Heritage in Danger, 32
Liuzza, C., 11
Lixinski, Lucas, 166
local distinctiveness, 129
local-level actors, 45
locals, dark heritage (of Finnish Lapland), 113–25
locations, categorization of, 67
Loism María, 13

Maastricht Treaty, 36
MacKinnon, D., 83
Mäkinen, Katja, 13
Making Culture, Changing Society (Foucault), 52

Malmo, Sweden, 134
managed landscapes, 65–80; Angkor World Heritage Site (Cambodia), 70–74; Angkor Zoning and Environmental Management Plan, 72–74; case studies, 69–70; heritage as scale, 66–69; value of Angkor, 75–76
management: cultural heritage, 66; environments, 97, 98, 103; heritage, 103, 104; urban, 72
mapping, 159
Marston, S., 4, 83
Massey, D., 3
materialit of klapa singing, 130
McAtackney, Laura, 115
McLuhan, Marshall, 141, 143, 144
media: concepts of, 143–45; topologies, 144
Medieval architecture, 131
Mediterranean cultural heritage, 134
Mediterranean identity in Croatia, 128–29, 133–35
Mediterranean klapa singing, 126–39
Member States, 45
memorabilia collectors, 120, 122
memories, 91
Meskell, L., 11
metacultural operations, 2
metadata, 55
Metsähallitus (the Finnish Forestry Commission), 120
Ministry of Culture (China), 26
Mistake Creek (Australia), 115
models of European cultural heritage, 45
modernism, 43
modernity, 142, 150
modernization, radio heritage (in Newfoundland), 150–52
monuments, Angkor World Heritage Site (Cambodia), 71, 72, 76
multidirectional power relations, 102–5
Mundaneum (Belgium), 40
Museo Casa Alcide De Gasperi (Italy), 39
museums, 51, 54
music: klapa singing (*see* klapa singing); ojkanje singing, 132; tamburitza, 132

Nanfang Zhoumo (Southern Weekly), 29
Nara Document on Authenticity (1994), 10
national identity, 1
nationalism, 149
National Television Board, 134
nation-building, klapa singing, 133–35
nation states, 1, 11
nativism, 152
Naxi Culture Research institution, 26
Nazis, 120, 122
The Neanderthal Prehistoric Site (Croatia), 40
networks, scale as, 7–8
Newfoundland: concepts of media, 143–45; Confederation, 149–50; history of radio in, 145–47; modernization, 150–52; radio as multidirectional, 147–48; radio heritage in, 140–55
New York Public Library, 54
Niggemann, Elisabeth, 54
non-governmental organizations (NGOs), 169
Norway: cultural environments, 99; documentation, 97
nostalgia, 129

'O Canada', 150
ojkanje singing, 132
Old Town of Lijiang, 22, 23, 27–30
Olomouc Premyslid Castle (Czech Republic), 40
Operation Barbarossa, 116
Our Lady of the Peña de Francia, 88
ownership, politics of scale, 160–63

Paasi, Anssi, 141
Pan-European Picnic Memorial Park (Hungary), 39
Peace of Westphalia (Germany), 41
Peace Palace (The Netherlands), 41
People's Republic of China (PRC), 23. *See also* China
performances, 82, 91
Pidä Lappi siistinä (Keep Lapland Tidy), 120
planning documents, 82

pluralism, 66
Pocius, Gerald, 152
policies, 12–15; affecting heritage, 15; cross-border regionalization policymaking, 81; cultural environments, 95–109; discourses, 103; European Union (EU), 36–49, 83; heritage, 26f; meaning of European significance, 38–44; promoting identity of European Union (EU), 46–47; top-down approach of policymaking, 32
Political Dimension of Cultural Heritage Conservation, 98
politics, 39; embeddedness of, 57; of heritage, 167, 168; of heritagization, 82; scalar, 81–94
politics of scale: concepts, 12–15; cultural heritage in China, 21–35; effects of representation, 166–68; European Union (EU) heritage, 36–49; Finland, 101; heritage and, 8–11; identification, 157–60; for intangible cultural heritage, 156–70; inventorying, 163–66; klapa singing, 129; listing, 163–66; ownership, 160–63; policies (EU heritage), 44–46; review of, 168–69
Poole, Nick, 56
portals, 54
Portugal, 81–94. *See also* BIN-SAL
postmodernism, 1
poststructuralism, 1
power, 1, 2, 160; of cultural heritage management, 66; multidirectional power relations, 102–5; scale as an instrument of, 5–6
practices, 12–15
preservation agendas, 165
private sphere, 114, 123
processes, scale as, 6–7
products, cross-border, 89, 90
professionals, heritage, 68
Provincial Department of Culture (China), 24, 28
public libraries, 58
public sphere, 114, 117, 123

radio heritage (in Newfoundland), 140–55; concepts of media, 143–45; Confederation, 149–50; history of radio in Newfoundland, 145–47; modernization, 150–52; radio as multidirectional, 147–48
ranking values, 67
Ratzel, Friedrich, 97
regional cultural environment programmes, 102–5
Regional Environmental Centres, 106
regions, 71; BIN-SAL (Beira Interior Norte-Salamanca), 84–89; cross-border regionalization, 81, 84
relationships: heritage-scale, 4; human-environment, 65; multidirectional power relations, 102–5
Renaissance architecture, 131
representation, effects of, 166–68
representations, 91
Representative List of Intangible Cultural Heritage of Humanity, 159, 163
Residencia de Estudiantes (Lithuania), 43
Residencia de Estudiantes (Spain), 40
Ritter, Carl, 97
rituals, 158
Robert Schuman's House (France), 40
romanticism, 129
rules, World Heritage List, 9
Russian doll structure of scale, 5
Russian Federation, 116

Saccone, D., 11
SACH (State Administration of Cultural Heritage), 23, 24
The Sagres Promontory (Portugal), 42
Sámi, 116, 120, 121
scalar affordances, klapa singing, 130–33
scalar categorization, 165
scalar mobilization, 27–30, 32
scalar politics, 81–94
scalar relations: concept of cultural environments, 99–102; cultural environment policies, 95–109; cultural landscapes to cultural environments, 97–99; Finland,

105–6; regional cultural environment programmes, 102–5
scale, 1–18, ix; Angkor World Heritage Site (Cambodia), 65–80; as an instrument of power, 5–6; definitions of, 4–8; dialogue of, 65; digital heritage, 50–62; governmentality and, 51–52; heritage as, 66–69; heritage-scale relationship, 4; as a hierarchy, 4–5, 6; making of heritage, 3; as a network, 7–8; politics of, 4; as a process, 6–7
scale jumping, 21, 31
scale of hierarchies, 117–22
scales of the heritage industry in China, 32
scaling processes, 168
sharing, 160
Smallwood, Joey, 140, 147, 148, 149, 150, 151f
Smith, L., 9, 10, 37
Smith, Laurajane, 160
Smith, N., 8, 22, 82
Smithsonian, 54
smuggling, 88
social agendas, 71
social construction of scale, 65–80
social management programmes, 162
social marginalization, 167
social movements, diversity, 8
Southern Weekly *(Nanfang Zhoumo)*, 29
space-biased media, 143
space(s), production of, 6
Spain, 84. *See also* BIN-SAL
Spanish-Portuguese border, 81–94
Stainforth, Elizabeth, 13
standardization, 57, 59
State Administration of Cultural Heritage (China), 29
State Council *(guowuyuan)*, 24
state parties, 162
St. Laurent, Louis, 140, 141f
stories, 91
storytelling, 158
Su, X., 29
sustainable development, 104

Sweden: cultural environments, 99; documentation, 97; heritage policies, 96
Swyngedouw, E., 6, 8
symbolic meanings, klapa singing, 130–33
symbols, 162, 163

tamburitza music, 132
Taylor, Peter, 82
territories, 71
tests, authenticity, 67
thematization of Croatia, 130
Thermal Waters, 88
Thomas, Suzie, 14
3 May 1791 Constitution (Poland), 42
time-biased media, 143
topics of klapa songs, 127
topologies, media, 144
tourism, 29, 72, 76, 77; Croatia, 129; Croatian National Tourist Board, 134, 135; dark, 114, 115; dark heritage (of Finnish Lapland), 113–25; in Finland, 119; klapa singing, 133–35
traditional culture *(chuantong wenhua)*, 23
traditional klapa, 127
traditions, 91
treaties, 36, 45
tribal drums, 143
triumphalism, 2
Tsing, Anna, 56–57, 59
Tuđman, F., 133
Turnbridge, J., 5, 9, 21, 140, 141
2003 Convention (UNESCO), 158, 159, 161, 162, 166

UN Conference on the Human Environment (1972), 104
UNESCO (United Nations Educational, Scientific and Cultural Organization), 3, 9, 10, 13, 14, 21, 69, 135; 2003 Convention, 158, 159, 161, 162, 166; functions of, 165; guidelines, 164; intangible cultural heritage, 156–70; symbols, 163; Urban Historic

Landscape (HUL), 96; World Heritage Committee, 24, 29, 98
Uneven Development (Smith), 22
Union of Lublin (Poland), 42
universal standards, 59
universal value, 159
upscaling, 30–32, 163
Urban Historic Landscape (HUL), 96
urban management, 72

validation processes, 164
value of Angkor World Heritage Site (Cambodia), 75–76
values, 66–69
Venice Charter for the Conservation and Restoration of Monuments and Sites (1964), 10, 25
visual representations, 82

Waffenbrüder (brothers in arms), 116
websites, 50, 54. *See also* digital heritage
Weiss, Lindsay M., 56
Wimmer, Joseph, 97
Windover, Michael, 14
wine, 85
Winter, Gordon, 149
Working Community of BIN-SAL, 84
World Commission on Environment and Development (WCED), 104
World Heritage, 23, 24, 158, 159

World Heritage Area, 69, 77
World Heritage Centre, 11, 29, 30
World Heritage Committee, 11, 22, 29, 98
World Heritage Committee of UNESCO, 24
World Heritage Convention (1972), 10, 98, 157
World Heritage List, 9, 10, 33, 71
World Heritage Sites: Angkor World Heritage Site (Cambodia), 65–80; Lijiang, China, 25, 27–30, 31
World Heritage System, 11, 22
World Tourism Organization, 26
World War I Eastern Front Cemetery No. 123 (Poland), 39
World War II, dark heritage (of Finnish Lapland), 113–25

Xi'an Declaration (2005), 27

Yleisradio, 118
Yugoslavia, 128

Zhu, Yujie, 12
zoning, Angkor Zoning and Environmental Management Plan, 72–74
Zoning and Environment Management Plan (ZEMP), 73, 74, 74*f*